PAPER
LION

BOOKS BY GEORGE PLIMPTON

The Rabbit's Umbrella • *Out of My League*
Paper Lion • *The Bogey Man* • *Mad Ducks and
Bears* • *American Journey: The Times of Robert Kennedy*
(with Jean Stein) • *One for the Record* • *One More
July* • *Shadow Box* • *Pierre's Book* (with Pierre
Etchebaster) • *A Sports Bestiary* (with Arnold Roth)
Edie: An American Biography (with Jean Stein) • *Sports!*
(with Neil Leifer) • *Fireworks: A History and
Celebration* • *Open Net* • *D.V.* (with Diana Vreeland and
Christopher Hemphill) • *The Curious Case of Sidd
Finch* • *The X Factor* • *The Best of Plimpton* • *Truman
Capote* • *Ernest Shackleton* • *Chronicles of Courage* (with
Jean Kennedy Smith) • *The Man in the Flying Lawn Chair*

EDITED BY GEORGE PLIMPTON

Writers at Work: The Paris Review Interviews,
volumes 1–9 • *The American Literary Anthology,* volumes
1–3 • *Poets at Work: The Paris Review Interviews* • *Beat
Writers at Work: The Paris Review Interviews* • *Women
Writers at Work: The Paris Review Interviews* • *Playwrights
at Work: The Paris Review Interviews* • *Latin American
Writers at Work: The Paris Review Interviews* • *The Writer's
Chapbook* • *The Paris Review Anthology* • *The Paris Review
Book of Heartbreak, Madness, etc.* • *The Norton Book of
Sports* • *As Told at the Explorers Club: More Than Fifty
Gripping Tales of Adventure* • *Home Run*

PAPER LION

CONFESSIONS OF A
LAST-STRING QUARTERBACK

GEORGE PLIMPTON

Little, Brown and Company
New York   Boston   London

Little, Brown and Company
Hachette Book Group
1290 Avenue of the Americas, New York, NY 10104
littlebrown.com

Originally published by Harper & Row, 1965
First Little, Brown edition, April 2016

Little, Brown and Company is a division of Hachette Book Group, Inc. The Little, Brown name and logo are trademarks of Hachette Book Group, Inc.

The publisher is not responsible for websites (or their content) that are not owned by the publisher.

The Hachette Speakers Bureau provides a wide range of authors for speaking events. To find out more, go to hachettespeakersbureau.com or call (866) 376-6591.

ISBN 978-0-316-28450-9
LCCN 2015951333

For a living dog is better than a dead lion.

—Eccles. 9:4

Foreword

by Nicholas Dawidoff

The problem with football writing has always been access, the fundamental elusiveness. How to overcome the crowd of armored players, the blur of motion, the anonymous wreckage after the tackle, the coded playbooks, the fenced-off team "facilities," the self-effacing conformity of it all? Secretive by nature, football defies anybody from the outside to get close enough to achieve the clarity and insight excellent writing requires.

In exclusion George Plimpton saw opportunity. Plimpton, the first editor of the *Paris Review,* was a privileged New Yorker who had spent his life in the most rarefied American communities. The quality that shines through *Paper Lion,* the greatest of all football books, is Plimpton's absolute conviction that he belongs. As a writer Plimpton was always more Paris than review, more safari-jacketed adventurer than urban belle-lettrist. That is to say, by procedural instinct he first walked among the fauna native to an exotic landscape — boxing rings, baseball diamonds, racetracks — and then returned to far East 72nd Street to convey their essence.

And so it was on fields strewn with (Detroit) Lions. Plimpton's solution to the problem of seeing football clearly was to get in the game. And while his playing pro football was assuredly a stunt, doing the daydream was also a terrific idea — so beautifully direct. Not only would participating in the Lions' training camp as a last-string quarterback help Plimpton to see behind the face mask, but it would also allow him to engage with the vicarious impulse at the heart of sporting spectatorship. Plimpton wrote *Paper Lion* in what was still a Walter Mitty era of armchair fandom when from the bleachers all reveries were plausible. The peerless baseball writer Roger Angell, who began covering his sport for *The New Yorker* by attending spring training in 1962, the year before Plimpton joined the Lions, said, "We used to think, with a little luck *we* could have been doing this. Nobody thinks that anymore. Today he'd get hurt." Angell considers it "amazing the Lions let him do it. They loved it. Could have been the opposite. He must have been extremely charming. George was very enthusiastic."

He was also an unlikely candidate for a mauling. A man about Harvard, the New Journalism cocktail circuit, and Kennedy administration skating parties (Muhammad Ali nicknamed him "Kennedy"), Plimpton's football pedigree was modest. He was built "along the lines of a stick" and had been cut from his high-school junior varsity. But all that was exactly the point here, and besides, Plimpton had other qualities. A youthful thirty-six when he joined the Lions, our man was tall, boyish, nervy, socially at ease in unfamiliar settings, and a person unlikely to allow his sense of self to become contingent on how well he played football. Among the Lions, Plimpton was always the confident, charming writer, glad to wear jersey number zero because he understood that his athletic incompetence was useful to his story.

All the best immersive reporters have a gift for self-fashioning, and Plimpton was a master. By 1963, he'd cultivated a patrician accent so affected even people who'd seen it all, like the writer Roy Blount, shook their heads in admiration. And yet Plimpton was also the sort of man capable of seamlessly dropping his y'alls from the moment he hit the Mason-Dixon Line. When Roger Angell was a boy growing up in New York, he admired the New York Giants' left-handed screwball pitcher Carl Hubbell above all players. Angell heard that the accumulated strains of breaking off his signature pitch meant that Hubbell's left palm faced permanently outward. So Angell began walking around with his arm to port similarly contorted. Angell's mother, alarmed, told him, "Don't do that, Rog." Angell recounted this to Plimpton, and soon enough word filtered to Angell of Plimpton, whose childhood love of Carl Hubbell was such that — get this! — he'd kept his arm bent in salutation until his mother told him to straighten up. Angell didn't hold this against Plimpton; inhabiting other people's lives was simply what Plimpton did.

At the Lions' training camp Plimpton insinuated himself with ease, retailing apocryphal tales of his amateur days as a member of the New-foundland Newfs. If his throwing arm was weak, come evening the Plimpton leg was stout enough to keep up with the big cats out at the Dearborn, Michigan, watering holes. Most people are susceptible to admiration, and the Lions quickly embraced the sustained attention of such a shimmering, seductive appreciator. They didn't care that he was lousy at football. They admired him for risking it, and for making what they did seem worthy of personal sacrifice, staying with them through the rugged hardships of camp. And Plimpton was sedulous about doing nothing to compromise the mission: "I behaved, of course."

I read *Paper Lion* first as a boy, and I still have my old childhood copy, a ninety-five-cent Pocket paperback. To look again at those disintegrating pages with their pale pink edges, some of them loosened from the spine and jammed back in haphazardly, is to recall what heady entry into an adult world it provided, a physical world of men. The pros were professionally accomplished at so many masculine arts: banter, beer drinking, vomiting (too much beer), games of chance, pranks, and post-curfew sneak-outs. There were exciting gambits like calling in to a popular restaurant under the name of the team owner to cadge a reservation (only to come upon said owner). There were women to meet out at dance halls, in tight slacks and mohair sweaters the color of pink spun sugar, and women to revel in from afar while watching them play tennis. And there were men playing football, so much football so memorably described.

The campus of the Cranbrook School where the Lions lived and trained was a gift to the writer, the contrast of rough game and sylvan setting one of the many juxtapositions that threads through *Paper Lion*, enlivening that central juxtaposition of amateur among professionals, elitist intellectual amid hard-hat muscle. Plimpton relates football as a game of intricate physical actions that are also often amusing because the players are so big, the actions so unique to the activity. After Plimpton compares centering a ball to a cow at milking, who could ever consider the hiker without thinking Holstein? Similarly, as soon as we observe massive men attempting to sleep as they overflow dormitory beds designed for teenage schoolboys, the scale of human we are dealing with becomes indelible.

Plimpton is a collector of small interactions in a volatile world. When I reached back into my old Pocket book, treats from the football day-to-day were extracted again in a rush: the account of former Lion coach Buddy Parker responding to losses by disrobing and dispensing with his (unlucky) suits of clothing, sometimes by stuffing costly jackets, ties, and trousers out the windows of speeding trains; the way players thought about the after-practice vats of lemonade awaiting them on those scorching Michigan summer days; the anxiety of the rookies forced to stand during meals and sing their school fight songs for the veterans; the steep alps of food the players put on their plates; the exaggerated reactions of headman George Wilson and the other Lion coaches during their downtime games of liars' poker; the reserve quarterback Earl Morrall generously throwing after-practice passes to a line of children — one of them a swift, sure-handed ball thief.

Football is the national passion, ever changing. Yet fifty years later *Paper Lion* still feels contemporary. That's because the book is a tour de force of vivid characters who become the Ur–football team. A football roster is scores of men, yet from just the few weeks Plimpton spent with the team, there's the necessary illusion of comprehensiveness; we feel we know them all. Several of the best were absent from Cranbrook that summer. The unruly lineman Big Daddy Lipscomb and the bantam-cock quarterback Bobby Layne had by then retired. Alex Karras, a near-sighted All-Pro defensive tackle, was famed within the team for his impromptu skits and monologues. But Karras had been suspended by the league for his underworld consortings. Plimpton clearly perceived it as an advantage that the trio was offstage; all three became entirely his. The players surrounding him provided as well, none better than Dick "Night Train" Lane, the Hall of Fame cornerback we meet up with in his dorm room dressed in a siren suit of his own design, listening to his wife Dinah Washington's R & B records on a portable stereo. Lane holds forth on the art of defense with a barrage of suffixy linguistic formulations—his "captainship"—that allow Plimpton to forever make him football's Lester Young. From these men we grasp football's strange high-low counterpoint—the big business of roughhousing. And while Plimpton may have behaved, he doesn't duck the trouble he sees, writing well, if without strong judgment, about race, addiction, and the ruthless ways of management. A very clear picture develops of how the day-to-day professional game works.

We get a very clear portrait of Plimpton too. Old Number Zero is a complicated proposition, a football ethnographer, a football interloper, and a football foil. The action in *Paper Lion* reaches an anticlimax with the five plays Plimpton quarterbacks at the team scrimmage held at Pontiac stadium, a stricken sequence that gives way to Plimpton's gradual realization that the fans didn't understand "the lunacy of my participation" and thought his ineptitude was a gag, a football Al Schacht routine. But Plimpton was a committed competitor. It's just that he saw the playing field delimits a bit more expansively than a hundred yards of gridiron.

For all the world-class athletes at Plimpton's literary disposal, *Paper Lion*'s top-billed performer is always Plimpton. His book is the culmination of a long game in which he is in unstated competition with all those Lion players, out to prove that his literary athleticism is even more entertaining than what they can muster on white-lined grass. He wins because he makes those forgotten practices involving distant players forever alive. Fleet, vain split end Gail Cogdill, lineman John Gordy called "the Bear" for a thick thatch of body hair, lady-killing defensive back Ricky LeBeau, the up-for-it utilityman Jim "Marine" Martin, the gregarious and tragic rookie lineman Lucien Reeberg—we remember them all because of skinny George. Of course Plimpton chose to be a quarterback. The quarterback is the writer, the one who makes it up, makes it happen. It was always going to be about him, and what lends the book its true imaginative distinction is Plimpton's inner life, those meandering within-the-helmet soliloquies, each of them funnier and more weirdly informative than the last.

As Plimpton recounts early on in *Paper Lion,* finding a football organization that would allow him to suit up was not easy. One team official told Plimpton, "You got to realize professional football is a serious business." Other teams thought the Lions were crazy to put themselves at risk by exposing themselves to a writer, but how provident for the Lions that they did. Such are the joys of the book, every Thanksgiving when the Lions play their traditional holiday game, generations of *Paper Lion* readers all over America take to their TVs to pull for the blue and silver.

Other writers' debts are on paper. By inventing an immersive genre, Plimpton gave otherwise obstructed observers the means for seeing distant subjects up close. As a young writer at *Sports Illustrated,* I traveled to Boston to talk hitting with Red Sox batting coach Walter Hriniak, an impresario of his time. It was challenging to understand the subtleties of Hriniak's methods, so at a certain point I asked if the coach might watch me hit a few and evaluate my swing. A look of dismay crossed his face. But fortunately for me there was a bystander who cried, "A Plimpton!" Just like that, Hriniak understood, and my encounter with the professional was assured.

PAPER
LION

CHAPTER 1

I decided finally to pack the football. It was a slightly used Spalding ball, an expensive one, with the information printed on it that it was "triple-lined and lock-stitched." Its sponsoring signature was that of Norman Van Brocklin, the ex–Philadelphia Eagle quarterback. It seemed a little deflated. I pressed it down hard against the shirts and was able to get the canvas suitcase cover zipped up around it. It was the bulkiest item in the suitcase, and the bulge of it was noticeable. I had two sweat suits in there, a pair of football shoes, some socks, a book on football formations written by a high-school coach, a sports coat and some trousers, and a few other things.

I was not sure what I was going to need at the training camp. The Detroit Lion officials had not sent me the sort of list one remembered from boys' camp — that one should bring a pillowcase, a mattress cover, a flashlight, a laundry bag, etc. I assumed I could buy what I was lacking at the nearest town. I carried the suitcase down to the street and went out to Kennedy airport to catch an airplane to Detroit. From there I would go by car an hour north to Cranbrook, a boys' private school near Bloomfield Hills, whose athletic facilities were being used by the Detroit Lions for their preseason training. I was going there as the Lions' "last-string quarterback" — as my friends referred to it — to join the team as an amateur to undergo firsthand the life of the professional and, hopefully, to describe the experience in a book.

I had written one such book—a recounting of my turbulent experiences pitching in Yankee Stadium in a postseason major-league All-Star game. *Out of My League* the book was called, and it described what happened to someone with the temerity to climb the field-box railings to try the sport oneself, just to see how one got along and what happened. The notion behind the book was to play out the fantasies, the daydreams that so many people have—seeing themselves on the center court at Wimbledon, or sinking long putts in the U.S. Open, or ripping through the Green Bay secondary. I had been able to arrange with the baseball game's promoters to play. Ernest Hemingway had thought it an odd if interesting experiment and he described the difficulties of my participation as "the dark side of the moon of Walter Mitty." Other friends were more critical. "Why do you want to embarrass yourself like that?" they asked. "It's terrible. Either you're the most frustrated athlete there ever was, or you're nuts."

"Well, the idea is also to get a firsthand knowledge of the professional athlete," I said. "By being one of them, in a sense—being a teammate."

"Sure," they said. "Some teammate. Well, all right, what are you going to do next?"

"The Detroit Lions are allowing me to go through training with them," I was able to say after I had worked it out with them. "They're going to let me play in a few games."

My friends were skeptical. "Sure, sure," they said.

During the earlier part of that July month I had been practicing strenuously with the Spalding ball. On New York City weekdays, with friends working in their offices, it was difficult finding someone with whom to throw; but I would take the ball out to Central Park, trotting along the paths in a sweat suit, bringing the knees up high, then launching into an occasional sprint, with the arm held out straight to ward off an imaginary tackler, and then in the open stretches, out in the meadows where two elderly men were helping some children fly a box kite, I would rear back and throw the ball. It would arch through the air, bounce down the field, and rock abruptly to a stop in the grass. I would fetch it. Then I would throw it again. Without someone to throw to, it was a melancholy practice—to throw a ball in a park meadow and then

Portrait of an NFL hopeful. *(Plimpton Estate)*

walk to it, and throw it again—and I did it in a sort of dull, bored way so that if anyone caught me at it, if one of the elderly men looked away from his box kite, it would appear that I had nothing better to do while awaiting the arrival of friends, obviously delayed in traffic, for a touch football game. Sometimes, I punted the ball. Once I kicked it off the side of my foot into the infield of a baseball game, and the black-shirted players began shouting, "Arriba! Arriba!" and waving their arms as if what had dropped down among them was a large buzzard. July was not the seasonal month to be carrying a football around in Central Park, and I didn't go out too often. I threw the ball around in my apartment, which is a sort of studio, long enough to allow a throw into an armchair from twenty or twenty-five feet away—keeping at it when I had the chance, if only to get used to the feel of the ball.

It was hot when I landed in Detroit. Many of those on hand to meet incoming planes were wearing shorts and dark sunglasses, some sporting cowboy hats with the Ford insignia. They meandered through the terminal, which was new and spacious, past glass cases which displayed machine parts revolving on small velvet-covered stands. Down on the lower level I rented a car, a red convertible, and I set out north along the main pike, called Telegraph Road, following directions for Bloomfield Hills. It is hard to go wrong. The country is flat, with the cranes standing in the fields amid the housing developments going up, and the bisecting roads are named for the number of miles out from the city limits—Seven-Mile Road, Eight-Mile Road, Fifteen-Mile Road— until about an hour out, when the country road names begin to appear on the turnpike signs, and the country itself begins to roll under big shade trees. I turned off for Bloomfield Hills, and the macadam road ran down through thick, tall woods, with an occasional glimpse of pond through the foliage.

I drove into the school parking lot, and carried my suitcase up through the school grounds toward a building which was indicated by an occasional directional arrow as the administration building. It was quiet and peaceful walking the brick-lined paths. The school buildings were ivy-covered, and everywhere sprinklers ticked back and forth on the lawns and flower beds.

In the administration building there was no sign of anyone around. I could hear a typewriter going somewhere, down a cloister, so I took my bag and followed along to the school office. Someone was typing in a cubicle there, and when I knocked and went in a woman spun around from her machine, blinking violently to dislodge a pair of pince-nez spectacles, which came off finally, and fell, suspended by a velvet ribbon around her neck.

She looked at me sharply.

"You are from . . . what country?" she asked.

I set my bag down. On the table beside her stood a row of badges of the type pinned on at conventions. One of them, turned slightly, had a name at the top which I could see and under it, in block letters, GHANA. Another card read IRAQ, and a third IVORY COAST.

"Yes?" she kept at me.

"Well, I'm from New York," I said hopelessly, turning my palms over.

She looked at me quizzically, and she said, "You are with the convention . . . with the bishops?"

"The *bishops?*"

She colored slightly. "Oh dear," she said. "I am in error. We have sixty Episcopalian bishops and other church people coming in for a convention . . . from all over the world. You are with . . . ?"

". . . the football people," I said.

"Yes," she said primly, recovering quickly. "The football people are in Page Hall." She gave me directions to the Lion public-relations office, where she thought someone might be able to take me in hand, squinting forward as she spoke, reaching finally for her pince-nez to give me a closer look through them.

I thanked her, took up my bag, and hurried from her scrutiny, finding Page Hall after a short walk through the school grounds, and then the public-relations office. Bud Erickson, the assistant general manager of the Lions, was in—personable, slow-talking, his hair cropped like an oarsman's, which gave him the appearance of being not long out of college—and with him was Friday Macklem, the team's equipment manager. He was older, thin, sand-blond, with amused eyes, and he wore pants as baggy as a comedian's. He had been the "man Friday" to his predecessor with the Lions, which is what they called him then, and the nickname had stuck. As he introduced us Erickson referred to him as the "guy who was the...ah...team humorist, in charge not only of equipment and uniforms and...ah...helmets, but also team *morale*."

"Naturally," Friday said. His manner was caustic. "*Your* morale may give me some trouble," he went on, grinning suddenly. "Bud's been telling me about you. I heard you're a writer turned footballer. You're going to play for us—making some sort of big comeback."

"That's right," I said.

He shook his head. "Well, I've been with Detroit for twenty-seven years, dishing out uniforms all those years, and I know if I'd ever been tempted *into* one, I wouldn't be around to tell of it, for sure."

"Did you get your insurance?" Erickson wanted to know. We had talked about that over the phone the week before.

"I got some sort of protection," I said. "It wasn't easy. The company tried to get Lloyd's of London to do it, but they backed off, not quite sure what it was all about."

"What sort of policy is it?" Erickson asked.

"It's a twenty-five-thousand coverage against death, dismemberment, or loss of sight," I said. "It cost me seventy-five dollars and the policy's only good for thirty days—which shows you what the insurance people think of my chances for the weeks ahead."

"Seems those people were trying to tell you something," said Friday. The two of them laughed.

"Don't give me away to the players," I said. "I'd like to be thought of as just another rookie, an odd one maybe, but no special favors or anything because I'm a writer. The point is to write about it firsthand."

Erickson asked if I'd had an easy trip out from New York.

"Until I got here," I said. "Up in the school office they took me for an Episcopalian bishop. Not too auspicious a start."

"Let's hope that's the worst thing that happens to you," said Friday.

After a while Erickson got my assigned room number out, and Friday said that he'd go along and show me the way. We went down the dormitory corridors, which were long and dark, with clocks up on the wall at the end, and bulletin boards, and past the rows of numbered doors, most of them ajar. We could glance in and see the small cubicle-sized rooms, each with its narrow bed with a kelly-green spread that looked as rough as cowhide, the cheap teak bureau, round wooden pegs on the drawers, the mirror on top, and then the varnished desk, which would have a round hole to set an ink bottle in, and alongside, on the floor, the big green metal wastepaper basket. The dormitory smell was familiar—faintly antiseptic, perhaps of laundry bags full of bed linen, or of damp linoleum, which lined the corridor floors and squeaked underfoot. The rooms all seemed empty. Quite a few veterans had arrived—Friday said—but they'd be off playing golf probably, the coaches for sure, and as for the rookies, they were all in, about fifteen of them, most of them bunked down up on the second floor.

My room was 122, on the ground floor. I hoisted my bag up on the bed, which was hard, with enough spring to bounce the bag back up. Friday cranked open the latticed window and the afternoon breeze began to come in past the tendrils of ivy. Some mourning doves were humming in the eaves. It was pleasant enough.

"At least you got a single room," Friday said. "Most everyone's in doubles. This being a boys' school, and everything sort of undersized, you get a three-hundred-pounder for a roommate and he's not far from over*flowing* a room."

It was true about everything being undersized. The hydraulic door jacks up in the corners of the doors had thick guards of wadding attached so the ballplayers wouldn't crack their heads. They had to bend down to reach the doorknobs. The chairs were small and creaked under their weight. The washroom sinks were two or three inches lower than usual; the mirrors were also set lower, so that the sight of a row of players hunched over those sinks, almost bent double to peer at their beards while they shaved, made them appear even more gargantuan than they were.

Friday said he'd come by at dinnertime, which was six-thirty, a few hours away, and take me along to the dining hall. He closed the door after him. I turned to my suitcase and unpacked it. I took out the football. At the end of the bed I set up the pillow, dropped back to the closed door, and whipped the ball into it. But the distance was too short to be of any value for practicing—just barely six feet.

I unpacked the rest of the bag. At the bottom were the football shoes I had bought in an army-navy store in Times Square. I took off my street shoes, and after kneading the football shoes back and forth in my hands I tugged them on. They were stiff when I bought them, and wearing them in Central Park had raised a number of painful blisters. I kept wearing them to soften the leather, and also to harden my feet. When I stood up and walked around, the round cleats left marks in the brown linoleum floor, so I flopped back on the rough bedspread.

I was going to look into the high-school coach's book on basic formations. But I was tired after the trip, and I fell asleep.

CHAPTER 2

M y arrival at Cranbrook brought me closer to active participation with a professional football team than I had been in four years of intermittent trying. It had been relatively easy to arrange to play in the baseball game that resulted in *Out of My League*. But it had been

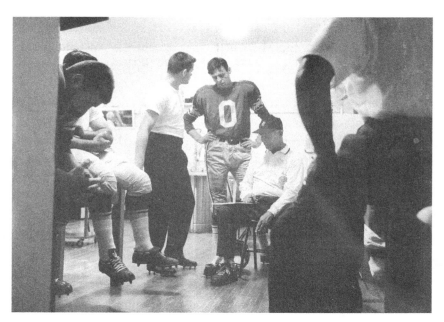

The author, number 0, prepares for a scrimmage in the Lions' locker room.
(Walter Iooss Jr.)

difficult with football—possibly, I supposed, because I could not approach the owners with quite the confidence I was able to muster when I asked to pitch. I had played a lot of baseball, but my football experience was limited. The school I went to in New York was English in character, and in the autumn, we played soccer rather than football. The "football song," which we sang lustily in school assembly, went as follows:

We do not mind
The winter's wind,
Nor weep o'er summer's bier,
Nor care a jot
If cold or hot
So long as football's here.

The other schools took us for sissies because we played soccer, and on the weekend some of us went out and played furious daylong games of tackle against them, and came home bruised and exhausted. I played end. I did not much like the clutter in the center of the line, or the physical contact, not being properly built for it, being very lean and thin, along the lines of a stick.

At prep school I kept at it for a while, playing end, but with neither the devotion nor skill to make the varsity, or even the junior varsity. At college I did other things, and the last tackle game I played in was the annual *Harvard Lampoon–Harvard Crimson* football game, in which thirty or forty people from each publication played to a side; two footballs were used, and big paper cups of beer were propped strategically around the field so a slug or two could be consumed on the fly.

My credentials as a football player may not have been of the first order. But I kept assuring myself that the purpose of my participation in professional football was not to represent the skilled performer but the average weekend athlete.

My first try was grandiose. I took a trip out to Los Angeles, to see if I could insert myself into the mid-January Pro Bowl game—the postseason spectacle which pits the best players of the Western and Eastern Conferences against each other. Red Hickey, who was the coach for the Western Conference All-Stars that year, had been described by an acquaintance of his as a most understanding coach. I was told he would surely accept my participation—it would amuse him.

With a letter of introduction I went to call on Red Hickey in his suite up in a midtown Los Angeles hotel.

"Sure," he said. "What can I do for you?"

I told him—somewhat haltingly, finding the proposal increasingly odd as I went on—that I wanted to train briefly with his team as a quarterback, never causing him any trouble, just staying on the periphery of things, and learning just enough to get by, and then trotting into the game itself in the Coliseum and calling three or four plays, just one *series,* I said, nothing much at all; then I'd be able to write about my experience and enlighten those who had wondered as a sort of daydream what would happen to them if they actually became bona fide quarterbacks playing in a pro game.

"Did I hear right?" Hickey asked. "You—with no experience— want to train and then *play*—in the Pro Bowl game?" He was incredulous.

"That's right," I said. "I wouldn't get in your way…"

"That's the damnedest thing I ever heard," he said. "Who put you up to this?"

"Well, I write for this magazine…" I began. *"Sports Illustrated."*

"They ought to know better." He stared briefly at me. "You're nuts, if you don't mind my saying."

"You mean it's impossible?" I asked. "I can't play?"

"Not a holy chance," he said. He looked nervous.

"I've come all the way out here," I said, somewhat frantically. "From *New York.*"

"A drink. You want a drink or something?" he said.

It was about three in the afternoon.

"Do you think I ought to try Buck Shaw?" Buck Shaw was the coach of the Eastern Conference team.

"Yes, yes," Hickey said. "That's the thing to do. You try Buck Shaw. Just the thing."

The interview ended. Hickey was very kind. He gave me a bench ticket for the game and I went to the practices and I met a number of his players, and sat around with them.

Whenever Hickey saw me in the hotel lobby, he'd nod his head, and once he called out, "There you are — my last-string quarterback..."

I said, "Yes, *sir*." I told him that I was ready to jump into uniform any time he changed his mind.

"Oh yes, oh yes," he said, and he drifted away. I really made him very nervous.

I never tried Buck Shaw. He was called the Gray Fox, a severe-looking man with a temper, I was told by the players, and he wouldn't go for the idea. It was too bad about him — the players said — that neither he nor Hickey would let me do it. The players thought it was a fine idea.

I kept at it. That spring I wrote to the New York Giants. I was a native New Yorker and a supporter of their club. I outlined what I hoped to do — train with them as a rookie quarterback — and after a while the front office wrote back to say that they would take my project under advisement with the coaches and see what could be done. They said that they might be interested. That gave me hope, and I began planning to set aside the end of July and August for a stay at Fairfield, Connecticut, where the Giants train. Occasionally, I called up the public-relations man at their office and he said, "Yes, there was interest — quite true," and he said that he'd let me know.

But I never heard anything, and as the summer wore on I began to worry. I called again.

"We brought it up at a meeting with the coaches," the publicity man said, "and while everybody thought the idea was just great, and there was a lot of enthusiasm *voiced,* I want you to understand, they turned down the project *flat.*"

"Oh," I said. "Well, how about all that enthusiasm?"

"The fact is," said the publicity man, "we got four quarterbacks, and the idea of a fifth hanging around—who'd have to take his turn, after all—that'd be too much for a coach to bear, I mean a guy'd be tempting a *coronary* carrying five quarterbacks on his team."

"I agree," I said truthfully. "Look," I continued, "I haven't got my heart set on being a quarterback really, I mean I'd settle for flanker back, why not? Where maybe I wouldn't cause as much confusion. Or tight end," I suggested. I was not sure what a "tight end" was, but I threw it in anyway.

"Look," said the publicity man, beginning to get an edge to his voice, "I did the best I could for you. You got to realize professional football is a serious business."

Having been refused by the Giants, I tried the other New York team—the Titans of the American Football League, then in their second year of operations. The team had not done well, either at the gate or in the league standings. Knowledgeable friends warned me that if my performance at their training camp had any flair, if I completed two or three passes, the coaches would not be likely to let me go. "Right off," I was told, "you throw some passes straight into the ground just so they won't get any ideas. You wouldn't want to hang around too long with those people."

I went to call on Harry Wismer, the wealthy sportscaster who formed the Titans and eventually went broke trying to keep them going. He ended up spending, by his own count, a million and a quarter dollars before he and the team went bust and the franchise was picked up by an entrepreneur, Sonny Werblin, who formed the New York Jets, who have done better. Wismer had troubles from the beginning, but still he was hearty enough in greeting me, and he showed me around his office, which was hung with framed photographs of himself shaking hands with mayors, athletes, and borough presidents, thin faces all smiling, but flat and two-dimensional in the photoflashes, like cardboard cutouts. He motioned me to a chair. He had on a bright-colored blazer, nearly orange it seemed to me, though there was a heavy thunderstorm going on outside and the afternoon light in his office was diffused and dim. He listened patiently to what I had in mind. As usual, the project seemed absurd as I explained it, particularly with the thunder, from time to time, accompanying it, and the heavy sluice of rain against the windowpanes. But he seemed enthusiastic enough when I had done. "Why not?" he said. "After all, what's a team without a last-string quarterback?

"You ever played much quarterback, kid?" he asked.

"No," I said.

"Well, you're going to have the best in the business out there at the camp showing you how, and of course that's . . ." The thunder came just as he was saying "Baugh," but his voice was resonant enough so that it carried through— *"Baugh!"*

"Yes," I called out. "Sammy Baugh. It's going to be a tremendous privilege."

" 'Privilege' is the word," he said. "Greatest quarterback who ever lived."

"I'm very fortunate," I said.

"Well, now," he said. The thunder murmured away. He slapped his desk with the flat of his hand and smiled broadly. It was the signal for me to leave. He told me he would check everything out with Baugh the next day—I wasn't to worry about a thing; all would be arranged. "We're glad to have you aboard," he said. He gave me a ballpoint pen with NEW YORK TITANS printed on it. I said good-bye and took the elevator down. I didn't have a raincoat with me, so I stood waiting in the doorway, watching the traffic move slowly up Park Avenue. The gutters were awash with rainwater. The temperature had dropped as the storm moved out, and it was cool and exhilarating after the heat. The project, after so long, seemed arranged, and the excitement was pleasant to savor. Behind me I heard the elevator doors sigh open. I turned, and saw Harry Wismer, coming along briskly, in a raincoat, working at the fastenings of an umbrella. As he came opposite, I said, "Hello, Mr. Wismer." I lifted a hand and smiled. He looked at me with no sign of recognition, and stepped outside. I guess he had other matters on his mind. He was an odd man: he used to say "Congratulations" to many people he met, on the grounds that they had probably done something they could be proud of.

I never saw or heard from him again, but I did get to know his secretary quite well over the phone. Her name was Rosemary. I would call up to see how progress was coming and I would say, "May I speak to Mr. Wismer, please?"

"Hello," she would say, recognizing my voice. She would apologize and say that Mr. Wismer was off somewhere, but he had me very much in mind and was going to mention the project to Sammy Baugh at the first opportunity and get the thing arranged. "He'll call you as soon as he comes in," Rosemary would say.

"Fine," I would say.

But he never did call, so every other day or so I would put in a call for him. After a while, when Rosemary answered the phone, I began to say, "Well, once again, this is the Great Arm calling…"

She would laugh pleasantly at the other end and tell me that Harry was out to lunch, or out at the training camp, or with the banks, or somewhere, and I would say that I was just checking in to get an estimate on when the Arm was going to be unleashed. . . .

"I'm sure everything will work out," she would say.

One day I telephoned and announced myself as usual: "The Great Arm calling…"

"I beg your pardon."

"The Great Arm," I said. "The Grrr…*eat* Arm! The answer to Baugh's headache…"

After a pause, the voice said, somewhat tentatively, "This is the New York Titans."

"Rosemary?"

"No, this is Miss Huron."

"I'm sorry," I said. I gave the new girl my name and asked if Mr. Wismer had any information for me.

The girl said carefully, "Of what specific nature is the information which you desire?"

"I'm supposed to be the last-string quarterback," I said. "I'm calling to find out when I'm supposed to report."

"One moment, please."

I could hear a murmur of voices in the background, and I heard someone say, "What's that... *last*-string quarterback?"

The girl's voice came on again: "We do not seem to be aware... Would you kindly spell your name, please?"

"Well... never mind," I said. I hung up. I decided I would wait for them to call me. They never did.

For a time that winter, I thought I was going to play for the Baltimore Colts. I had been introduced to Carroll Rosenbloom, the Colt owner, at a skating party the Robert F. Kennedys gave one evening at a lighted outdoor rink in Chevy Chase near Washington. A furious hockey game was going on at the time — despite a cold misty rain — a small beach ball being used as a puck, and the contending teams, about twenty to a side, including Ethel Kennedy, seven months pregnant, were equipped with brooms. I was off the ice momentarily. I have bad ankles for skating, which collapse painfully, my ankle bones just off the ice except when I am simply gliding, when I am able to keep the blades upright. I was sitting on the bench with my skates off, kneading my feet and working my toes comfortably. We had already had a relay race, carrying balloons for batons, and I had done the length of the ice and fallen, socking up against the boards, after handing the balloon on to a girl with a black babushka hat. She set sail back up the ice, moving well against her opponent, the balloon in attendance, swaying and skipping behind her, but then halfway down the rink the string slipped through her mittens and the balloon, helium filled, the size of a pumpkin, rose slowly up into the mist. The girl braked and stood, her head thrown back, watching the balloon rise; she reached up an arm with a long mitten at the end of it, and she made an utterly poignant hop, perhaps an inch or so off the ice, as if the force of her determination would soar her up to retrieve the balloon — forty feet or so in the air by then, caught in a slow wind current, and moving laterally toward the frozen tennis courts. The girls at the party were very serious competitors. Occasionally, one would skate off the rink, from the hockey, breathing with difficulty, and sit down hard on the bench and rest her forehead against her broomstick. We would talk until she got her breath back, and then she'd tug her scarf tight, and glide out on the ice toward the beach ball, with the crowd around it, flailing at it, and she would hold her broomstick in front of her warily.

Suddenly, play stopped. Someone was down on the ice, a crowd collecting around him — Ed Guthman it was, the attorney general's press secretary — and it developed he had broken his collarbone in a bad fall. It was sure to be Guthman, curiously prone to disasters of this nature: he has a short, flat, triangular nose, nearly a parody of a prizefighter's, which was pushed in years ago when he took off his catcher's mask to shout out something to his pitcher, who it happened had just completed the follow-through of a pitch that caught Guthman just as he removed his mask, *pop,* right on his nose. He was always being hit with objects, or falling off things, or into things, and when his skates went out from under him, and he gyrated slightly before his shoulder hit the ice, he had time to think *"Again"* before the bone snapped and he felt the pain. After a while he was helped to his feet, and he was propelled slowly off the ice. His face was pulled tight with pain. Beside him skated the attorney general. "All right!" he called out, as they approached the bench. "Let's hear it for Ed." We stood and applauded, with the muffled sounds of wet-soaked mittens, and the press secretary was helped past the bench into the clubhouse.

On the rink, the hockey game started up again in the rain. I began putting on my skates. Through a big plate-glass window I could see Guthman sitting in the clubhouse waiting for transportation to the hospital — holding his arm to his chest, sitting bolt upright and still to ease the pain. Rosenbloom arrived then, late for the party, hurrying into the clubhouse. A friend sitting next to me on the bench pointed him out through the window. "That's Rosenbloom of the Colts," he said. "Maybe he's a good bet for your football project." We watched him pick up his skates at the rental counter and glance uneasily at Guthman. He came outside and sat with us on the bench. We were introduced. He smiled at me briefly, then squinted out at the rink. "What the hell," he said. "That's not *curling* going on out there, is it? What are all those brooms for?"

"Hockey," we said.

"Oh," he said. "Of course, if the Kennedys went in for curling, that's the way they'd play it." He leaned forward. The flailing was going on at the other end of the rink. "Is that Ethel out there in that carnage, for God's sake?" He leaned back and nodded toward the clubhouse windows. "What happened to the guy sitting in the vestibule?"

"That's Ed Guthman," I said. "They think he's snapped his collarbone."

Rosenbloom said, "It takes a little time to get used to this. I mean I've just come from a little dinner in Georgetown — the usual thing, cocktails, pleasant light conversation, candlelight, a little brandy in the library, small room, you know, and paneled. And now..." he said with a vague gesture, "...well, *this*. And in the *rain,* what's more." He took off his shoes and put them neatly under the bench.

"Perhaps," said my friend, "an appropriate moment to tell you that George, here, wants to play for the Colts."

Rosenbloom looked at me sharply. "I'm going batty. You're not serious," he said.

I said I was, and as he worked his feet into his skates, loosening the laces, I explained once again what I wanted to do. He was attentive, despite his struggle with his skates, and when he had them on, the two of us up and moving gingerly over the duckboards toward the ice, he said, "I don't see why it can't be arranged...that is, if we survive this," he said, gesturing toward the melee, where there was considerable yelling going on. "I don't see much point in moving into that mess without a broom," he said hopefully. I thought of offering him mine, but I think he would have declined it.

So for a while I became a strong Baltimore supporter. I studied up on their players, telling people I was going to play with them, and as the spring arrived I purchased a football and threw it around the apartment, into armchairs, and occasionally down on the street with a friend, and at night, coming home, I would break into a trot, bringing the knees up high, and at other times, relaxing. I would think about what was coming, the excitement beginning to collect, until I would have to go out to an art gallery or a movie to keep my mind off it.

But the Colt people, it turned out, were just as difficult to settle anything with as Harry Wismer and his Titans, and it was more expensive, besides, having to telephone Baltimore to find out no one knew anything. Rosenbloom always seemed to be away "traveling." I wrote a few letters finally, and then one day a note from Rosenbloom came in the mail. He wrote we would have to defer the project for a year. Baltimore had a new coaching staff, headed by Don Shula, newly arrived from Detroit, and it was going to be important to keep things as simple as possible for them. Did I understand? Of course I did, I wrote back, wishing him luck for the coming season, and I stopped throwing footballs around my apartment and the broken-field running late at night in the streets. I could wait another year, I thought.

Not long after, though, I met one of the directors of the Detroit Lions. He said he'd put in a good word for me with the club officials, and he recommended that I write George Wilson, the head coach of the Lions, to see what he might say. He was encouraging. He said that there were two types of teams in the league—each reflecting the head coach's disposition. Some were primarily no-nonsense, tight, stiff organizations, which would be averse to any such idea as mine, and others, relatively few, were disposed toward something that might catch their fancy— "loose" was the word.

The Lion team was still reflecting its fame in the past as a tough roughneck outfit; that was not to say that it was undisciplined, but that it was a *player's* team, molded by such "rounders"—which was the old football term for the hell-raisers—as their quarterback Bobby Layne. Indeed, the year before, the deportment had reached the stage of public scandal: six Lions had been fined heavily by the commissioner's office, some of them two thousand dollars, for gambling. They had placed their bets, actually, on a team not their own in a postseason game — the championship game between Green Bay and New York. The league rules forbade it, in any case, and the commissioner levied the fines. For placing a series of small bets during the season, Alex Karras, their great defensive tackle, had been suspended indefinitely. These offenses had nothing to do with Wilson's tenets of coaching, my Detroit friend was hasty to point out. Paul Hornung, the Green Bay superstar, had been suspended along with Karras from a team guided by the hand of Vince Lombardi, who was tough and dictatorial.

I wrote George Wilson to see what would happen. It was much the same letter I'd sent the other clubs, telling them that I would just hang around the periphery of things and not bother anyone, just try to participate enough to get the feel of things in an atmosphere which was denied the general public, but which they wondered about.

To my surprise George Wilson wrote back and said he thought the idea was interesting. He invited me out to the training camp at the end of July for the three-week training session. He said that there would be an intra-squad game up in Pontiac in early August, a big night game that might be a possibility for my participation. Then, the first exhibition game was against the Cleveland Browns a week later. His letter was short. It ended with the hope that I was in good shape.

I looked at the letter for a time. That same day I began throwing the Spalding football around the room again, and I went out and bought the stiff-leather football shoes.

CHAPTER 3

Friday came by at six-thirty and woke me up. I swung my legs off the bed and stood up, the football shoes indenting the linoleum floor.

"I fell asleep in them," I said lamely, sitting down to change into my street shoes.

We walked across the terrace of Page Hall to the dining hall. The system there was self-service, a buffet steam table in the kitchen which we passed by with plastic trays, loading on the food, and then we walked on out to the dining hall, which was vaulted and high-ceilinged, designed like an English manor hall, with an aisle down the middle, and long tables on either side. The baronial effect was heightened by the rows of Episcopal bishops sitting at the far end of the hall. Many of them were in clerical outfits, and the roar of conversation rose from that end. An area of empty chairs and tables in the center of the hall separated them from the Lions, who were sitting up at the kitchen end, just a few of them, in T-shirts, with sloping, powerful shoulders bent over their plastic trays, most of them sitting alone.

"Rookies," said Friday. "They all sit on the right of the aisle. Veterans on the left. Segregation. Coaches can sit anywhere."

A big man in a gray business suit motioned us to join him.

"That's Gil Mains," said Friday. "He used to play a great tackle for us, until he got hurt against San Francisco. He's an insurance man now, working the area, I guess—that's why he dropped by—brought in over a million dollars' worth of policies last year."

We sat down with him. I was between them, and after we had been introduced and had chatted a while Mains leaned across and asked, "Friday, what about the rookies this year?"

"Well," said Friday, eyes shining, so one sensed a set piece of monologue coming up, "I want to tell you this is the greatest crop of rookies we've ever seen—they've sent down nothing but all-Americans."

"That's great," said Mains. "How many of them are going to stick with the team?"

"None of them, of course," said Friday. "But this is still the greatest crop of rookies ever sent along—every one an all-American, and I just don't know how our scouts continue to do it year after year.

"Hey!" said Friday, motioning at me. "You know what this guy's going to be doing in the next weeks, up in Pontiac for the first big scrimmage and on August tenth against the Cleveland Browns?"

"No, what?" Mains looked at me.

"Well, he's going to be down there on the field. Doing what do you think?"

"Head linesman," said Mains.

"Guess again."

"I don't know...maybe he's some kind of promoter or master of ceremonies?"

"Come off it!"

"What the hell," said Mains, exasperated. "Maybe he leads the bands between the halves. You mean he's actually on the field?"

"Right," said Friday.

"He's a referee."

"No," said Friday. "He's a quarterback, our quarterback, the new one, just fresh off the campus. Talk about what a great job our scouts have done—Nussbaumer and the rest of them..." He was delighted. He whacked his fork against the plastic tray.

Mains stared at me.

"It's true in a way," I said, explaining it to him. "Don't let on to the others," I said. "I'm here from a semipro team known as the Newfoundland Newfs, if anyone's curious. Don't give me away."

Friday said, "Show him that limb of yours, Gil. Show him what sort of thing can happen."

Mains reached down and rolled up his pant leg, turning in his chair awkwardly, his leg stiff, to show me.

"Take a look at this," he said.

Two long half-moon scars ran down either side of his knee, which no longer had the outlines of a kneecap, but seemed as shapeless and large in his leg as if two or three handfuls of socks had been sewn in there.

"Holy smoke," I said.

He took out a pencil and showed me on a napkin what had happened—the cartilage removed, which is not too serious, but on both sides of the knee the ligaments had been torn away (he had been blocked on the blind side during a kickoff play in San Francisco), and, since ligaments will not grow or mend, complicated grafts had to be done. He will never walk normally. It was not easy to look at his knee, much less the napkin design of what had happened to its interior.

"Maybe Gil is trying to tell you something," said Friday.

"I'll say," I said.

"It was the cleats that caught," Mains said.

"Perhaps I should wear sneakers," I said. "I can ride into town and pick some up."

"That'd be welshing on it," said Friday. "You come down to the gym tomorrow, and we'll get you outfitted."

Mains talked about his injuries. He had an unfortunate empathy with San Francisco: he had never been hurt in the slightest playing against any of the other clubs in the league; in games against the 49ers, he had fractured his jaw, an arm, a right leg, and finally his left knee had been torn on the kickoff play which put him out of football for good.

"It's hard to be out of it," he said. "I always look in on the Lions when I get the chance."

Around us, our end of the dining room was beginning to fill. A crowd of veterans came in. I recognized some of them from their pictures in the Lion fact book. Their conversation was lively. Their attention seemed concentrated on the rookies across the aisle. A finger would come up and point, as if what was in view were heads of beef. The rookies were conscious of the scrutiny; they ate sullenly, bent over their food. Suddenly, one of the veterans motioned across the aisle. "On your feet, rookie!" he was calling. "Sing!"

"What's this?" I asked Friday.

"Watch," he said. "They're calling on the rookies to sing their school songs."

A rookie, his face pale, his jaw working on a vestige of food, climbed laboriously onto his chair. He put his hand over his heart and sang in a low, embarrassed monotone.

Here are the Razorbacks, pride of old Arkansas,
Never in duty lax, ready to fight.
We have the winning team, see how our colors gleam,
Always they'll be . . . ah . . . supreme, the red and white.

No applause greeted his rendition. He climbed down from the chair, and dug a spoon, which he had clutched in his left hand while he sang, into his deep-dish apple pie.

Friday explained that the hazing—the singing of school songs mostly—was a tradition fomented originally by Bobby Layne, the Lion quarterback and team leader through the fifties. The dining room at mealtime was his special province. The rookies would rip through their meals to get out of the dining hall before he came in to eat. If he was already at the table, latecomers coming in with their trays from the buffet would peer in the swinging doors and they'd try to gauge where Layne was in his meal—whether he was just starting in, in which case they could sit down and bolt their meal, or whether he was done, and about to push back his chair, pat his belly, and look around for some fun. In that case, the rookie would slide his meal—steak, potatoes, bread, and a slice of pie, all of it—into a paper bag and go out and eat in the woods. They ate in the woods because often Layne after supper would come down the corridors and rout the rookies out for a concert on the quadrangle lawn in front of Page Hall. "We're going out to *chirp*," he would call loudly.

Rookies had to perform various stunts and chores. Wayne Walker, a big linebacker sitting opposite, overhearing us talk about Layne, leaned across and told us that in his rookie year during training camp Layne stopped him late at night in the corridor—Walker was padding down to the washroom in his pajamas to brush his teeth—and ordered him to provide him with a pizza pie. "I want a pizza pie, boy, and I want it hot and I want it fast," he said, jabbing his finger at Walker's chest for emphasis. Walker had arrived in camp the day before, and had hardly settled himself in. He had no idea where the nearest town was, or how to get there, or whether there was a pizza palace in it. But he did what he was supposed to.

"You'd turn up buffalo steaks for that guy," he said.

From their table a group of veterans were shouting across. "Friday! Friday!"

He looked up from his ice cream.

"That a rookie sitting beside you?"

Friday looked at me. "A rookie?" Friday called back. "*I'll* say. You mean you guys don't recognize your own top *draft* choice?"

"On your chair, rook," they were calling.

"Get up there," Friday whispered back.

"Christ, Friday," I whispered to him under my breath. "I don't *know* my college song. I haven't thought about it for years."

"Just squawk something. Nobody'll know the difference."

"Sing anything!" Mains said, looking at me with a big grin.

I climbed up on my chair. It was very high and precarious balanced there; I could see the bishops clustered down at the far end of the hall, one or two with their heads craned around. I put my hand over my heart and sang:

Crimson in triumph flashing
'Til that last white line is past.
er... We'll fight for the name of Harvard
'Til... that last white line is past...

fading it away at the end, since all of it had gone wrong, and I climbed down off the chair and looked into my plastic tray.

"That's the shortest damn college...not much *body* to that song," said Friday.

"They took me by surprise," I said.

No one seemed much put out. Everybody went on eating, though perhaps one or two heads came up at the name of the college, an institution with little identification with professional football. Nobody put down their forks to listen. It was apparent that the singing was secondary to the indignity to which the rookie was put; he was being embarrassed so that he would keep the rigorous caste system firmly in mind. After my inept performance, Lucien Reeberg, a big three-hundred-pound black rookie from the Bronx, was ordered up on his chair, and without any self-consciousness he boomed out the song of his alma mater—which was Hampton Institute—with great gusto, a high, tenor voice coming out of all that bulk with no hesitations as he coursed through a song full of "thee's" and "thou's" and "hail, sweet mother," etc.—but when he sat down, quite pleased, it was to the quiet clicking of cutlery against the plastic trays, no approbation at all, except from the bishops down at the far end of the hall, one or two of whom half stood and turned to hear.

Then next up was a tall, spindly fellow who was sitting alone, down at the end of his table toward the wall. He got up on his chair slowly and you could see he was in trouble. His features constricted swiftly in concentration, then relaxed, and he peered moodily down the hall at the bishops. Occasionally, his hand would drift up toward his heart, but it would drop away, and we knew the words had not come. Then a tremendous smile would burst onto his face, and die away instantly, and he would lift his melancholy face and peer into the shadows of the vaulted ceiling. We heard him say, "Oh my," and then after shifting his feet he said, *"Shee-it,"* and maneuvered himself out of the chair and sat down. But there was no complaint from the veterans at his lapse of memory. He had paid his obligation to the system simply by getting up. Friday whispered that his name was Jake Greer. He came from a small southwestern college.

Friday told me that Bobby Layne had been much tougher in his day on rookies who had difficulty remembering or performing their songs. "Hum it, man," he would have said scornfully to Greer. "Everybody quiet now. We're going to hear the rookie *hum* his school anthem."

Or he would have said: "Well, if you don't know the school song, let's have your school yell...a *yell*, please."

"You mean..." the rookie would say, "what the cheerleaders...?"

"Right."

The rookie would shift uneasily in his chair.

"Rah!" he would shout tentatively. "Rah. Rah. Rah...Rah. Rah," his eyes fixed in a mournful face, his arms jerking oddly, as if strings from the vaulted ceiling were being manipulated by an unseen puppeteer.

"Hold on," Layne would call. "What was that?"

"That was the locomotive cheer...sir."

"What?"

"That's what they call it...the loco..."

"How many rah's in that yell?"

The rookie would look at the ceiling.

"It speeds up toward the end of the cheer, but I reckon there must be, altogether, maybe *fifty* of them."

"Fifty!"

"Just about, I reckon."

"What other cheers do you have?"

"Well, we had one" — the rookie was very embarrassed — "we had one that goes:

They ain't no flies on us,
They ain't no flies on us,
There may be one or two on you,
But there ain't no flies on us.

"We heard some great yells," Friday recalled. "Thanks to Layne. I remember one that come out of Roosevelt High School in Gary, Indiana. He got some poor guy up on his chair, shouting it.

When you'se up, you'se up.
When you'se down, you'se down.
When you'se up 'gainst Roosevelt
You'se is upside down.
Hey Ray Roosevelt!

When Layne left the Lions, traded to the Pittsburgh Steelers, his hazing methods were continued, though less rigorously. When Alex Karras came onto the club, after his own rookie year, during which he barely spoke a word, he became the unofficial hazing master. But he used the dining room less as a hazing ground than as a stage to display his own theatrical tendencies. He banged the water glass for silence so he could deliver his own speeches, skits, or monologues; even a request for chocolate syrup for his ice cream, which could have been fulfilled by raising a finger to a passing waitress, was given a performance. He would rap his water glass loudly and signal out the dining-room matron. "Mrs. Page!" he would shout. "Mrs. Page, having consumed a salad, your salad, with a little shrimp in it, is it too much for me to ask, as a red-blooded American, a voter, with a wife back home, a dog lying by the hearth, a parakeet in a wire cage, is it too much for me to ask for a beaker of chocolate syrup to pour on my ice cream? Mrs. Page, give me chocolate syrup or give me death!"

"He's a great loss," Friday was saying. "It's hard to think of the dining room here at Cranbrook without him in it — doing some crazy act." He shook his head sorrowfully. "Right, Wayno?"

Wayne Walker, sitting opposite, said, "No one like him."

The desultory singing went on until all the rookies had performed, nearly fifteen of them, rising one after the other, to sing their songs with their hands over their hearts. All of them remembered. Only Jake Greer had been unable to come up with his song.

Afterward, Greer was standing out on the terrace outside the dining hall, just after supper, a toothpick working in his mouth with just the tip of it showing, and as I came up he turned away to look out over the school grounds; I grinned at him. "You had a little trouble there with your song," I said, meaning to commiserate with him.

He looked back at me, stricken, and he got himself set, and began to *sing,* having recalled his school song apparently, and taking me for a veteran. He had a very high, gentle voice, and as for the song, it too had a "thee" in it, and a "sweet mother," etc., but he did not get much of it done, because I leaned toward him, after my surprise, and said, "Oh no, not on my account!"

He stopped. "She just warn't coming to me back in there," he said in a rush. "She was at the do', just scratching to get in, but she warn't *comin'* in"—his head shaking in exasperation—"and I know my school song—my!—why we sing it every time the team wins, down there on the field, and that season y'know, we only lose once."

It was very much on his mind, so I said, "Well, I didn't do no good neither," letting the language go in some subconscious deference to his concern. "I messed up."

"You sanged?" he said, surprised. "My." His toothpick began to work. "She was sure at the do'," he said, reminiscing again about his own troubles. "But she warn't comin' in"—his head shaking again, the toothpick whisking busily.

CHAPTER 4

The evening class, the first of the training season, was scheduled for eight o'clock. I met the coaches a half hour before. Friday took me up to their dormitory common room on the second floor—a small room with a big refrigerator in one corner, some armchairs, and a card table with some open decks lying on it. George Wilson said, "Welcome to the Lions." He was a wide-shouldered, dark-haired, deeply tanned man with a voice of curious resonance—which the players said reminded them of someone speaking up through a long iron pipe. He and the other coaches had been playing golf. All of them wore golfing hats with crossed club-sticks insignia on the front. Wilson introduced me to them, as they stood there waiting, some with diagram charts under their arms, to go down for the evening class: Scooter McLean, the backfield coach, who spoke with the accents of South Boston, a slight, wiry man with a gentle, worried face who had been a mercurial runner for the Chicago Bears in Wilson's time, and had a spell, an unsuccessful one, as the Green Bay Packer head coach; then Aldo Forte, the big pleasant-faced line coach who had also played for the Bears; and Don Doll, a soft-spoken man with fading, close-cropped hair, a newcomer to the Lions that year, a former defensive backfield star for them just a few years before, who had come to take over that department from Don Shula, an enormously popular assistant coach who had gone to the Baltimore Colts as their head coach; Bob Nussbaumer, who coached the offensive ends and flankers, and was nicknamed "the Hawk" for a bird-of-prey profile and a manner which was imperious and quick. Finally there was Les Bingaman, who coached the big interior defensive linemen; he was huge himself in shapeless purple trousers, his shoulders rounded and enormous, supporting a chubby small boy's face with blue eyes in it, and slicked with sandy-colored hair. I shook hands with all of them.

Wilson said, "Well, I hope you have an interesting time with us. We'll try to help you as best we can."

But almost immediately there was a problem. I went down across the quadrangle for the first class. Wilson saw me standing at the classroom door, which faced outside onto a courtyard with a fountain in the middle, and he came over and said, "Hold on now. You can't go in there. That's closed to the press."

I looked at him blankly.

"What is this?" he asked.

"Well, I wanted to do this," I said. "Stick with the rookies throughout, the classes, the scrimmages, all of it . . . just as if I were one of them."

I spoke very rapidly. Once more, it seemed I was going to be barred. But Wilson then saw exactly what I wanted to do—I think the first time he'd really put his mind to it. I could sense him turning it over—how much my activities might be a diversion to his objectives. The coaches crowded around him, at the door.

"All right," he said abruptly. "But you get too much on anyone's nerves, and you go home."

I said that I understood. I went to the back of the classroom and sat down. Not many of the players had noticed the confusion at the door. The playbooks were being handed out and they were looking into them.

A roll call was read. At the end of it Aldo Forte asked if anyone's name had been left off. I said nothing, and I saw George Wilson standing at the side of the classroom grinning. He picked up two playbooks and brought them over.

"If you're going to do this right," he said, "you'd better have these."

The two books were heavy, stiff-covered loose-leaf notebooks — one for the offensive team, the other for the defensive. Each had index tabs listing such categories as screens, goal line, double wings, and, in the back, blank pages for diagramming plays. The plays were drawn on the blackboard or thrown up on a screen by a projector for the players to copy down — the theory being that the assignments on a given play could be more formidably ingrained by having the player draw them into his own textbook.

I read in them a bit, keeping half an ear on Aldo Forte and Scooter McLean, who had lists to go through and announcements to make. The book for the offense was arranged by topics in the order of importance. Its first page led off with the heading "Two Minutes," and a first paragraph which read: "Probably the most important part of a ball game is two minutes to go in either half. It is not only imperative for the team captain to know when time is out, and whether the clock starts with the snap or with the Referee's whistle, but for each individual also. Time-outs must be saved for these periods. A team that can handle itself through this period without confusion and frustration will be the champion."

A list of important points to remember about those two minutes followed — such as "After the fourth time-out, clock starts with Referee's whistle."

I turned the pages to find that next in line of importance was the category "Third Down Situation." The text began: "The ability of a team to succeed on third down (either offensively or defensively) is the key to winning football. . . . The good clubs in the league today are the ones who excel on third down situations."

The third category of importance ran under the heading "Severe Penalties and Their Avoidance." First on the list was "Running into Kicker." The text warned: "A foul is often called if you just touch the kicker. This penalty is unpardonable." Also high on the list was "off-side or holding on 4th down kicks," about which the text commenced coldly: "There is no excuse for this foul."

Other than an index of "basic terminology" there was not much else in the offense book. The rest of the pages were blank for diagramming plays. A young football fan coming across one of these books by chance would be disappointed — finding a few admonitions that are impressed on every high-school player, and not much else. Obviously, the book increased in content and value as the players diagrammed their plays. I learned that three or four were taught at each evening class, so that by the time the training season was over almost a hundred plays would be drawn into the book. Naturally, the penalty for losing a playbook was high — with some clubs as much as a three-hundred-dollar fine. The players kept close tabs on them, and they were urged to browse through them at every opportunity to learn not only their own assignments on a given play, but also their teammates', so that they had a more complete picture of a play's operation. The books were as much an organizational symbol as the Lion decal that the regulars wore on their team blazers. When a player was cut from the squad, the coaches reached for his playbook.

The defensive book was more interesting. Besides the usual admonitions about penalties, and the importance of the third down, and playing superior football for the last two minutes of each half, the book included page after page of statistics, graphs, and charts, and a long section showing assignments for individual players against specific offensive plays. The young football fan might not have understood much of what was in it, but it would have suited his confidence that professional football is a complex and heady business. Furthermore, it seemed to be written with a zest missing in the offense book — perhaps indicative of Detroit's great tradition of defense. The defense had always received the adulation of the Detroit fans — Les Bingaman in his day, then the defensive backs known as Chris's Crew (headed by the linebacker Jack Christiansen) in the early fifties, and then Joe Schmidt up through the mid-sixties with the assistance of such as Roger Brown, Alex Karras, Night Train Lane, Yale Lary, and the others. When Tobin Rote passed the team brilliantly to a championship in 1957, it was still the defense which held the fans' fancy: they swarmed on the field and carried off Joe Schmidt and the other mainstays of the defensive unit. Two or three of them went for Rote, but not enough, so that he sagged awkwardly off their shoulders.

I spent some time looking through the section on terminology, knowing that I'd hear some of the words down on the field and in the classroom as time went on — "Brown" (an offensive designation which means that the fullback blocks to the weak side), "Slotback" (any back who is set inside a spread end), "Crackback" (flanker back blocks back on the linebacker), "Slow" (off-side end blocks on passes) — all these terms used on the offense. As for the defensive terms, the two that caught my fancy were "port" and "star," which are designations of defensive areas, left and right — the terms derived, obviously, if curiously, from the nautical port and starboard.

The main defenses were listed as red (which was man-to-man on the potential pass receivers), blue (which was a zone defense), a 4-2, a 4-3, and what was called a green 5-1. There were others, but these were the basic defenses — all of which entailed different responsibilities for the defensive personnel. For example, the instructions in the playbook for the left linebacker on blue coverage read as follows: "Delay the end — don't permit inside release unless there is a close flare to your side. You are responsible for strong side turn zone. Get to your area fast, 10–12 yards deep. Look into quarterback's eyes."

The middle linebacker had the following responsibilities: "Strong side hook zone. Responsible for any close flare or 'T' flare — flow away — favor your weak side — be alert for strong side end crossing. With roll-out or run-pass, replace your strong side linebacker. If rushing the passer, 'red-dogging,' call 'Jumbo!' to your tackles to let them know you are gone, and they will drive and pinch the middle."

The reading, what little of it I could understand, made me feel somewhat uncomfortable — the knowledge that in a few days the linebackers would be jumping around behind their linemen trying to look into my eyes to see if I was going to tip my plays. I was not at ease about such phrases as "pinch the middle" and about the linebacker's cry "Jumbo!" —

to signify, apparently, that the red dog was on—the linebacker's bulling rush toward the quarterback.

"How are you coming?" It was George Wilson hanging over the back of my chair.

"Just great," I heard my voice saying to him. "I'm so damn appreciative." I pointed at the phrase which instructed the linebackers to look into the quarterback's eyes. "They won't be learning anything from me," I said. "They'll be shut tight."

Wilson grinned.

"We break the team into groups now," Wilson said. "After the team announcements. You can stick with anyone you want—go with the defense if you'd like, down the hall, or stick here with the offense. I'd take a few plays down in your book, just like everyone else, and down on the field we'll work out the plays you can do best. We've got a big scrimmage coming up in Pontiac, and you'll want to be set for it."

Thereafter, I stuck with the offense most of the time, which Nussbaumer, Forte, and McLean taught, though from time to time I went off to listen to the other components for a while—to Don Doll with the defensive backs, drawing his fastidious, absolutely precise diagrams on the board. Behind him was Night Train Lane, a fervid kibitzer, tilting forward on his chair legs to raise a hand and offer a comment: "Co'ah, co'ah...the way Ah see it, the angle come..." Down the hall a few doors was Les Bingaman, the chalk snapping off in his hand as he scribbled the quick big circles and arrows of his diagrams; the big linemen, with a haunch or two slid out of the schoolboy chairs, bent over their books, filling in the play. It was such an odd equation to make, and one I never adjusted to, between the classroom work, the scratch of chalk and pencils on those near-somnambulant summer evenings with the sound of the fountains outside, and the ticking of water sprinklers—between that and what the symbols on the blackboard actually stood for—that an arrow on a blackboard between two mild-looking circles depicting a halfback's line of direction actually entailed, in effect, the twisting frantic rush of a back between the heft and surge of three-hundred-pound linemen.

At the first session for the offensive team Aldo Forte said he wanted to give a brief outline of how the offense play numbers and signals worked.

"The system we use is very simple," Forte said. He drew seven circles on a line across the board. "There's your front line," he said. "The holes between the linemen are numbered from the left, starting out beyond left end, eight-six-four-two-one over the center, then three-five-seven and nine out along the right to beyond the right end. Your backs are numbered one, two, three and four." He drew a circle for the T-formation quarterback (1) just behind the circle designating the team's center, and then split diagonally behind the quarterback he drew two circles for the backs (2) and (4). "The number three back is the flanker," he said. "The flanker is positioned either out at the eight hole on the left, or he's flanked out at the nine hole on the right. The first number of the quarterback's call in the huddle tells the three back where to go. 'Three left' means he positions left, 'three right' to the right. Got that?"

Forte's procedure was to pepper his instruction with questions and to ask for assurances that the class understood him. "Right?" he would ask, looking from face to face, and then once assured he'd say, "Right," and turn back to his blackboard.

"Now the next number that the quarterback calls in the huddle tells who's going to get the ball from him and where he's going to go with it. If he says 'Twenty-three' "—he wrote down 23 on the board—"it means that the two back will take a handoff and run straight forward into the three hole just to the right of center—" he tapped the spot with his chalk—"a straight-ahead power play." He drew an arrow to mark the direction of the three back. "There it is," he said. "One of the oldest plays in football. Once again: the quarterback calls it in the huddle by saying 'Three right' (which positions the flanker), 'twenty-three' (who's going to carry the ball and where), he gives the hike signal, 'on two,' let's say, and then he calls 'Break!' and here in Detroit we have the players give a sharp clap of the hands—in unison—to bring everyone smartly up to the line.

"Now," said Forte. "Sometimes the play the quarterback calls will include information for the linemen on their blocking assignments. Our off-tackle run to the right side, for example, is called as follows: 'Three right, forty-seven, *near oh pinch*.' Those last three words indicate to the offensive tackle and end that they double-team and block on the defensive end, which will clear the seven hole for the four back to get through.

"Now as for passing—all pass plays are indicated by the word 'green.' The quarterback says: 'Three right (or left)'—for his flanker—then 'green,' and then he gives the action for his primary receiver: 'nine turn,' for example, which means that the right end goes through the nine hole, downfield, and turns...buttonhooks. Clear? Right.

"I'm giving this to you very sketchily," Forte said. "Very sketchily. So you get the idea. Right? OK. *Now.* How does the quarterback call the signals up on the line? First of all, he starts his call with a sequence of three numbers, meaningless numbers—eighty-eight, twenty-one, sixty-six, they could be. This sequence doesn't mean anything *unless*"—Forte pointed his chalk at us—"the quarterback doesn't like the defensive alignment against the play he's called in the huddle, and he decides to check it off, call an audible. To do this, he uses the same number of the play he called in the huddle to begin the sequence. That is, if he's checking off a 'twenty-three roll,' for example, the first number he calls is 'twenty-three.' That checks off the play. He's got to call it out clear so everyone knows...all the way out to the flanker. The next number he calls is the *new* play—'forty-two,' for example, which will take the ball to the other side of the center. He calls out one more number, which doesn't indicate anything, just any old number, and then he begins the count. Here at Detroit we use a rhythm cadence: *hut*-one *hut*-two *hut*-three *hut*-four—very snappy—and if the hike signal is three, everybody shoves off on the *hut* just before three—'bam!'"—Forte drove his fist into his palm—"giving us just that little extra rush and drive..."

With the different teams the signals varied. At Cleveland, when Paul

39

Brown was there, the quarterback called, "Ready, set, let's go, one, two, three…" The year after I was with Detroit, the Lions changed the count to what was called a "staggered" sequence—an innovation which became popular throughout the league. "Go" was the operative word. If the quarterback said "on four" in the huddle, the center would hike the ball the fourth time he heard the word "go." The quarterback was not harnessed to a rhythm in his call. He could call "Go!" wait a few seconds, then "Go-go"—as if calling off the names of the discotheques that were springing up at the time—then wait until he felt just right before his fourth "Go!" and the clap of the ball back into his palm. The advantage of the staggered count was that the quarterback could get the ball when it was most advantageous to him. If one of the opposition jumped offside, he could rip off his "go's" to get the ball and catch him for a penalty before he could hop back across the line. Equivalently, if he was faced with a shifting defense he could wait until it moved into a compromised position, then get to his last "go" and unleash the play at the most propitious moment. The disadvantage of the staggered count was that it denied the linemen and backs the split second of motion they could get on the opposition with the rhythm count when they knew exactly when the hike was coming and could pop off their stance at the *hut* of whatever the hike number was. With the staggered count the offense, with the exception of the quarterback, was as much in the dark as to when to shove off as the defense.

George Wilson came by again.

"How are you getting along?" he asked. "Getting the plays down?"

"It's not easy," I said. "I think I'll steer clear of the audibles."

He said, "It'll all be clearer down on the field. You got anything to wear down there?"

"I have a sweatshirt," I said. "And some socks and all."

He said, "Friday'll fix you up tomorrow morning. You get yourself over to the gym early and he'll outfit you."

Later, when the classes were over, I saw him motion to Friday and start talking to him, nodding over at me. I was beginning to feel a part of things.

But the most gratifying sense of being attached came when my name was installed on the roll call which was read at the beginning of each class. My name was inserted after that of the big fullback Nick Pietrosante.

"Yo," he said when the coaches called his name, and then mine came.

"Here," I said, just right, matter-of-factly, absolutely perfectly, as if it was nothing at all to be there.

CHAPTER 5

The next morning, just after breakfast, I walked over to the gymnasium to get outfitted. Practice was called for ten o'clock. Friday was there, in the locker room, and he took me in hand. I had my own equipment with me—the shoes from the army-navy store, the sweat suit, the socks, the rest of it—in case any of it could be used—and Friday took a look and said, "Well, you can take that stuff and dump it somewhere. You come with me."

We went down a corridor to the basketball court, passing under a framed life-sized color photograph of Pete Dawkins, the Army halfback, who went on as a Rhodes scholar to play rugby in Oxford—Cranbrook's most illustrious graduate, the color in the photograph fading and the surface badly scratched, his face patched with color like a circus clown's.

Friday had the equipment laid out in separate piles on the gymnasium floor—shoulder pads, knee pads, thigh pads, belts, helmets, shoelaces, and so forth, and we went from one pile to another, Friday as officious as Mole in *The Wind in the Willows,* putting together an outfit. There were over a dozen separate items. "Now these shoulder pads," Friday said, "used to belong to Doak Walker. Here, you slip them on *this* way."

"I see," I said. I strung myself into them.

"Lift up your arms, like you're throwing the ball."

The pads, smaller and lighter than a lineman's, seemed to restrict movement somewhat, in fact extensively, but Friday seemed satisfied. "Of course," he said, "I've not got anything here that's going to be of much use to you, since what you need is a suit of armor. I haven't got none of those around."

"Of course not," I said.

He handed me an elasticized padded garment he referred to as a "wraparound girdle"—"to protect the hips." I looked at it speculatively, not sure how to get into it.

"Don't mind being confused about the equipment," Friday said. "Let me tell you, a few years back, some rich Detroit bozo sent his son here to try out with the Lions. He arranged it somehow. The poor fellow wasn't worth much, missed it in every profession he tried, ten or a dozen of them since getting out of school, so his father thought he'd try him at *football,* for Chrissake, starting him out at the *top,* one might say, getting him in here with the pros. Well, this poor fat fellow—he'd've weighed three hundred pound, easy—didn't know from nothing, couldn't catch the ball, hardly *throw* it, and as for his weight, he didn't know how to use it: they pushed him around like he was on rollers.

"When the first scrimmage came up, this fellow put on the same sort wraparound girdle you got there, but he thought this back part here which covers the base of the spine"—Friday pointed out a reinforced section of the equipment—"was supposed to cover his *john,* for Chrissakes, so he got the thing on backwards, for Chrissakes, and the guy must have been in *agony* down there on the field, moving around like a sort of spastic ape."

I was grateful for Friday's story. I was confused by the girdle, and I might easily have put it on the way the young three-hundred-pounder tried it, which he probably sensed.

"What happened to him, Friday?" I asked.

"He got shoved around something fierce. Of course, the team dropped him. A big, confused fellow. Hated football and couldn't take it. I suppose he went home and said, 'Well, Dad, I didn't make it, y'know, failed *again,*' and I suppose his father looked at him hard and then crossed 'football' off some crazy master list he kept of professions he wanted his son to try."

We finished the outfitting, and Friday led me back up to the locker room, my arms weighed down with paraphernalia so I could barely see over the top, on which was the hard silver helmet with the decal of the blue lion.

The author, helmet in place, observes the game keenly from the bench. *(Walter Iooss Jr.)*

From the beginning I had trouble getting into the helmet. The procedure was to stick the thumbs in the helmet's ear holes and stretch the helmet out as it came down over the head, a matter of lateral pull, easy enough if you practiced isometrics, but I never had the strength to get my ears quite clear, so they were bent double inside the helmet once it was on. I would work a finger up inside to get the ears upright again, a painful procedure and noisy, the sounds sharp in the confines of the hard shell of the helmet as I twisted and murmured, until it was done, the ears ringing softly, quiet then in the helmet, secure as being in a turret. Then I would look out beyond the bars of the nose guard—the "cage" the players call it—to see what was going on outside, my eyes still watering slightly. It was more difficult to get the helmet off. The first helmet Friday Macklem gave me was too small—a helmet was supposed to fit snugly to afford the best protection—and when I tried it on in front of my locker I yelled as it came over my ears. Wayne Walker, the big linebacker, happened to be chatting with me at the time. He was one of the few players who knew of my amateur status. He had read my baseball book and remembered my name.

"How's she feel?"

"Feels fine. Snug," I replied. "Once you get the thing on."

I tried to take it off. I got my thumbs in the ear holes and tried to budge the helmet loose.

"I'm stuck in here," I said simply.

Walked began to grin. He looked down the locker-room aisle for other players who would have enjoyed the dilemma. Mercifully, none were on hand.

"*Damn!*" I said. "I can't budge this thing."

"You'll get used to it," said Walker.

"Gee*zus!*" I was really straining to get it off.

"You're truly married to pro football," said Walker. "After a while you'll never know that you got it on."

The helmet came away finally, leaving my ears inflamed and raw, the side of my head furrowed. "Enough to make me quit the game," I said.

No contact work was planned the first day. I put on the blue shorts, a T-shirt, white socks, and the football shoes Friday had given me, which were worn and comfortable. I followed the other players out the back of the gym down to the practice field—down through a small pine grove, past the school tennis courts, on which, even at that early hour, a pretty girl in shorts was banging a ball up against a backstop. She stopped briefly to watch our group go by through the pines.

The practice fields were vast, four or five football fields separated by rows of tall, widely spaced trees. Off in the distance were a pair of baseball backstops, for softball perhaps, since no base paths marred the long expanse of green. A few distant sprinklers were working, throwing up long enormous curves of water as they turned.

We were early. A number of players were lying around on the grass. Most of them were rookies, but there were some veterans, who were the ones talking easily. It was peaceful, the earth still cool from the night dew. There was gossip about players, always the name linked with a height and a weight ("This guy, Logan Fox, oh he'll go six feet five, run maybe two thirty-four, well against Boston College this time, he..."), and often his speed ("...does the hundred in nine oh three"), and they talked about coaches, and how tough they were, and with calisthenics coming up in a half hour or so, the rookies wondered what the Detroit exercises would be. At Chicago, one of them said, running through the grillwork of ropes, which was one of the standard exercises they had in all the camps, was easy because big Doug Atkins would step on the ropes going through and press them down to within an inch or so of the ground. They stayed down there too. No spring left in them after *that* guy stepped on them. That's what he had heard.

"What's he weigh?" someone wanted to know.

"Atkins? 'Bout two seven oh. He's six eight. Big as six barns."

The footballs arrived. One of the centers brought them down in a blue sack and spilled them out on the grass. Some of the players got up and began tossing them back and forth, limbering up. I noticed that the big linemen could hardly throw the ball: their arms seemed stiff, hinged like thick poles to the bulge of muscles along the backs of their shoulders. They threw the ball in an overhand lob motion—like tossing a grenade. They didn't catch the ball particularly well, either, which made my spirits rise. The ball would drop and bounce. But their hands were enormous. They picked up the ball with one hand and it seemed to fit in the palm.

When the quarterbacks and halfbacks started throwing the ball, it was another matter—the footballs traveling on a line and with distance. I went and stood alongside Earl Morrall, the second-line quarterback. He had a close-cropped haircut and a friendly face, and he kept up a lively chatter. He was one of the two quarterbacks the Lions had, his reputation that of being a superb "reliever" for Milt Plum, who was the first-line quarterback. Plum stood opposite—fifteen yards downfield, tall, his dark hair neatly groomed above a face that shone with a pale, curiously high-polished skin that did not seem to weather. Next to him, John Gonzaga, an offensive guard, was grizzled by comparison. He was a veteran to whom I had introduced myself that morning. He had the locker next to mine. Even at that distance, alongside Plum, I could see his arm tattoo, which was a large quizzical-looking cartoon-character duck on his biceps, and underneath in dark blue letters against his skin the question WHO ME?

When I played baseball in my stint in Yankee Stadium I had difficulty getting anyone to warm up with. Not recognizing me, the players took me for a batboy, I had assumed, and they wouldn't throw the ball to me though I stood in beside them, waiting, tapping my glove speculatively. So I found a batboy and warmed up with him. The football players had no such compunction. They saw me in the team practice togs, and assumed I was one of them. Plum threw me the ball immediately—the nose slightly down as it came, and its spiral perfect so that it seemed to slip through the air and was at my hands and almost through my fingers to my chest before I had time to react. And yet his motion, directly overhead, was as nonchalant as if he had been waving at someone across the street.

There was no mistaking a professional quarterback's throw—one had the sense, seeing it come, of a projectile rather than a football. I found it nearly impossible to imitate with my own throws. The grips varied, and there was no standard hold that could produce those perfect hard spirals. Otto Graham, the great Cleveland quarterback, threw the ball with his thumb on the laces. Plum held the ball much further toward the end than Morrall. Both of them at different stages of the training showed me their grips, and the arc of the arm in the throw, but they agreed one had to work out one's own style. The object was to get the ball to the receiver; there were great quarterbacks who rarely threw the classic pass: Bobby Layne's passes invariably wobbled, and Frankie Albert, the 49er quarterback, had been known to throw the ball end over end to his receiver. Still, it was galling not to be able to do it correctly. Sometimes the ball would leap off the fingertips — I had done it right — and the receiver would nod his head. But the next time something would go wrong, and sometimes the players watching would call "quack-quack-quack!" to bring attention to its fluttery flight.

I made my first mistake as a rookie after Plum threw me the ball — not two minutes having gone by of my physical participation. I caught the ball and looked for Gonzaga, next to Plum, to throw to; someone had called his name, and he had turned away. So I threw the ball back to Plum. I pegged it pretty hard. Plum looked startled, but he caught it. Morrall, alongside me, looked over and said: "Up here we don't throw to a quarterback like that. Throw it to the other guy. He'll shovel it to the quarterback. Or if you *do* throw it to the quarterback, toss it underhand."

He said it perfectly kindly. I had learned my first lesson. The precaution was against anything happening to the quarterback, even a jammed finger from catching a ball. His person was inviolate — a coddled piece of equipment that was not subjected as much to the physical wear of the training. If a quarterback was brought down in a scrimmage, the coaches would call, "Go easy, go easy..." When Clark Shaughnessy was installing his new T formation at Stanford, he was so nervous he might lose Frankie Albert through injury that involuntarily he would blow his whistle just before the start of a play in the practice scrimmages.

While the limbering up was going on, and about fifteen minutes before the coaches' whistles blew for the calisthenics, the kicking teams began to practice—Wayne Walker and Jim Martin alternating at field-goal attempts, starting at the twenty-five-yard line and moving the ball back from the goalposts five yards at a time until they were trying fifty- and fifty-five-yard kicks from their own territory.

Over by the sidelines Yale Lary and Pat Studstill practiced their punting. I went over and watched. I never tired of it—standing downfield from them and watching the ball arch up to the height of the tall rows of elms and sycamores bordering the football fields. The kicker's foot seemed to impart a liveliness to the ball so that it bore up to a height where the properties of the ball itself seemed to change—it seemed a toy against the sky, a feather-light object about the size of a baseball hanging almost motionless, far up, at the apex of its trajectory. I would be sixty or so yards downfield to retrieve, waiting with Tommy Watkins, who did the punt returns in the games, and he would say, "OK, you take it," and I would look up, almost straight up, and the football would begin to reestablish its properties—growing abruptly larger in its vertical drop as I tottered around under it, and then with the faint whew-whew-whew of its laces turning it would be on me, as large and heavy as a dead goose knocked from the sky, so that as I hauled it in to my chest I would let out an involuntary grunt.

Watkins himself seemed to do it with the ease of a shortstop handling an easy pop fly. But as I watched the ball sail down to him from those elm-high heights I would shake my head, thinking that however easy it was for him to catch the ball, the feat was tempered by the thought of the big linemen coming down and reaching for him. "In a game..." I said.

Watkins once told me: "You think of the ball *first*, and *then* what's coming for you down the field. Reverse the order, and you've got yourself a fumble, sure'n shooting."

Occasionally, I would stand upfield next to Yale Lary and watch him swing his leg into the ball and sail it up on those long flights. There was nothing about his kicking leg to distinguish it. Lary was wiry, built like a European soccer player, though perhaps a bit heavier—180 pounds. He was very fast, and played defensive safety in addition to his kicking. Size seemed to have little to do with kicking ability. Bobby Green, the Cardinal kicker, Lary's closest rival the previous year, weighed only 150 pounds. Lary's skill had come naturally. In junior high school when he was about eleven he outkicked everyone — the ability was always there, and it was a question of tuning it up: like speed or like the quarterback's arm, he said; it's natural, and it can be improved, if only to a certain degree. He practiced in the street outside his house. The streetlights would go on, and he would punt the ball up through the cover of darkness, gone, and then forty or fifty yards down the street it would suddenly reenter the streetlights' glow, startlingly white, and bounce erratically on the macadam and rock to a rest. He would stroll down the street, stepping off the yards to check his progress, to retrieve the ball and kick it back up into the night sky toward his front gate.

He wore out footballs, practicing; the bladder would protrude and be stuffed back in and a patch put on, but it would pop finally. For a long time, he remembered, he owned a yellow ball the color of a lemon which had the staying power of a cement block. It lasted a couple of seasons. The nose of the football disintegrated first, since a perfectly kicked ball has about the same trajectory as a howitzer shell — that is to say a long climb to the apogee and then a steep vertical drop in which the nose is pointed straight down, indeed is pointed slightly back toward the kicker so that the ball when it lands will cartwheel rapidly downfield and add to the kick's length. Lary averaged forty-six or forty-seven yards a kick during a season (the lengths of the kick measured from the line of scrimmage, of course), which is usually the best in the league. Sammy Baugh of the Redskins had the annual record, fifty-one yards, but as a tailback he did some quick-kicking, which catches the defenses in tight against the line and allows the ball to roll unencumbered. He had a number of these the year he won his record kicking championship. Lary's longest kick was a seventy-four-yarder against Cleveland in 1953. Desperation may have added a dozen yards or so on that punt — the snap from center was a poor one which bounced well in front of him, and he had to rush to field it: he was only just able to fly the ball up over the fingertips of the incoming linemen.

It was always frustrating to watch the ball soar into the air from Lary's foot, and then try to do it oneself—which suddenly imbued the ball with a lead center, replacing the life that was in it; it was like punting a large dead bird in comparison. I envied the kicker's skill. It seemed so simple. Milt Plum once told me about a Bunyanesque character who had turned up at a Cleveland practice when he was with that team. He was very young, spindly, with a happy-go-lucky high-school face working hard at a stick of gum, and afterward no one was sure whether he'd been sent by a scout or had just stepped out from the spectators lining the practice field. The calisthenics had not yet started. The players were spread across the field tossing footballs back and forth, and the field-goal units were practicing. A football rolled near this fellow. He picked it up and looked at it speculatively, twisted it slightly to get the laces right, a look of schoolboy concentration caught at his face, and he stepped forward and kicked a long, high spiral which came down, the football's nose over in the perpendicular drop of the perfect kick, seventy yards away. A ball coming off the kicker's foot correctly makes a sharp though thumping, gourdlike sound that, reverberating, seems to hang in the air. Hearing that, the players standing nearby could turn in time to see the ball soar up, for a cataleptic instant a part of height and air, before its nose turned over and its trajectory became vertical.

"Jesus," someone said.

Another ball was tossed to him, which he turned over, inspecting it as if it were an object he had not seen before; he worked his gum furiously, and then with simple ease he lofted up another punt, quite similar to his first—the same hollow *thonk* of sound, the ball poised against the sky before the nose went down and it dropped straight. The coaches came and stood around.

"Well, what happened then?" I asked.

"I never saw such kicking," Plum said. "I don't remember whether the guy had kicking shoes, maybe a pair of sneakers, whatever he had on when he walked out to practice. I don't think there was one of the punts less than sixty yards."

"Was he signed up?" I asked. "What became of him?"

"That one time was all I saw of him," Plum said. "There must have been some technicality. He might have been in college, y'know, which made him ineligible. Our coaches must have kept an eye on him, praying he'd come to them when he got his degree. He may never have gotten one—he was a goofy sort of guy—and maybe the Army got him afterwards, or maybe kicking a football bored him finally. My, he could kick a football," Plum said, shaking his head, thinking back to that summer afternoon.

At ten o'clock the coaches arrived, coming across the field in a group, most of them carrying clipboards. All of us—almost sixty men— gathered around while Nussbaumer, the Hawk, checked a roll call. He announced that anyone straggling down late through the pines from the gym would be fined. He then divided the group into five sections— the defensive linemen, the defensive backs, the offensive linemen, the flankers and ends, and the quarterbacks and backs. The centers stayed with the latter group—the quarterbacks and backs—and so did I.

First, the coaches sent off each section at a time up the length of the field twice and back to limber up—two hundred yards at a fast dogtrot that didn't seem to bother anyone. I didn't mind it. Many of the players carried on conversations as they ran—regulars who had just arrived the night before being filled in on camp talk.

The squad then circled Nussbaumer, who directed the calisthenics. The exercises were easier than I had thought they were going to be. They started with simple stretching exercises—hands on hips and swaying from side to side ten times, that was all, then touching the toes perhaps ten times, which was followed by a stretching exercise for the muscles of the calves. Everybody flopped to the ground then, on their backs, and the stretching exercises continued: hauling the knees up, first one, then the other, then both, to the chin. A bicycling leg exercise came next, followed by a tougher drill, which was to stiffen the leg and touch with one toe, then the other, the ground behind the head; one had to rear back on one's shoulders to do so. That exercise was not easy, and neither was the next, which was to turn over on the stomach and, arching the back, rock up and down on the stomach, from head to foot, like the curve of a rocking-chair leg—an exercise that was supposed to strengthen the stomach muscles. The exercise was easy for the big men, who could rock on their ample stomachs like inflated beach-toy sea horses. But the receivers and defensive backs, the thinner men, would groan and carry on as they tried, complaining, the spectators already collecting along the sidelines gawking and pointing, until Nussbaumer would order a few push-ups. Then he'd leap up and lead everyone in quick jumping-jack exercises, everyone shouting the cadences because the exercise was the last of the morning, and it was a relief to be done with them.

The squad then headed for the "ropes"—a long grid of roped squares, raised about a foot off the ground—the exercise course that they had spoken earlier of Atkins having lowered—and we ran through it a number of times, the coaches urging us on. Here, the heavier men, Roger Brown and Lucien Reeberg, the three-hundred-pounders, had a more difficult time, having to hoist their bodies through the course in a series of quick little jumps. Their speed along the ground—that is, running flat out—was awesomely impressive, but the grid squares held them up and made them pick up their feet and hop, which they did cumbersomely and slowly.

The grid course was the last of the conditioning exercises—only about twenty minutes of them altogether—and the squad would then separate into its component parts: the offensive backs and quarterbacks stayed with Scooter McLean; the defensive backs moved to an adjacent field with Don Doll; the offensive linemen went down to the blocking machines with Aldo Forte; and the defensive linemen headed to an area where they immediately started contact work—what were called "nutcracker" workouts—and the distant thump of men colliding would drift up from their drills.

As the morning wore on, the various units would begin to gather together: the flankers and ends would trot over with the Hawk and join the quarterbacks and backs, and together they would run through play patterns. Then the offensive linemen would appear, which would

Running the ropes. In front of George is Jim Martin, a utility man of great value who could fill in at a number of positions and was a top-rate field goal kicker. *(Walter Iooss Jr.)*

complete the offensive unit. On the adjacent field the defensive people would be similarly forming, and when its components were together and it had drilled for a while as a unit, it would come across to join the offense, running in a big bunch, and the offense, seeing them come, would float down a few derisive moos and beef-cattle sounds in appreciation of their heft, and the entire squad would be together.

The sun was high then. It was about eleven-thirty in the morning. The players would pass the white translucent plastic water bottles among them, and the spectators, thick along the sidelines, stood under the big shade trees. The last half hour or so, with the squad together, was used for scrimmaging, or if there was no contact work, which was the procedure for the first few days, the team ran through its plays — the ones we had learned the night before in class — the players moving into both offensive and defensive positions in relays. Morning practice was over at noon. The afternoon practice, which followed exactly the same procedures and timetable, began at two-thirty and ran for two hours.

During the practices I stayed with Scooter McLean and the offensive backfield most of the time, sticking close behind the two quarterbacks. McLean would motion them over to say, "Now, you quarterbacks… I want to make sure…" and he would make sharp, quick motions with his hands to show them the line of the play he was describing. I sidled along behind. My distance from the two quarterbacks was about that of the best man from the bridegroom at a church wedding — a discreet distance — but I was close enough to keep an ear on the instruction.

CHAPTER 6

I had come to Cranbrook hoping vaguely to maintain anonymity and be thought of as a rookie, and treated as one. I knew my pretense would break down, but to start I had a mild fiction prepared for those who asked where I'd played ball. I was to say that I had played for some years in an obscure east Canadian semipro league for a team called the Newfoundland Newfs. The team had always finished in the league cellar, but I'd had ten years of experience with the Newfs. It had been suggested that if I made a horrible mistake at Cranbrook — that if I fell down, or ran the wrong way, or threw a pass end over end rather than in a spiral, or kicked the ball over my head — I was to cry out loudly, "Well, *that's* the way we used to do it with the Newfoundland Newfs!"

I never had the temerity to pretend I was something that I wasn't. The team caught on quickly enough: Wayne Walker had read my baseball book, and I suppose he talked about it to the others. The Harvard song set a few to wondering, I suppose. My manner of speaking caught their ear — an eastern seaboard cosmopolitan accent that they thought was "British." They delighted in imitating my quarterback signal calling. After practice I'd hear them yelling the numbers in the shower: "...fawty-foah, fawty-tew." The swear words I used also caught their ear. I never learned to master obscenities, to use them with ease and without self-consciousness. The swearing around my house was limited to such bland expressions as "My Lord," "Shoot," and an occasional "Ye gods and little fishes" from my mother; at school, and later in the Army, I never caught on enough to do it with proficiency. I can throw out an obscenity if pressed, but it sounds wrong, just as anything that is not done out of habit often seems awkward. Besides, good swearing is used as a form of punctuation, not necessarily as a response to pain or insult, and is utilized by experts to lend a sentence a certain zest, like a sprinkling of paprika. Someone at training camp would come up with an innocuous request — "Like to go down to town and have a beer and pizza?" — and in the course of the asking he could slip in six or seven obscenities, and if there were some polysyllabic words in his sentence he could slide a few functional words in between the syllables. Sometimes, particularly when the training season drew to a close, the players would tone down on the swearing to keep the habit from slopping over into their home life or out in public. Substitute words were found to help the easing off. The word "bent" was used for a while.

Someone would shout: "Get *bent,* you son of a bitch."

Throughout the incampment I remained faithful to my feeble supply. I would run downfield for a pass, and if it slipped off my fingers I would say, "Shoot!"

The players looked over. One of them said, "Man, dropping that ball really *tore* that guy — he feels it."

I knew there would be some kidding about that. So, at the dinner table later that evening, a player would lean across at his teammate and say loud enough so I could hear: "Whatja say when the tornado blew the roof off the toolshed?"

"Shoot!"

"And you look in the house and there's your wife with the milkman."

"Why I say 'Shoot' just like that. 'Shoot!'"

"And your dog, Spot, he comes tear-assin' off the porch and sinks his teeth into your leg. Whatja say then?"

"Shoot! Spot, whatja do that for? Shoot."

They would look at me, grinning, and I would say, "If it wasn't for those bishops sitting down there, I'd give you an earful."

"Holy mackerel," one of them said.

I use that expression too. Friday made me feel better. He told me that Bo McMillin, the former Detroit coach, and formerly of Centre

The author shares a laugh with his teammates at Lion training camp at Cranbrook Academy. *(Walter Iooss Jr.)*

College's famous Praying Colonels, had only one phrase he used in moments of stress: "Oh my side and body!" he would shout.

But it was down on the practice field most particularly that my activities did not support the fiction of being a practicing quarterback. I usually carried a little notebook with me—to jot down what I saw. When I was called on to run a play I'd toss the notebook down and trot in among the players, and then look for it when I'd done with the play. Sometimes, tired of scribbling, if I wasn't wearing my helmet I'd drop the notebook in it and leave it lying on the grass with the others so that I was sure where it was. But most of the time I carried the notebook. Terry Barr, one of the team captains, saw me writing in it the first day he came down to practice, and he said his jaw dropped. He had an idea I was a rookie with a short memory.

He told me later that at lunch that day he had turned to one of the regulars and said, "Well, that's a great bunch of rookies. Just beautiful. You seen the guy with the notebook?"

"No."

"They got a rookie down there who carries a notebook around. He scribbles in it. If you ask me why, I'd have to say because the guy can't *remember* things. What else could it be?" He shook his head. "Where the hell do you suppose they dredge up these rookies from."

"You sure the guy's a rookie?"

"He's got the right gear on. And the coaches seem interested in him. I see Don Doll call on him to run a pass pattern. Flanker back position, he wants him to try. Well this guy *jumps* when he hears Doll's voice, and he runs around like a shot rabbit trying to find a place to put his notebook. He puts it in his helmet, which is lying there, but then they want him to wear his helmet—they've got a defense unit working—so he throws the notebook out, and a pencil, and he *strains* that helmet on. Lord, I've never seen anybody struggle with a helmet like that . . . it's like to *kill* him."

"Did he catch the pass?"

"Christ, I don't know. Out of the corner of my eye it looks to me like the guy runs like the forward end of a giraffe. But I couldn't resist it. I sidled over to take a look at that notebook, lying open there in the grass, and I look down and I read in this big nervous handwriting: 'Jake Greer chews toothpicks while running pass patterns.' "

"What the hell does that mean?"

"What it says, I guess. You think it's code?"

"Don't ask me."

Whatever doubts the players had about me were dispelled the first day George Wilson sent me in to a play as a quarterback. The first day of practice he had asked what position I had figured on playing.

"Well, quarterback," I said. "I guess that's the essence of the game, isn't it?"

"How about flanker or split end?" he said. "You're not likely to get into too much trouble unless you catch the ball."

Other players had agreed with him. On my trip to California to try to play in the Pro Bowl game, I had talked to Raymond Berry, the great Baltimore end, about survival, and he had said that I would survive a scrimmage if I played his position—out on the flank—and was sure to stay out of what he referred to as the "pit." The "pit"—as he described it—was an area along the line of scrimmage, perhaps ten yards deep, where at the snap of the ball the Neanderthal struggle began between the big 270, -80, -90-pound linemen. The struggle went on within a relatively restricted area, which was possible to avoid. Berry himself, when he told me this, had wandered into the "pit" only three times in his career—coming back to catch poorly thrown buttonhook passes falling short—and he spoke of each instance as one might speak of a serious automobile accident, the particulars embalmed in his memory in absolute clarity: that it was *that* year, in *this* city, at such and such a game, during such and such a quarter, when so-and-so, the quarterback, threw the ball short, his arm jogged by a red-dogging linebacker, so that Berry had to run out of his pattern back toward the scrimmage line so many yards to catch it, and it was so-and-so, the big 290-pounder who reached an arm out of the ruck of the pit and got him. Being hit, of course, could not be avoided unless—and Berry smiled—you dropped the ball, or ran out-of-bounds if you *did* catch it, but downfield it wasn't so bad: it was one thing to be hit by a safety man or a deep defensive back, who are relatively light, since the positions require speed and agility, and quite another to be caught by someone out of the pit who weighs nearly three hundred pounds.

"One thing to remember when you get hit," Berry had told me in his soft Texas accent, "is to try to fall in the fetus position, curl up around the ball, and keep your limbs from being extended, because there'll be other people coming up out of the pit to see you don't *move* any, and one of them landing on an arm that's outstretched, y'know, can *snap* it."

"Right," I said.

"But the big thing is just stay out of that area."

"Sure," I said truthfully.

So I told Wilson that Raymond Berry had indeed advised me to play flanker on end. I told him about Berry's concept of the "pit."

He laughed. "That's good," he said. "Well, what do you say? It's up to you."

"I still think quarterback. It's the position everyone would want to read about."

"You'll be standing right at the edge of the pit — just teetering there," said Wilson, grinning.

"I'll back away quick enough," I said. "And I'm not going to run into it. What's that fine dictum of Van Brocklin — that a quarterback only runs out of sheer terror?"

Wilson did not give me much time to change my mind. On the fourth or fifth day of practice — the backfields running through play patterns without contact from the defense — Wilson suddenly called out: "OK, George. In you go. Let's have the twenty-three roll. You've got it in your playbook. You know how it works."

I dropped my notebook.

I *did* know what to do from the class the night before — that is, I knew how the play was supposed to run, but I had no idea where my hands were supposed to go, exactly — as I stood up behind the center to receive the ball. I had never stood in against a center, my hands groping under his backside, in the odd near-coupling stance of the T-formation quarterback.

If I had persisted with my story about the Newfoundland Newfs, I could have excused my ignorance by explaining that our attack there was single wing, that we had yet to adapt to the T formation — too "newfangled" our coach had thought it. I said no such thing, of course. I was very embarrassed. Even the most self-absorbed of the rookies would recognize that an impostor was in their midst — a quarterback who didn't know how to accept the snap from center.

I took a few tentative steps toward Bob Whitlow, the center, waiting patiently over the ball. I suddenly blurted out: "Well, damn it, coach, I don't know *where* to put my . . . I just don't know . . ."

The coaches all crowded around to advise, and together we moved up on Whitlow, who was now peering nervously over his shoulder like a cow about to be milked.

It was demonstrated to me: The right hand, the top of it, rests up against the center's backside as he bends over the ball—medically, against the perineum, the pelvic floor, just down from the base of the spine—with the hand lifted and applying enough pressure for the center to know where it is, exactly, so he can swing the ball there with power. The quarterback's left hand is hinged with the right, the heels and thumbs together, the angle between the two kept sufficiently wide for the ball to slap flush against the right hand, the laces turned so they automatically land right under the fingertips, the ball set for throwing, as the left closes behind it for control. Some quarterbacks reverse the position of the hands, keeping the left hand on top. Otto Graham of the Browns was a notable example, accepting the snap from center that way, and he always assumed the habit was a carryover from his early baseball-playing days, catching the ball with the left hand and trapping it with the right.

At the signal, the center swings the ball back and up, generating as much power as he can, so that his rump bucks with the effort and the ball slams into the quarterback's palm with a *pop* that can be heard across a practice field. At Notre Dame, I was told, the image that the coaches fixed in the centers' minds was to try to make the quarterback's hand bleed—"Make that boy *bleed!*" the coaches shouted at them, and there was a rumor that if you *could,* the coaches bought you a suit of clothes.

I tried receiving the snap a few times from Whitlow, everyone standing around and taking it easy. I had my left hand get in the way the first time, not sufficiently open, so that my fingers got jammed when Whitlow brought the ball up, and I yelped and skittered away, running in small aimless circles until the pain began to let loose. I kept the angle between my hands wide after that and after a while I got used to receiving the snap, practicing afterward as much as I could with anyone who would center me the ball.

But as for my anonymity—it ended that day with my stumbling approach toward the center. I could lope through the pass patterns without giving myself away. But not the quarterback position. The veterans looked over that night in the dining hall, and began joshing: "Well, damn it, coach...I just don't know...I don't know where..."

There wasn't much I could say. It killed them.

CHAPTER 7

Down on the field after a day or so, the players, who had been so many ciphers, one indistinguishable from another, began to take on identifying characteristics. Some were obvious. One was struck by the odd disparity of the football players' physiques—more than in any other team sport—from the lean, near-emaciated stringiness of the defensive backs and flankers to the bulwarked heft of the linemen, many with pronounced bellies, who were set close to the ground, like cabbages. The range would be from such a player as Del Shofner, the Giant flanker, lanky, sallow, with ulcers, who has been described as looking like a saxophone player after a hard one-night stand—from Shofner to Brown, the three-hundred-pounder of the Lions, the bulge of his thighs so enormous that to get one leg past the other produced a waddle of such distinction that the players seeing him in the locker room or emerging from the shower jawed at him about it, and imitated his walk.

Down on the practice field I would see Brown and the other big men endlessly circling the field after practice—distant figures against the trees, trying to remove a pound or two, so that their bulk could be moved with more agility.

The running styles were as different as the physical characteristics. Dick Compton, a small Texan scatback, ran with sharp exhalations when he had the ball, *ah-ah-ah,* like piston strokes—a habit he had picked up in high school which he felt gave power to his run. He could be heard across the width of a field. "The Gasper," some of the players called him, and he was also nicknamed "Roadrunner"—after the quick-running desert bird of his home state. Jake Greer also had a distinctive run—moving his spindly body in leaps like a high jumper moving for the crossbar, high, bouncy steps, and then he stretched out fast, and when he got to the defending back he feinted with his small high-boned head, sometimes with a tiny bit of toothpick working in it. Then he'd fly on past or off at an angle, his hands splayed out wide, looking back for the ball homing in to intercept his line of flight, and then he'd *miss* it—good moves but bad hands in those early training sessions, they said—and the shouts would go up, "Squeeze that thing, baby," "Hands, man, hands." Greer would circle back, stricken, staring into his big hands as if they had betrayed him as he bent down to pick up the ball. His face would remain long and melancholy, and when his signal came up again, Scooter McLean would shout: "Look like you want it, Al, come *on*, baby."

He had come up from the Southwestern Athletic Conference, which has small colleges—Prairie View, Grambling, Mississippi Vocational—but very good teams: the year Greer graduated from his college, Jackson State, six of his teammates went on into the professional leagues. Greer had almost impossible competition at Detroit—Terry Barr and Pat Studstill at the flanker back position, and Gail Cogdill at the weak-side end. The only reason that Greer was there at all, and kept around, was that Barr's knee had been badly injured the year before and was of uncertain strength.

The coaches were readily identifiable on the field—all of them with clipboards except George Wilson, and golfing hats, whistles dangling from cords, and they wore big rubber-ribbed shoes that seemed outsized on all of them except Les Bingaman, whose heft was proportionally matched. He was lighter that year. He had come to camp on a diet which had lost him seventy pounds. One year he came to camp weighing more than the training-room scale allowed for; he was weighed on a thousand-pound-capacity machine in the Ypsilanti feed-and-grain store, and he weighed eight ounces short of 350 pounds. That summer he was known as the "two biggest men in northern Michigan." He had played middle guard for Detroit, a position which became obsolete when the emphasis moved to passes and a more mobile attack. Buddy Parker, who was the Lion coach then, said that Bingaman was so good that he never had to position a linebacker behind him. He had extraordinary speed for such a large man. Parker used to say that he was one of the team's fastest men for eight, perhaps even nine yards. The player next to him in the line properly symbolized the great defenses that Detroit had always been noted for: he was a guard called Thurman McGraw, who was so strong that on one occasion, shoeing a horse on a Colorado ranch, he lifted the right hind leg too high, and over the horse went. That was a story Bingaman told. Everyone called Bingaman "Bingo," and down on the field he had a strange cry, like a bird's, to exhort his linemen, calling, "Here we go," which came out, "Hibby-go, hibby-go, hibby-go"— repeated endlessly.

It was easy to spot George Wilson. He was usually in the middle of the field, almost always alone, wearing slick-pressed purple knee-length shorts, and socks drawn halfway up his calves. Occasionally, he talked to a reporter, or the coaches collected around him. The procedures all seemed to have been set, the timetables established, so that he only seemed to keep half an eye on what was taking place. He would walk with his head down, seeming to inspect the ground before he moved a shoe onto it, and then after the deliberation a foot would move forward, and he would plod slowly in an aimless turn among his players as if unaware of their presence. He had strategy in mind, I always assumed, some master design that was going to dismay the opposition in the next game. Occasionally, he would look up at an end flaring for a pass and he'd call out something, but more likely he would turn away from what he'd seen and the ruminating would begin again. It could have been something else: he could have had his bank balance on his mind, or the girl his son was taking out in the family coupé, or the crabgrass problem on his lawn.

He had been with most of his associates since his Chicago Bear days, and it was apparent that he rarely interfered with them: each knew what he was supposed to do. Their day began with a meeting at 9:15, just after breakfast. Wilson presided and scheduled what was to be done during the day. Just before lunch, they had a short fifteen-minute meeting to discuss the morning's practice and to check the various rookies' showings. A few minutes after 2:00, they met again to prepare the afternoon practice session. At 5:15 another meeting was held to discuss the afternoon's session and to plan the next day's program. The last meeting of the day was at 7:10, when the staff decided what would be presented at the 8:00 players' meeting. So they had five official meetings called during the day, and an evening meeting with the players, and after the 5:15 meeting they were down in a bar on the Pontiac pike relaxing and playing liars' poker. After the evening meeting they started a pinochle game up in the second-floor rooms in the dormitory. That often lasted until midnight. They were always together, a strong sense of camaraderie knitting the group, and their operation was a cooperative one, Wilson in charge, but the authority being delegated. The assistants managed the evening meetings; Wilson made the introductory remarks and then prowled around in the back of the classrooms. It was not the standard practice around the league. Some of the head coaches involved themselves with every detail. They said of Pop Ivy, the Cardinal coach, that he handed out the players' equipment in the morning for practice and at the end of the day ran the projection machine at the team meetings.

Wilson's nickname was "Pine Tree" after a song which he was supposed to give a great rendition, though I never heard him sing it. Almost everyone called him George, though the rookies, of course, referred to him as "the Coach."

The team nicknames were colorful, many of them, and they made it easier to identify the players, since many of them were based on physical characteristics. When Daryl Sanders, a tall, shy rookie with a white streak in his hair about an inch wide, arrived in camp the players spent a day wondering how this phenomenon could be worked into a nickname. There were the dull possibilities, "Whitey" and so forth, but then Wayne Walker came tearing down the dormitory corridor, very excited, and he had come up with "Skunk," which stuck for a while, poor Sanders.

Roger Brown, the great three-hundred-pound tackle, was nick-named "Rhinofoot" and sometimes they called him "Haystack." The suspended guard Alex Karras was often called "the Hog," a name that had been suddenly arrived at on a bus when a teammate turned on Karras in a storm of ribbing and referred to him as a Cincinnati dancing pig. John Gordy, the All-Pro offensive guard, was called "the Bear" for being heavily thatched with body hair, though for his prenom he was often called "the Bathroom," especially by Joe Schmidt. Schmidt would stick his head in the door and say, "Where's the Bathroom at?" I would answer, "The last time I saw the Bathroom he was playing pinochle."

Schmidt would say, "Well, tell the Bathroom, if you see him, to get his ass on down to the Monk's room."

"Sure," I'd say.

"The Monk" was Pat Studstill, so called because of the capuchin monkey resemblance, with black, close-cropped hair that stood up stiff and brush-heavy above a small, pinched face that might have belonged to a Sicilian ascetic. He kept it in repose, poker-faced, tight-lipped, and then it would erupt in motion as he'd suddenly belt out the first line of a bossa nova: "Fly me to the moon," yelling the phrase in the high moun-tain twang, drawing out on the word "moon," holding it for quite a peg, and then he'd snap it off short. It was the only line of the song he remembered, or chose to sing, and after a while he'd let loose with it again, particularly if he was in the dormitory showers, where the tile walls gave resonance and tone to his voice.

Carl Brettschneider was called "the Badger," presumably for his belligerent attitude on the field. He had a big pale face that never seemed to darken under the hot summer sun; he was a lively prankster, and good company off the field. But in play he was unpredictable, with a killer reputation, and occasionally he had been removed from a game altogether. On one occasion he was removed for kicking the Philadelphia player, Dan Burroughs, in the belly. "He *punted* him, for Chrissake," I was told. "Damn wonder Burroughs didn't sail up into the sky, spiraling."

Other names were derived from personal habits. Bud Erickson, from public relations, was known as "Uh-Uh" by the players, because of his halting speech, and when they talked about general manager Edwin Anderson the players often made a strange, belching sound, imitating his sonorous manner of speaking. Don Doll, who coached the defensive backs, had been in camp just long enough for the team to discover that he neither smoked, drank, nor swore and he got himself tagged with the nickname "Coop"—for Gary Cooper. "I heard the Coop say 'Heck!' today," said Wayne Walker. "No! No!" said the players, throwing up their hands in horror.

Night Train Lane, of course, owned the most famous nickname in camp, given him in his Los Angeles Rams days for a phonograph record he liked to play.

Jim Martin, a utility player, the field-goal specialist and reserve center, was "Marine"; he was a veteran not only of that service, a Bronze Star winner, but of considerable tenure on the Lions—voted the most valuable player on the 1959 championship team, elected to play in the Pro Bowl that year, which is rare for a utility man. He was an absolutely dedicated player, always pep-talking down on the field, and he was one of the team leaders—almost a billboard caricature of his nickname, with his blond crew cut, his broad tough features, an erect carriage, and a puffed-out chest. In the shower, with the cold water sluicing down, he drummed his chest with his fists and made howler-monkey sounds. On his biceps was a large Marine Corps tattoo with the anchors and the Marine motto, "Death Before Dishonor." I was told that at a cocktail party one of the teachers at Cranbrook had given, to which a few of the Lions had been invited—a hot evening, out on the lawn—one of the wives had come up to Martin and said, "Now. Who are you?" He had told her, and she said, "Look at that," touching the blue design on his biceps. "My, my. 'Death Before Dishonor.'" She took a quick sip of her fruit punch and pressed down on the biceps. "Just suppose, Mr. Martin," she said, "I asked you to dishonor me," cocking her head at him. He looked at her, and he was very polite, but he said, "Death, ma'am, before *that!*" and she couldn't tell whether he was serious or not. So she threw the fruit punch at him. The glass was empty, and the only thing that came out of it was a strawberry, which sailed over his shoulder.

Two players owned titular nicknames. Wayne Walker was called "the King"—but that was a tribute to his sartorial elegance more than an indication of rank. Hoots would go up along the corridor when he came sashaying past the doors in a powder-blue outfit tailored to his big frame, grinning, ready for a night on the town. Joe Schmidt had the other titular name. "The Old Man" he was called—in deference to his position as the team leader. Officially, the Lions had four captains, two from the offense—Terry Barr, the flanker, and Jim Gibbons, the strong-side end—and two from the defense—Night Train Lane, who in his strange argot referred to his position as the "captainship," and then Joe Schmidt. No team in the league had as many captains, and when the four of them marched out abreast to meet the opposing captain in the pre-game meeting at midfield they seemed to belong to another part of the ceremonies—a close-order drill team perhaps, in football outfits, striding out to do some intricate maneuvers before the flag-raising ceremony.

Schmidt's was not the flamboyant cock-of-the-walk leadership that typified Bobby Layne's years with the Lions. But the same competitiveness glowed in him. On the practice field he stayed down with the quarterbacks when the rest of the players were moving up for the gym, and for minutes at a time, off by himself, he practiced the crab-scuttling movements of the linebacker—lateral, and up and down the field, the quick starting and turning that the linebackers must be able to do to keep on top of the offensive maneuvers. Defeat or sloppiness of performance affected him profoundly. In 1952, when he was the captain of a run-of-the-mill Pitt team, his coach, Red Dawson, prevailed on him to give the pep talk before the Notre Dame game and left the dressing room to give him free scope to say anything he wanted. Schmidt told his teammates in so many words: "You guys whip Notre Dame, or, so help me, I'll whip you." His team went out to upset Notre Dame 22–19, and afterward one of the Pitt players said, "We were more scared of Joe Schmidt than the Irish."

Off the field he was calm, almost shy. His face was large and wide, with pale eyes, he had thin yellow-blond hair, and in street clothes, dressed to go to Detroit, he wore very narrow collars clasped in front with a tiepin, perhaps a sartorial trick to make his neck seem longer. He had a size 18 neck, so the Detroit Lion fact sheet said, but its length was inconsiderable: his head seemed set immediately on his shoulders, like a stone Aztec head on a wall. Schmidt himself joked about it. He said he had been six feet three inches when he came to the Lions, with a fine neck, not swanlike, but evident enough, and during his playing years of diving and bulling his way through blockers his head had been driven down a few inches into his body, like a cartoon character bopped with a sledgehammer. He was getting down to an even six feet. He felt that he perhaps had further to go — that a few more years of active play would see his head hammered down so that his neck disappeared completely, then his chin would go, tucked away in the clavicular cavity, eventually his mouth (after a Green Bay game), and they'd have to feed him in some complicated way, and then his nose would disappear, and finally, when just his eyes peeked out of his body, like a man going under in quicksand, he would announce his retirement and apply for the players' pension fund.

There were always rough jokes made about players with short necks. "Look at that guy," someone would say. "He's got to unbutton his shirt to blow his nose."

Almost all of Schmidt's weight was in his torso. His legs were surprisingly spindly. He told me that when he was at Pitt, the coach had this notion that all good football players were thick-calved. At the beginning of spring training he lined up all the candidates according to position and walked down behind them and assigned them to teams depending on how big and powerful the backs of their legs were. It was embarrassing for Schmidt, who ended up on the third team. He was the captain that year too, which embarrassed the coach, who was quickly disabused of this theory. Schmidt said impassively, "Well, you have to let those guys work things out for themselves."

As its true leader Schmidt was the Lions' "Main Man"—that was the current term for it when I was there. The league itself had its "Main Men." At that time there were three at the most—Schmidt, Jimmy Brown, and John Unitas. I remember standing with Unitas at a dance following a Pro Bowl game one year. He had not played because of a knee injury sustained during the season, but he was in Los Angeles for the game. A player would come around, an absolute star in his own right, perhaps even the "Main Man" on his own team, and he would see Unitas leaning against the wall, looking on, and he would say, "Hey, Main Man, how's it?" or something as innocuous, just to pay court, to drift by and acknowledge who the number one man was, this despite a humility and politeness on his own part that leads Unitas to refer to everyone, short of a teenager, as "sir." The terms changed—the Big Guy, the Leader, the Big Stud, the Old Man, the Boss Man—whatever the title, it was one of tribute.

There were some players, of course, who had been known not to show deference to the Main Man. When Joe Don Looney, the odd and troubled star who had caused such consternation to a number of coaching staffs throughout the league, came to Detroit and began cutting practice, the Detroit coaches, who were unable to impress him, sent Joe Schmidt around to talk to him. Schmidt found him sitting cross-legged on the bed in his room, a big Indian blanket pulled up over him, and his high-fidelity equipment turned up full volume.

Schmidt turned the music down, Looney watching him from the hood of his blanket, his eyes flickering.

"Joe Don," began Schmidt easily. "A football player has certain responsibilities. Practice is one of them. You'd have no *kind* of team if the players didn't report for practice. You can see that. I haven't missed, or been late for, a practice in thirteen years...."

"Thirteen years!" exclaimed Looney.

Schmidt supposed that he was beginning to make an impression.

"Man, you need a break," Looney went on. "You'd better take an afternoon off. Take my word for it."

Failure was so galling to Schmidt that his reaction to it was thought by some to have damaged the overall team effort. Bob Scholtz, the big center, told me that the team character, in a certain sense, had been formed by what happened in a game in Green Bay in 1962. With a minute and forty-six seconds left, the Lions were leading 7–6. The victory, which seemed so close, would ultimately have given the Lions the league championship that year. They had possession of the ball on their own forty-nine-yard line; it was third down with eight yards to go. Before the series of plays which got the Lions to the forty-nine, Joe Schmidt had come off the field with the defensive team and, as he passed Milt Plum, going in to quarterback the offense, he called to him to run out the clock as much as he could with running plays. Even if he had to kick the ball over to Green Bay, the defense was very strong and would be able to contain the Packers' final rush. His point was that Plum could rely on the defense and therefore did not have to take chances with passes and possibly lose the ball in his own territory. Plum, who had his own ideas, began the series back on his own twenty-two. Mixed in with his running plays he threw three passes, two of which were complete, one on a third-down play which got them a first down on the thirty-four, and the second, also on third down, which got them a first down on the forty-seven. The third pass was thrown out-of-bounds; Plum, while being judicious, was inviting trouble by throwing the ball at all, of course, but possession was surely worth the risk at that stage. Green Bay had only to score a field goal for a win, and only had to reach the vicinity of the Detroit forty-yard line to make a try for it.

With the ball on the forty-nine, and the minute and forty-six seconds to go, possession was still very much on Plum's mind. He could have used the third down for a running play, which would have kept the clock running, and then, presuming the play had not fetched the first down, Yale Lary, the best punter in the league, would have kicked the ball on fourth down deep to the Packers. Green Bay would have had a little more than a minute and the one time-out they had remaining to move up to field-goal range. The onus would have been on Schmidt and the defense. No one knows what would have happened because Plum decided to pass once more to try to get another first down. Herb Adderley, the Green Bay left cornerback, intercepted and the Detroit players moving in their offensive patterns suddenly heard the cry go up from the Packers, "Bingo! Bingo! Bingo!" to indicate their players should start blocking every Lion jersey in sight. Adderley slipped down the sidelines in front of the Packer bench, all of them jumping insanely as if on pogo sticks, their heavy-weather capes billowing like wings, and was wrestled down on the Detroit twenty-two-yard line. The Packers ran a few plays to keep the clock moving, and with thirty-six seconds to go Paul Hornung kicked the field goal that won the game.

It took Joe Schmidt a long time to get over it, and perhaps he never did. For many games thereafter, when Plum and Schmidt passed each other on the field as the defensive unit came off and the offensive players were taking over, Schmidt would say disdainfully: "Pass, Milt, three times, and then punt."

I said, "That doesn't seem...ah...to represent the qualities one would expect in a captain. I mean Plum's confidence wouldn't exactly stand up..."

"The quality that makes Schmidt a leader," Bob Scholtz said, "is his absolute honesty. Everybody knows that. Johnny Unitas is the same. The guy never said anything, ever, he didn't believe in. Schmidt took that for a dumb-ass call in that Packer game, and there's no way in his book it can be rubbed out. His reaction may have hurt the team, sure, in some subtle way. The balance between offense and defense has never been right here at Detroit. A team is as skittish as a herd of animals — like gazelles — and a wrong word or decision can rile them up so they never can really be set straight again. That's what a coach is supposed to do. Maybe Wilson won't be able to do it, set everything right, to get that exact harmony where you don't have to worry about anything but winning. So they'll bring in somebody else to see what he can do."

"How about Bobby Layne?" I asked.

"Well, there's a case," someone else said. "You think *Schmidt* may have been rough."

He went on to say that Layne was a different team leader from Schmidt—with brass rather than dignity, and cocky rather than forthright. He didn't get along particularly well with Buddy Parker, who was head coach at that time, but they accepted each other. Layne's methods, which were hardhanded often, worked with most of the players, because he was admired by the veterans and held in awe by the rookies, though the cussings-out he was likely to give embittered some of them, so that they'd sulk and their performances would dip accordingly.

When Hopalong Cassady arrived as a rookie halfback with a considerable reputation from Ohio State, he tried to buck Layne, apparently to assert his independence, and he suffered for it. In one of the early scrimmages he made an excuse for a play Layne had bawled him out for, and Layne grabbed him and took him up to Parker, like a teacher hauling a miscreant before the headmaster, and shouted that he didn't want to see the fellow around, ever, not ever again, not on the field or anywhere, and Parker listened without a word. The Lions didn't let Cassady go (he was a high-priced rookie), but what must have astonished him was Parker's silence. It indicated who the field general of the Lions was, if not the supreme commander.

For reasons of his own, Cassady refused to be intimidated. Not long after, he announced loudly on the practice field, after being cut down in a running play, that the blocking was nothing but crap, and that his blockers at Ohio State had been superior. He called it out obviously as a challenge. The players getting up off the ground hunched their pads into place on their shoulders, and they stared at him. On his way to the huddle Layne signaled across the scrimmage line to the defensive team — a nod of the head to the defensive captain, some such signal — and in his own huddle he called Cassady's number to handle the ball, and by some prearranged sign he indicated to the rest of the team that the "club rush" was to be executed. The club rush was a punitive tactic in which the offensive linemen by design allowed the defense to storm through unopposed, and the blockers stepped aside so that the ball carrier was unprotected, and it was simply a question of which lineman, ripping at full speed, got to him first, and how many piled on afterward. The coaches turned away when the club rush was called, and they looked off at the line of trees, or at the spectators, hoping that the internal strife was not too evident, and that what the spectators thought they were seeing, eyes slightly popped and mouths ajar at the violence, was just another blown play, with one or two of the players missing their assignments. Particularly they hoped that the victim of the club rush had survived, and when they turned back there was very nearly the temptation to peek out between their fingers, grimacing, as if an expensive vase had been dropped and they hardly dared to look.

"That's pretty damn callous," I said. "My sympathies are with Cassady. God Almighty!"

"That wasn't the end of it either," my informant told me. "They reckoned he squawked too much — a parrot — so they put crackers, graham crackers, and such things in his bed at night. They led him a right lively time."

"Just damn childish," I said.

The veteran nodded. "It'd seem so, for sure. But you had to remember that Layne broke the rookies like a broncobuster, and while maybe you didn't like how he did it, he put a team together, and they'd do anything for him. Ask Joe Schmidt or John Gordy. They were scared of the guy. Others liked him. Whichever it was, they played a great game for him. They'd do *anything* for him. He was about the most popular man in Detroit, I'll tell you. There was the time when the police got him on a charge of drunken driving. It was pretty serious. He could have been forced to sit out part of the season. There was a big uproar from the fans.

They'd have lynched the arresting officer if he'd stuck to his story. So he admitted that he might have mistaken Layne's Texas drawl for the drunken stammering he'd picked him up for. Layne got off, and that year a sign sat around the dormitory: 'I'm not drunk. I'm just from Texas.' He was like he came out of a movie," the player said. "You ever see him play?"

"With the Pittsburgh Steelers, his last year."

"Well, you remember. When he played, no one ever watched anyone else on the field but him. He had that cocky walk when he came out of the huddle, almost a duck walk because of that pot he had. And then you could see his face. He didn't wear a face bar, yet the guy had all his teeth. Then he wore a shrunken old-fashioned helmet that looked like he swiped it off the head of Red Grange, one of those old-timers. It sat up high on his head, and you could...well, *recognize* him. You didn't have to look at the guy's number and reach for your program to find out who he was. He had a *face* for you to look at. Then he had these thin little shoulder pads, not much more than a piece of cardboard they were, and he didn't bother about any of the other pads, so that when he was out there he looked like a human being. Next to him, all those guys with shoulder pads pushing up to their ears, and the bulge of pads around the calves and the thighs, and the twin bars of the helmets so that you can't even see that there's a human being in there, they look like a bunch of space cadets.

"And then the man's confidence. He was the best quarterback there ever was with two minutes to go, which is when you have to cut the mustard. When that was the situation, he could move the ball with a team of Girl Scouts. Players used to say something about Layne which is the best description of him, and accurate."

"What was that?"

"That he never lost a game, really—that time just ran out on him a few times. That's not a bad man to have around as a leader."

"No question about that," I said.

CHAPTER 8

What I learned in the classroom and down on the training field I practiced when I had the opportunity. Walking in the school grounds, or down by the lake where there were no witnesses, I would practice the seven quick steps back from the center on a pass play. In my room I would hold my hands open, with the heels of the palms together, up against the bottom of an open bureau drawer the way they were supposed to rest against the center's backside, and I would practice calling the count. As soon as I was up in the morning, I got the Spalding out of the clothing alcove and I practiced the handoffs in my room, calling the count, then spinning, and sticking my arm out at an imaginary fullback ripping by.

Once the door swung open, and Bertha, one of the Cranbrook cleaning women, came in with a dusting mop and caught me at it.

"Don't let me be disturbing you," she said. "You keep right on with what you're doing."

I sat on the edge of the bed. "Practicing on the sly," I said.

She began sliding her mop around. She wrote verse for the local paper—invariably about flowers. I had tried to persuade her to jot something down about her job, about the clutter she turned up in the Cranbrook rooms—a comparison, perhaps, between schoolboy clutter and what she cleaned out of a professional football player's room. I said the readers would be interested.

"Here, practicing a simple spin handoff to Nick Pietrosante, I have not turned fast enough to get the ball to him. He has had to reach for it, most likely in vain. In a game, the procedure for the quarterback in this event is to try to follow the full-back into the line." *(Walter Iooss Jr.)*

She had said, "What's the difference between two messes?" She reflected. There was some, of course: cleaning up after football players was usually cigarette butts, cigars, and half-eaten fruit. The schoolboys didn't loll around in bed, she said, and throw peach pits. But then the boys had pets, and that was worse than peach pits.

"Bertha," I asked, "a football player ever bring a pet to camp with him?"

She drew back in alarm. "I don't look forward to the day they do," she said. "Imagine what they might take it into their heads to care and feed."

"That'd be a good subject," I said, thinking of her poetry.

"Come on," she said, squinting her eyes. But she was fond of the Detroit players and as she dusted she talked about them with enthusiasm.

The one who drove her almost crazy was Gil Mains, the big tackle whose knee had been destroyed. "He's gone now, but he was...oh *my!*" Her face glowed with remembrance. "I'm a nervous type," she said. "So what does he do when I come in for work in the morning but stand in the corridor and shout that if I got home from the bars earlier I'd do my job better." She shook her head. "Why, I never had a drink in my life, not so much as a drop, and he's shouting, 'Bertha—the Booze Hound—open the windows—the fumes!—she's coming,' carrying on so you could hear him fifty miles away. You can imagine what the authorities up in the school office must have thought. Oh, he was everything that was the devil, and then he'd come and hoist me up near to the ceiling in his arms, you know, and carry on, and I'd go just crazy mad at him. I never knew what he was going to be up to. Threw a firecracker at my heels once, scared me half to heaven.

"I know," she said, prompting me. "I should write a poem—a sonnet, or something," she said, giggling, "about Mr. Mains."

"You should," I said.

She finished dusting. "Look." She fished in her cleaning apron. "I have a new one." She took out a clipping.

The daffodils are butter yellow, I read. *The wind sweeps...* etc.

"That's very nice," I said.

When she left, I went back to my practicing. I needed it. I was worked into the quarterbacking rotation with Plum and Morrall only rarely. Down on the training field, I worked the plays on the sidelines or behind the goalposts with Friday Macklem's and the trainer Millard Kelly's assistants when they weren't busy—four or five boys, the oldest working their summers at a pittance to build up pocket money for their school or college year. We had some spirited sessions, the puzzled spectators occasionally turning to look since I was indistinguishable from the bona fide Lions on the field—being in the same practice clothes—and it was difficult to understand why I was working with a group of boys who ran gravely in the patterns of the plays I was learning. "Injured, that guy is," I overheard someone say. "Damn shame, isn't it?"

The youngest of my sideline squad was Artie Morante, going on ten years old. The son of the superintendent of the girls' division of the Cranbrook School, he had been coming to practice for two years. July, at the end of the month, was the best time, when he would walk up through the school grounds and across the girls' hockey fields, and, hearing the voices on the fields that had been empty, he would come up through the border of trees and see the blocking sleds there on the school varsity field, and the tackling dummy hanging from a steel-bar gibbet like a pirate in chains, and everywhere the footballs moving through the air, or rocking and bouncing on the grass, the players jogging after them, everything at an easy pace, and one or two would spot him and call, "Hey, Artie baby. Look who's here. How much you weigh this year, Artie?"

"Seventy-one."

During the practice he would stick around Friday Macklem and help him if he could. He'd fill the pliable plastic water bottles, carry them out when the time-outs were called, and watch the players tilt their heads and press a stream of the warm salted water through the thin spouts against the roof of the mouth, and then spit it out on the grass. For him, it was terrific being a part of what was going on, carrying the bottles and the knotted towels that had ice in them and which the players would drape around the backs of their necks. When the field-goal units practiced, he would get under the goalposts and chase after the balls kicked beyond the end zones. The proper attitude was not even to notice the kids standing among the spectators. He was delighted when I would motion to the others of my small squad and we would head off behind the goalposts to practice my plays. "Let's try the twenty-three roll," he would pipe, so I would call it in the huddle, bending far down to get the signal to him, and he would play the two back and churn into the number three hole with the ball clutched to his chest.

The best part for all of us was after practice when the quarterbacks stayed late. When they had finished practicing pass patterns with their ends and flankers, they would throw to anyone who would run out in the patterns. A crowd of kids would stand on the sidelines, ten or twelve of them, waiting. The wait was long. At first, the centers would stay to snap the ball back for a while, and when they had gone the quarterbacks would slap the ball with the palms of their hands to signal the receivers to start downfield, and then drop back those exact seven yards, stop with that half-dance step to set themselves, and whip the ball on a line to their targets. By and by, the receivers—Barr, Cogdill, Gibbons, Studstill, and the rest of them—would drift away toward the gym. The quarterbacks could never seem to get enough practice throwing the ball. Sometimes, they would even throw each other passes, which also gave them the exercise of running downfield and sprinting for the ball. Don Doll, who occasionally stayed to help me with the plays, said, "Watch. A quarterback'll never catch another quarterback's pass." We watched Morrall throw a long spiral to Plum. Sure enough, Plum didn't catch it. He had an excuse. "Came right out of those trees," he called. "Lost it against those trees, Earl."

"Absolutely instinctive," said Doll. "Of course, they're careful about their fingers, careful not to jam them, so they haven't what you'd call confident hands."

We watched Morrall drop a Plum pass. He swore cheerfully. "Right on target, Milt," he called up the field. "Too much juice on it for me."

I said to Doll, "My hands haven't been all that confident either. I'm glad to know the reason."

"Quarterbacks are often freaks," Doll said, "like baseball pitchers. Over at Cleveland, Frank Ryan, who's the quarterback there, used to say that his coordination was so bad that when he picked up a dart and looked for the board the people standing around would start running."

"Thanks for all the excuses," I said.

Often I did some practicing with Bob Whitlow, the center, receiving the snap, and I'd throw a few. If the ball was near Cogdill or Barr, or any of the others, it would be gathered in. It was like throwing into a net.

The last to leave was always Earl Morrall. He stayed to give the kids their chance, and he would motion to Artie Morante to take up position on the imaginary line of scrimmage at the flanker position. "Go on out on the divide, Artie baby...great hands, baby," he would encourage him, and then he'd slap the ball between his hands to signal the hike, then loft it like a balloon. Artie would chug down under it and haul it in like a man catching a suitcase tossed out a window, and he would hold it clutched to his chest, an object about a quarter his size, and keep on going downfield apace, savoring his success before turning and trotting back.

Morrall never seemed to tire of throwing passes, whoever the receiver. He was pressing Plum hard for the starting position. The players said he was "throwing the hell out of the ball." They joshed him because earlier that spring he had lost part of his big toe to a power lawn mower (he had joked that he needed to lose a couple of pounds, but it was a tough way to do it), and the odd thing was that his passing seemed to have improved as a result—perhaps because he set up to pass in a slightly different stance in deference to the injury. The trajectory of the ball seemed to flatten, and a built-in wobble which had always distinguished the flight of the ball disappeared. He thought perhaps it was because he was releasing the ball quicker or later, it didn't matter which since he wasn't going to dissect his form to find out: he just wanted to keep throwing the ball, to groove his newfound skill.

That first pass was the signal for the boys on the sidelines to line up, one behind the other, some of them moving pop-eyed and tentative, watching the big quarterback, waiting for him to give a signal of acquiescence. "Get on up there, Slim," Morrall would call out. "Try a flare," he'd say, explaining with an arc of his hand where the receiver was to go.

The boys followed his direction with great determination and the awe of being thrown to by a professional quarterback. It was a mixed bag of receivers. I was among them, rearing above them, but taking my turn for the practice, and the fun of it. One of them, one of Friday's assistants, wore heavy glasses which sometimes slipped off when he made his cut and looked back for the ball. The glasses would fly off, and in mid-flight his hands would fly up to protect his head; he would stumble along, cringing, as if the football were a swarm of bees. Another of the boys left a loafer behind where *he* cut, simply stepping out of his shoe and leaving it behind in the grass as he moved in bizarre, determined flight for the ball.

Once I saw a full-grown man, wearing a seersucker jacket and a straw hat with a colored band around it, sidle for the line of youngsters, and he got in it for a while, then dropped out; then he made up his mind and stepped in again, and though he wore an embarrassed smile he stuck to it, and wearing both coat and hat he cut downfield for his pass and got it. He went over the grass with quick bouncing strides, but his hat stayed on, and his grin changed afterward from embarrassment to accomplishment. He looked at the ball as he ran back toward Morrall, chuckling at his audacity, and then he flipped it back and headed for the sidelines, still shaking his head.

One afternoon, a tall boy wearing black chino trousers joined the line of receivers. He was very fast, and the first passes he caught were short buttonhooks and flares; he was sure-handed with them, and tossed the ball back toward Morrall with an underhand shovel motion that was nonchalant and professional. He seemed to want no part of the easy, joking camaraderie that existed around Morrall in those post-practice sessions. When a receiver's loafer would drop off, or the boy losing his glasses would cringe down to escape the ball he suddenly couldn't see, I could hear him mutter under his breath, "Come *ahn,* come *ahn!*" as he took his place on the line. Morrall didn't offer him his usual words of encouragement. He seemed to pitch the ball hard to shame him perhaps, to knock his attitude off a peg or so, but the boy held on to the passes, and he would turn and deliver the little underhand flip to sail the ball back up toward Morrall. He was about seventeen, I guess. He must have been a star on his school team.

When his turn came up again, he said, "Hey, throw me a long one."

Morrall dropped back his seven yards and bounced up on his toes twice, waiting a while to get his receiver far downfield, and, meaning to make him stretch, he finally threw the ball about sixty or seventy yards, a long arching spiral like a perfect low punt. We watched the boy in the chino trousers running like a sprinter for it, his arms pumping, and then we saw the arms come up, the ball settle into his palms, and he kept on going, his legs still pumping high, and whisked through a hedgerow at the end of the field, like a ferret into a bush, and was gone with a twenty-two-dollar official Duke ball, only slightly scuffed.

Everybody was embarrassed. There was no hope of catching him. He had a hundred yards' start on us before anyone had recovered from the astonishment of seeing him keep going, and no one of us could have matched his speed. Friday's assistant blinked behind his glasses. He would have to explain why the blue sacks contained one less football. But most of the concern was over Morrall—what he would say. The kids stared at him wondering—as if the boy in the black chinos was a responsibility of theirs. Would it be thought an act of betrayal—an affront to his kindness in staying down to throw passes to them? They watched him stoop for a blade of grass and chew it solemnly—gazing off at the distant hedges where his receiver had disappeared. He shrugged his shoulders.

"Helluva catch," he said. "That guy was moving so fast he was having his troubles slowing *down*." He shook his head in appreciation. "A pair of hands, I want to say. Come on, Artie baby. Where's my boy?" He picked up another football and slapped it hard. "A flare, Artie baby, on three. Let's see some action." He began to bark the signals. "Hut-one... hut-two... hut-*three*," and when Artie began to run downfield the others formed their line eagerly. The theft was dismissed from mind, and it was almost possible to hear a sigh of relief go up.

Finally, Morrall would say, "That's it, everyone. Do six laps and go home." It was greeted with a groan.

"They'd stay until the moon came up—and they'd play by its light," Morrall told me as we walked across the field for the gymnasium. He looked back over his shoulder. "And I'm not so far from wanting to stay down myself. There are not so many better ways of fooling around."

CHAPTER 9

The morning of the first contact work—with everyone in full gear except for those with gimpy legs or ankles—George Wilson motioned me over after the calisthenics.

"We're scrimmaging today," he said. "Your ankles taped?"

"Sure," I said.

"Well, we're going to get you blooded today," he said.

"...today?" I asked.

"Don't forget to wear your helmet," he said. "Scooter will tell you what play to call." He turned away. "Don't forget about that helmet," he said over his shoulder.

I said, "I think I'll slip into it right now."

When the scrimmaging began a little after eleven, I did in fact get into my helmet as I waited on the sidelines with the others—wanting to be done with the effort of putting it on—grimacing as it came down over my ears and flapped them down against the side of my head. I worked them upright with my fingers. Inside, it was quiet, but the first sounds of the scrimmage out in front of me on the field were sharp and concussive—the odd whack of football gear when the lines came together sounded like someone shaking a sack of venetian blinds. The spectators on the sidelines gave a gasp at the violence of the contact seen from as close as they were. Inside the helmet I felt my own jaw drop slightly and my eyes widen.

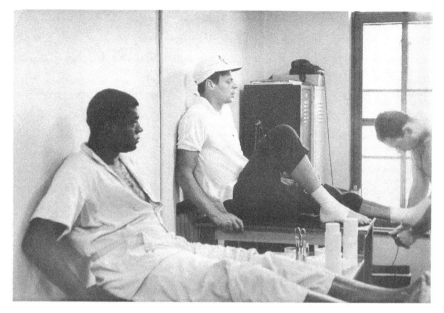

Taping the ankles was an essential part of pre-practice procedure. Waiting his turn is Night Train Lane, wearing a jumpsuit of his own design. *(Walter Iooss Jr.)*

"Listen to that crowd," said Roger Brown, standing alongside. "That play shook 'em. Look at them back away."

I turned to see that some girls who had been lolling at the sidelines as if seated around a picnic blanket were getting up, reaching down for their handbags.

After ten plays or so had been run, all basic running plays—the quarterbacks, Morrall and Plum, in rotation and giving handoffs to the backs driving into the line—George Wilson began motioning to the sidelines, waving his arms.

"Who's he looking for?" said one of the regulars.

I stepped out where I could be seen more easily, and Wilson increased his waving.

"Watch this," I murmured, and began running out toward them.

Then something happened that I remembered for a long time.

Behind me, on the sidelines, the regulars, after a quick word among themselves, came hurrying after me of their own volition, wanting to see that I got the best protection. I was unaware as I came running toward the huddling rookies that I was leading ten regulars behind. There were quickly about twenty men in the huddle, and some pushing and murmuring as the rookies were replaced: "...Right, rook, out you go," and I could hear George Wilson calling out, "What's going on there?"

Everything got sorted out finally, and in the huddle I called the signal that Scooter McLean, standing off to one side with his clipboard, had whispered to me to run: "Twenty-six near oh pinch, on two, break!" I called—a play in which I was supposed to spin and give the ball to the two back, who then slanted off for the number six hole.

As I walked up to the line behind Whitlow, the center, I was suddenly conscious of Raymond Berry's description of the "pit." The big broad backs of the linemen, hunkered down in their position, seemed sprung from the earth itself. Across the line the linebackers, close up to their edge of the pit, were shouting "Jumbo! Jumbo! Jumbo!" It was a jarring cry to hear—the code cry that I knew indicated that a red dog had been called, and I was going to be rushed.

The defensive code words varied. When Jim Ninowski, a former Lion quarterback, was traded from Detroit to Cleveland, the defensive signals, which Ninowski knew, of course, had to be changed when the two teams met. It was decided to change them from colors to girls' names—one of them Ninowski's young wife's name, Judy, I think it was—and he would call his play in the huddle and come up behind his center to hear the linebackers across the line all hollering "Judy! Judy! Judy!" The Lions hoped that might shake him somewhat. I had only the vaguest idea what those code words meant, and could not have used the information to advantage anyway, since I knew no checkoff plays.

I cleared my throat and began the signals. The count began with the three meaningless numbers. I had to be careful not to begin with the same number as the designated play. That indicated the play was

A step too slow on the handoff, the author fumbles just before taking a hit. *(Walter Iooss Jr.)*

checked off, and that an audible was being called. "Sixteen," I called. "Seventeen, ninety-nine!" Then I started the cadence, "*Hut*-one, *hut*-two!" shrilled above the chorus of "Jumbo's" across the line, and at "two" the snap back came. I began to turn without a proper grip on the ball, moving too nervously, and I fumbled the ball, gaping at it, mouth ajar, as it fell and bounced twice, once away from me, then back, and rocked back and forth gaily at my feet. I flung myself on it, my subconscious shrilling "Fetus! Fetus!" as I tried to draw myself in like a frightened chinch bug, remembering Raymond Berry's advice on being trapped in the pit by the big linemen, and I heard the sharp strange whack of gear, the grunts, and then a quick sudden weight whooshed the air out of me.

Dave Lloyd, a 250-pound defenseman, had got through the line and pounced on me to make sure I wasn't going to get up and run. A whistle blew and I clambered up past him, seeing him grin inside his helmet, to discover that the quick sense of surprise that I had survived was replaced by a pullulation of fury that I had not done better. I shouted lustily at my clumsiness, hopping mad, near to throwing the ball into the ground, and eager to form a huddle to call another play and try again. The players were all standing up, some with their helmets off, many with big grins, and I heard someone calling, "Hey, man, hey, man," and someone else, John Gordy, I think, because he said it all the time, called out, "Beautiful — hey, real beauti*ful*" — sensing, then, that an initiation had been performed, a blooding ceremony, as George Wilson had wished. Lloyd said, "Welcome to pro ball" — something in his tone which made the comment not only in reference to the quick horror of what had happened when I fumbled, but in appreciation that I had gone through something that made me, if tenuously, one of them; they stood for a while on the field watching me savor it.

But the trouble was that the confidence that came with being blooded did not last long. After ten minutes, kneeling on the sidelines quaking with eagerness to be called again, one would feel it begin to seep away, and the afternoon would pass, and what confidence was left would edge away, skirting the discomfiture and insecurity that waited, as palpable as cat burglars, to move in.

I said to Joe Schmidt on the sidelines just after my play, still in the throes of my excitement and talking about it too much: "I got the feel of it out there. I suppose it could have finished me...I mean the humiliation...but I got the reverse — confidence."

He nodded.

"It was really something," I said.

"Sure," he said.

"The best thing was how the regulars all jumped in."

He was grinning. "The defense would've killed you if you'd hung on to the ball. You can't throw the ball away like that. You've got to give us defense people a chance to get to you."

The other two first-string linebackers, Walker and Brettschneider, were standing with Schmidt. They nodded and grinned. They always seemed to stand together, as if their skill at defense as the three line-backers was such a corporate undertaking that it bound them together even off the field. The scrimmage began again. Their attention shifted to it immediately. They were watching the rookies substituting at their positions. "That's crud," one of them said, gauging his replacement. "Look at that!" he said scornfully. Their attention was completely taken up by it. He pointed at some maneuver the rookie had made which was too subtle for me to catch.

I asked, "Will you straighten him out—whatever it is he did wrong?"

"You must be kidding," Brettschneider said. "They're after our jobs, boy."

"But they're your teammates—common cause," I said tentatively. I was startled.

"Crap," one of them said.

Wayne Walker pointed at the rookie who had taken over at his position. "Look at Clark's stance," he said. "It's wrong for a linebacker. He's got his arms hanging down as he waits. When the lineman busts through to him he's got to bring those hands up to stave him off, which loses him a half second or so of motion. He should wait with those hands up—all set to fend..."

"But you won't tell him?" I asked.

"Hell no," said Schmidt. "He'll learn quick enough. He'll get hit on his ass and he'll learn."

"That's the damnedest thing," I said.

Schmidt looked across. He could sense my disillusionment, particularly after the display of the regulars coming into the scrimmage to help me. "I'll tell you," he said. "When I came up in 1953 the team was hot off the 1952 championship. But it was a team getting on, long in the tooth, and Buddy Parker traded some of the regulars to put in rookies and first-year men. When he traded Flanagan, the middle linebacker, a lot of the regulars broke down and *cried,* I want to tell you, and when I took over his position they took it out on me as if I was responsible.

They wouldn't have anything to do with me. I went through six league games as a regular and no one talked to me. I played the game, dressed, and then I went home to my apartment and looked at the wall.

"Veterans don't love rookies," he went on. "It's as simple as that. You always read in the paper that some young rookie coming up says he couldn't've done it if it hadn't been for some ol' pappy-guy veteran who took him aside and said, 'No, son, up here we do it this way,' and then showing him. Well, that's crap, you'd better believe it. A regular, particularly an old-timer, will do almost anything to hold on to his position short of murder. They say that Big Daddy Lipscomb used to get into these horrible fights, close to *kill* these guys during the training season when he was with Los Angeles, really beat up on them, and everybody'd say, 'Boy, Big Daddy's got a mean temper this year.' Then the coaches look around and find that cooler than hell he'd been beating up on the guys trying for his position so that finally there wasn't anybody at his position *but* Big Daddy."

"I was thinking how the offense—the regulars—came in to help me," I said.

Brettschneider, who had been listening and nodding, said, "You're not quite what we'd think of being a 'threat'! But you start completing some passes and hanging on to the ball, and doing something sensational, and you'll see if you get anything but the back of their hand from Plum or Morrall. You threaten them for their jobs and you'd be like to get a time bomb in your soup. You've got to be a son of a bitch to play this game right."

"Well, not completely," I said, considering it.

If the attitudes the veteran held about the rookie were scorn and suspicion, the reaction of the rookie in consideration of the veteran was invariably awe. When the veterans—Schmidt and the rest of them— trotted in to scrimmage, the rookies stood on the sidelines watching silently, engrossed, and one could sense them soaking up information for their own use. Even playing against a veteran, they found it difficult to reduce an idol or a player of great reputation to corporeal status. John

Gordy, one of the offensive guards, told me that in his first league game, which was against the Colts, the coaches sent him in at the beginning of the second half to try to stop the Colt tackle, Art Donovan, who had spent much of the early part of the afternoon in the Detroit backfield. "They found me in the corner of the locker room," Gordy said. "Aldo Forte kept yelling, 'Gordy! Gordy!' and I kept answering, but in such a small voice that the fellow on the next stool couldn't've heard me.

"I'd seen Donovan in the game films, and I knew all about him, and it just seemed crazy that I was going in there. I went out for that second half and *tried*—you could say *that*. Once, Donovan felt that I was holding him, and he told me right then that if I tried anything like that again why he was going to remove my head from my body. You know what I said? I said, 'Yes, sir!'

"That was the sort of respect you had for the great ones," Gordy said. "And you felt it even if you were in the field hitting hard. That same rookie year I was going to play opposite Jesse Richardson in a game. The coaches told me that he'd been playing that position since the third grade. He'll play it straight, the coaches told me. So don't bug him. Play it straight yourself, they told me. He knows the position so well he'll take advantage of any funny stuff you try. You get him riled up with funny stuff and he'll kill you. That's what they say. So I go in there, and this guy holds me, and gouges me, and I get kicked around, and I say what *is* this, what *is* going on? Why there was a moment in the game when he knocked my helmet up in the air and he grabbed it and hit me with it. We could see it afterward in the game films—the helmet pop off, and this guy reaching for it, and belting me by the strap. The rest of the guys watching the film broke up laughing. I mean you could see this guy was really having himself a time. So I said to Forte: 'Aldo, that guy Richardson really been playing since the third grade?' So Aldo tells me that Richardson had been moved to the other side of the line. I was playing against a rookie. They forgot to tell me."

The only rookie down on the practice field who seemed unabashed was Lucien Reeberg, the big three-hundred-pound Negro who had bellowed out his song in the dining-room hazing without any self-consciousness. He was the only rookie who said very much—a cheery high voice urging everyone on—a pepper talk that one felt was probably a veteran's prerogative. He attracted attention. He got on the veterans' nerves. I wondered if he wasn't cocky enough to get a club rush lowered on him—remembering how Bobby Layne had done it to Hopalong Cassady to indicate a rookie's proper station. The second or third day of practice, with some light contact work going on, Reeberg hit the man opposite him, Larry Vargo, a tight end in his second year with the Lions, harder than called for. Vargo said, "Watch yourself, fat man. You thinking you're Sonny Liston?"

Reeberg looked at him. Both men had small tight grins.

"I'll whup you like Cassius Clay, if you want it," Reeberg said. "I don't get beat, man."

I was grinning too, assuming they were fooling around, mimicking the two heavyweights. I sidled over.

"You're going to get it, fat man," said Vargo. He began moving around Reeberg, watching him. The other veterans began moving around. "You ever see so much ass on a fat man?" I heard one of them say. They were going to make sure that Vargo, one of them, a veteran, wasn't humiliated. I was aware that the grin was still on my face, stuck on there foolishly. Someone brushed by me. Reeberg said, "I don't get beat...by *no*body." He looked at the circle of veterans.

"Fat lip for a fat man," someone else said.

Millard Kelly, the trainer, ripped in between them, leaning against Reeberg's arms. "Crazy? Crazy?" he called at them.

"He says I pushed him too hard," Reeberg said, his voice high and querulous like a child arguing in a playground argument; it was difficult to tell if his voice was natural, or if he was taunting Vargo.

"Settle it here," Kelly said, straining up against him, "and you'll be on the next train out, the both of you."

The tempers began to cool. The veterans stared at Reeberg, but they stopped milling around him. Curiously, the reaction began to settle most strongly in Kelly. His mouth opened and shut like a piece of silent machinery. He was almost quivering with rage, or perhaps at the thought of his temerity in stepping in between the two big players.

"Crazy! Crazy!" he kept hissing between his teeth. "Bunch of god-damn adolescents — the bunch of you, like fooling with pistol triggers."

When the practice was over, Reeberg tried to patch it up with Vargo. He walked along beside him on the way to the gym, trying to explain in his high voice that he was trying his best and didn't mean to do no wrong. Vargo was embarrassed to have a rookie hanging around him. He knew the veterans walking along behind were grinning. He said, "OK, OK," and he began to trot quite hard for the gym, his speed picking up. But Reeberg kept right up with him, his voice still going, and his weight bouncing as he ran. The players behind shook their heads and laughed.

CHAPTER 10

That day George Wilson dropped into my room after the afternoon practice and asked if I would join his coaching staff for a drink four or five miles down the road. "Bring your wallet," he said. They would be playing a variety of liars' poker with dollar bills. That was the ritual after afternoon practice — the players and coaches would shower and shave, and with an hour or so to spend before the evening meal they would set out in cars for various bars and inns along Route 22, each clique, or "click" as it was pronounced, to its respective place, its sanctity then carefully respected by the others. I saw Earl Morrall and some players behind him start to come into the coaches' hideout, just coming on it by chance, and he turned and herded the others out as if he had stumbled into a boudoir. As for the rookies, they rarely left camp. They would wander into the dormitory common room and loll about waiting for supper, watching the Detroit Tigers absorb another loss on television, which they were doing with great regularity that season.

It was dark and cool in the coaches' bar, and pleasant. They had a corner table reserved, and there was always good-natured joshing with the waitress as they sat down. The drinks they ordered seemed surprisingly exotic to me — whiskey sours, manhattans, and orange blossoms. Scooter McLean drank the orange blossoms. Bingaman, who was off alcohol, had a special glass mug the waitress would set in front of him. He drank water, and it must have held nearly a quart.

The liars' poker was started almost immediately. It was a relatively simple game: Each player would fork up a dollar for the pot, and then draw out someone else's dollar, which would become his "playing" dollar. The value of this "card" was determined by its serial number, specifically by the number of like figures. The idea of the game was to try to guess how many similar numbers there were around the table. The winner after a series of bidding rounds would be the player with the highest successful bid. The most powerful dollar you could hold would be one with eight nines in the serial number (which was always to eight places), and the least valuable, one in which there were no two numbers alike. A dollar with a serial number which was a consecutive run from one to eight would be a rotten bill indeed to hold in liars' poker.

After everyone had studied his dollar, the bidding would start. George Wilson would take a sip from his fancy drink, squint at his dollar bill, and he would say, "No fooling around, I bid six threes!"

His bid indicated very little. He might or might not have a three in his hand. A chorus of disbelief and pungent comment would rise from around the table, and when it had died down the player at his left, Scooter McLean say, would offer *his* bid. He had the option of passing or continuing the bid—which always had to be higher up the scale in value than the one preceding—or, if he didn't believe that Wilson could put together the requisite number of threes from his own and the other hands, he could challenge Wilson to produce them. It being likely that more than six threes could be found in the bills around the table, McLean would undoubtedly continue the bidding. "Six eights," he might say.

Next to him, Les Bingaman would scowl and mumble at his dollar, and then pass. If it was passed all around the table it was equivalent to challenging the last bidder.

Aldo Forte, sitting next, with perhaps four threes in his dollar bill, would stare at Wilson, wondering if the original six threes bid was honest. If it was, he could bid high, and perhaps rake in the kitty—three threes at least from Wilson, four in his own hand, that was seven, and he ought to pick up four or five from the rest of the players.

"Eleven threes!"

"Mother of God," Scooter McLean would say, and from the noise rising from the corner table, and from the hoots of derision and approbation one might have thought a group of children were hot at slapjack or go fish. It was very much part of the ritual of the game to exaggerate one's reactions. Bingaman would bang his tankard, and turn heavily and sulkily from the table. McLean was querulous, Doll and Nussbaumer were caustic, and Wilson would say happily, "You wouldn't think, looking at that fine open face of Aldo's, that there could be so much *deceit* in the man."

The reactions would level off eventually, and the bidding would continue. Sitting next, and being new at it, and thus conservative, I would pass, and Nussbaumer, the Hawk, next to me, after a considerable study, would pass too, and also Larry Gersh, a Chicago tailor and a friend of Wilson, who was close to the coaches and one of their group, *he* would pass, and perhaps Aldo's bid of eleven threes would get passed around the table.

The tabulation came next — full of suspense, and usually preceded by a round of drinks.

"How many threes?" Aldo would ask me.

I would put my bill down on the table and look to be sure, and say, "No threes, Aldo."

"Hawk?"

"I got two threes."

"Larry?"

"Nothing here at all."

Don Doll had two.

"That's four. George?"

Wilson would peer at his bill, and he'd say, "Well, Aldo, old scout, lemme just take another look — I got so many of your threes here..." savoring his delight, and then he'd announce: "Fancy that, there's not a *one in my hand,* not one blessed three."

"He'd show his bill to Aldo, who would peer at it, disbelieving and disappointed. Another gust of noise would swirl around, and amid a babble of comment and commiseration McLean would turn up with one three and Bingaman with one as well, which with the four threes in his own hand made a total for Aldo of ten around the table, just one off his bid. That meant he had lost, and Aldo would fork up the equivalent of the kitty and each of us would win a dollar. If he had won—found eleven or more threes around the table—each of us would have given up his dollar to him. Each game took longer than I have described. In an hour, and before it was time to get back to Cranbrook for supper, three or four games might be completed. I never saw such agonizing, and because their actions were exaggerated it was inevitable that watching them play, one came to an appraisal of character. Scooter McLean played a mercurial, nervous, almost feminine game, with small clucks and nods of the head, like a hen, and losing seemed to hurt him. There was sympathy for him when he lost rather than the usual good-natured derision. The Hawk's game was calculated and severe. I suspected he was the winner over the long run. His attention was close, and his judgment of each bid, which he would recapitulate aloud and at length, was sound, though he was perhaps oversuspicious. He assumed all the players were lying. Losing seemed to make him impatient, as if there were something wrong with the game itself for not matching his careful synopsis.

Don Doll's game was somewhat akin to the Hawk's—careful, thorough, very serious, though perhaps more conservative. It was his first year with the coaching staff, and perhaps extravagance should be contained. Larry Gersh, the tailor, played a vague, confused game, and he seemed harried by its complexities, so that he occasionally erupted in short cries of anguish. Most of the joshing was leveled at him; his attitude seemed to be to play the clown.

Aldo Forte's game was quite different—matter-of-fact and solid, and I suspect he lied about his serial number less than the others, and was likely to accept their bids without suspicion. Bingaman played an ambitious, confident game, though it would be hard to imagine otherwise, his physical presence being what it was—his enormous rounded shoulders, the oversized glass tankard at his elbow, and his dollar hidden in a big clump of hands. He was a fast player, and he spoke in a quick rush of words, as if at one time he had had a stutter, which he had learned to overcome by getting his sentences out in one quick breath.

It was difficult to learn much from George Wilson's play. He had the most fun with the game, full of comment, and his play was haphazard and difficult to categorize, as if the occasion was what he took pleasure in—to sit in that cool bar, after the heat of those August practice afternoons, with his confederates and relax in that camaraderie. His was the strong character at the table. For all the piques of play, it was obvious the staff got along well; a strongly knit group with Wilson surely its leader—though it was never deference that was indicated, but respect, subtle but evident.

I drove back to camp from the bar with Larry Gersh, the team tailor. He had been associated with the Lions since the days of Buddy Parker, Wilson's predecessor. He had been part of what Parker called his "hex team," which included Gersh; John Francis Burke, a Hollywood florist; and Wallace "Boots" Lewis, a seventy-year-old crap-shooting Negro who ran a shoe-shine stand in the off-season and who when pressed about his age would cry, "Ah'm just a boy, just a growin' boy." Of the three, Gersh had stayed on with George Wilson, who became the head coach when Parker abruptly left the team. He was a very likable figure in the camp, always with the coaches, a regular in their card games, and a constant butt of comments by the veterans, who kidded him about the quality of the suits he had made up for them. They would say, "Larry, what's with this—the fly zipper in the small of the back of this coat...!"

As a tailor, Gersh was a very important personage in his days with the Buddy Parker entourage. Parker was superstitious to the point of spookiness. His habit was to throw away a suit every game his team lost, get rid of it in a rage. It was very profitable for Gersh. Gersh told me that in a Pullman compartment on a train coming back from a loss to

Cleveland, Parker had tried to get rid of all his clothing as the train was pulling out of the Cleveland railroad yards. He rang for the porter.

"Give me a hand with this window," he said. "Damn thing's stuck."

The porter said, "Suh, it's mighty cold out there. Below freezin'."

"Give me a hand."

"You want some fresh air, I can turn on the li'l *fan* heah."

Parker, straining up against the window, opened it by himself. A rush of fine powdered snow swept into the compartment. "Stand back," Parker said. He picked up his brown felt hat and scaled it into the night. He ripped off his tie and flung it out. "Hand me that overcoat."

"Suh?"

"That overcoat—hanging on the peg."

The porter took it down, but he held it draped carefully over his arm.

"Suh, you have any objections," he said, "if the disposing of the coat is taken care of by *me?*"

"Get rid of it," Parker said.

The porter slipped out into the corridor to store the overcoat somewhere. He was gone just momentarily. Parker began straining out of his suit coat, but the rage left him suddenly, and he sat down and put the heels of his hands to his temples. The porter returned, a little breathless. He cast a speculative eye at Parker, according to Gersh, measuring the suit coat and trousers. The two men were about the same size.

"Anything else I can help you with, suh?" he said, looking at Parker.

Gersh cut in: "You can give me a hand getting the window shut."

The two got it closed. A few tiny flakes of snow sparkled on Parker's shoulders and in his hair before melting. He began trembling. A loss in December was not the best thing for his health. Gersh said that coming back from losses out of town Parker would step out of the plane or onto the station platform with everyone else bundled up in greatcoats, with scarves, the wind whipping at them, and Parker would be hatless, in his shirtsleeves, with perhaps a shoe gone.

"That's incredible," I said.

"He was bothered by just about everything when the Lions lost,"

Gersh said. "I remember after losing a game to the Packers he fired Bud Erickson—temporarily, of course—for assigning him to Room 94 in a Green Bay hotel because the two numbers added up to 13, yelling at him from the steps of the airplane as the team was standing around waiting to get on. Very embarrassing."

"What happened when he won?"

"Well, he was in great humor then," Gersh said. "He never washed, felt he'd wash the good luck off, and he always wore the same suit, which, of course, wasn't so good for me. It's a curious Detroit phenomenon—this business of superstition," Gersh went on. "When Bo McMillin was the coach he made these amazing arrangements and designs with *hairpins,* for God's sake, and no one could disturb them. I expect something like that to sneak out in George Wilson any day. The pressure does it," he said. He turned the car into the Cranbrook parking lot and we walked in to dinner.

The rookies held Gersh in awe. He was a harbinger, in a sense, of success—to those who were going to make it with the Lions. Being privy to the coaches' conversations and thus their assessments of the rookies, he was aware of which were doing well and likely to stick with the team. Whereupon, he would drop into a rookie's room and ask to measure him for a Lion team blazer. I don't know whether he did this unthinkingly or not. The rookie would leap up with a cry, and by the time Gersh had finished with him he might have ordered two or three additional suits in the throes of his delight. They said, "The Hawk in your room, and you're dead; Gersh, with a tape, and it's life." One evening he dropped in to measure Red Ryder, the Miami fullback, for a blazer, and Ryder was so excited he could hardly stand up. But looking on was Jim Simon, a big rookie end, also from Miami, and Larry bustled around Ryder with his tape measure as if Simon wasn't in the room. He lay on his bed watching the tailor bleakly. Gersh left the room finally, when he was done, without a word to Simon, who thought he was done. He made the team eventually, but he told me that the low point of the training was that evening. He said he would have given one thousand dollars if Gersh had turned to him and said, "Well, you look like a forty-two long to me. Why don't you just stand up here and we'll just check you out with the tape?"

The rookies had other hints about how they were doing. Some were minor, but the smallest slight was sufficient to worry them and cause them to slope around the corridors, moping. They'd check the bulletin board for notice of publicity shots to be taken. If they weren't listed — if their photograph wasn't wanted — they felt they were in trouble.

A more useful indication was the attention of the coaches. If the rookie was suddenly not being yelled at, or suggestions were no longer flung at him, it did not mean that he was doing everything right — though he *hoped* that's what their lack of attention meant — but that the coaches just were not interested in him anymore.

It preyed on their minds constantly. Lucien Reeberg, the big tackle, even tried *me* for a hint.

He'd come in the room and sag down into the chair and ask: "How do you think I did today?"

"Lord, Lucien, I don't know."

Reeberg looked around. "What are all these papers?" he asked.

"Manuscripts," I explained. "I'm an editor — when I'm not quarterbacking — of a literary magazine, the *Paris Review*. It gets edited on the fly, so to speak. That's typical of such magazines — they're done out of the editor's briefcase, wherever he happens to be — though I doubt one has ever been edited out of a football training camp."

Reeberg picked up a short story, peered at it briefly, and dropped it back on the desk.

"Look at this," he said. He showed me a letter. It was from a preacher, a Reverend Albert Reed, who had seen a picture of Lucien in the *Arkansas Gazette* and felt that someone of such proportions would be a natural prizefighter. "I would like to see you begin immediately," the letter read, "to first give this suggestion a serious study, and then decide that this is your opportunity to make a few million dollars. I believe that *you* should be our future Champion Heavyweight fighter."

"Well," I said, "there aren't many people around who get letters like this." I folded it and passed it back to him. He held the letter lightly, his mind abstracted, then slapped it against his knee. "Hey," he said brightly, "d'ja think I did all right out there today?"

"Well, Lucien..."

"Did I *look* all right?"

"Lucien, I'm not much of a judge."

"D'ja *think* I looked all right?"

"Well..."

"D'ja *hear* anything?"

"The coaches are still yelling at you out there—that's for sure," I said. "Bingaman keeps telling you to 'rock ass, Lucien, baby, rock ass'—which I guess means they're still interested."

"You think so? You sure?"

"Damn it, Lucien..."

"Well, have you heard any rumors?"

"Sure," I said. "They were talking about sending Roger Brown to the Houston Oilers. Reeberg will anchor the whole right side of the line... that's what they were saying."

"What?" Reeberg was anxious enough to believe anything.

"Lord, Lucien," I said. "I don't know, honest. Has Gersh measured you for a blazer?"

"No," said Reeberg. "Someone as big as me, with all the yards they'd have to use in a suit, you'd think Gersh might put in a good word for me." He looked at me hopefully.

"Well, that's a thought," I said.

CHAPTER 11

The first squad cuts were made on the sixth day of practice. Lucien Reeberg survived. The coaches had a last look during the morning scrimmage, and then they called the players over they had to let go. One of them was Dick McMacken, a big 265-pound tackle from Huron College, who lived nearby, I guess, because two or three of his family came to see him scrimmage that lovely Saturday morning — an older man, his father perhaps, and a girl holding a youngster. I noticed them because I saw them come down to the field together with McMacken. The girl, his wife presumably, sat under a tree up on a knoll a distance from the playing field so their little daughter could roam without getting trampled by the spectators watching the practice. The older man stood on the sidelines. After the practice Aldo Forte motioned the tackle over, the two of them standing alone while the rest of the squad trooped up toward the pines and the gymnasium beyond. The father edged along the sidelines. For a second or so, he might have been pleased that a coach had singled out his son for a complimentary word or so. But a slump in McMacken's stature suggested that he was being let go. His head was down. Forte was talking to him earnestly. They shook hands at the end, and McMacken turned slowly for the gym. The girl joined him, their child roaming on ahead, switching a little stick at the grass, and the older man came quickly across, and they walked up together. They were trying to comfort him. The girl, who seemed very small beside him, leaned her head briefly against the biceps of his arm, and the older man whacked him on the rump.

I walked up to the gym with Don Doll. I asked him what would happen to a player like McMacken on being let go. He told me that Detroit tries to help them. Calls are made around the country to try to place them. The coaches were recommending McMacken for a semipro team where he could make fifty dollars a night and get himself in better shape than when he arrived. Then it would be up to him. That was his trouble. He had arrived out of shape, and was weakened trying to get his weight down, and thus was pushed around. Doll, who thinks a lot about physical fitness and whose weight hasn't changed a quarter of a pound in ten years, perhaps more, said that he just couldn't understand. "The guy has the whole spring to get ready, and into the summer, and he *knows* when he gets here he's going to be playing for all the marbles. So what happens. He gets here and *begins* what he should have begun back in June."

"What do they say when you tell them you've got no place for them?"

"They worry about the future," Doll said. "Where they're going to go, what they're going to do. They put a lot of stake in sticking with this club. Then the bottom drops out."

He looked after McMacken with the lovely girl in close to him. "He just cheated himself, that's all." Doll's voice was tight and furious, and I had the sense that he was about to kick the ground in frustration. "Why the heck didn't he come set to do a *job?* Then his girl wouldn't be saying to him, 'Don't worry, honey, everything's going to be all right, don't worry, honey.' . . . Why it makes you just *sick,* that's all."

He seemed much angrier than McMacken up ahead.

We walked along silently for a while—by the pond that was very low and still as metal, with dragonflies resting in clusters on the blue-green water-lily pads, and through the pines up by the tennis courts, and finally Doll said that the hardest thing in coaching was to let players go. It was easier in the beginning of the training season when they could be let go for obvious reasons—lack of physical equipment, or attitude—but when the season got under way and two or three good men had to be cut to get the squad down to the thirty-seven-man limit, that was when the profession of coaching was for the birds. Doll said that in his day the awful process was referred to as "the Turk"—he supposed in reference to the cut of a Turkish scimitar. " 'The night of the Turk,' that was what we called it," he said. "The Turk is coming. Nowadays," he went on, "the rookies refer to it as the 'Squeaky Shoes'—'the Squeaky Shoes are coming down the hall, *tonight,* men.' "

Doll said that when he and the Hawk would come down the dormitory corridor and look in a rookie's room, just offhandedly, the rookie would rise up off the bed as if an electric charge had gone off.

"You'll be seeing some of them," Doll said, "nights of the Squeaky Shoes."

When I got back to the dormitory I discovered that Dean Look had been let go. I was sorry to see him go. I had got to know him at the rookie table at meals (he had warned me not to drink milk: "... Cuts down your wind," he had said), and we had played some cards—bridge—with Milt Plum and Tommy Watkins. An articulate, quick-witted athlete, he already had a considerable career of barnstorming behind him—great years as a halfback at Michigan State, two years as a bonus player in the Chicago White Sox baseball organization, and then, shifting back to football, a year with the New York Titans of the American Football League. He used to tell me about life with the Titans—the team I almost played for. It had been nothing but bickering on the practice field, he said, mostly because the plays, both offensive and defensive, were improvised right on the spot, just as they might be in a Central Park touch football game. "You go here, and you cut over here, and the rest of you guys go deep in case no one's open and I'll throw the hell out of it"—it was that sort of thing.

Look had played quarterback for them and, hit on the blind side in a game against Denver, he suffered a concussion and a fractured vertebra. He was trying to return as a defensive cornerman. He had cleared out his room and left within an hour of shaking hands with George Wilson.

The days of the squad cuts made everyone uncomfortable—the empty beds and the missing faces—and I felt it strongly. The effect of insecurity was stronger on my fellow rookies, of course, who had so much at stake. But I felt it during those early days, after the first squad cuts, when after the afternoon practice there was nothing to do, and we sloped around, yawning with nervousness, trying to occupy ourselves as best we could. Everyone tried to keep his mind off the future. One found things to do. At the end of each dormitory corridor were the school bulletin boards. Lists and announcements from the preceding school year were still tacked up there—laundry-collecting schedules, regulations, a list of boys allowed by parental permission to smoke. One could stare at the bulletin board for a long time. That helped the tedium. One of the names on the smoking lists was Abdulhadi Al-Awadhi. I wondered about him—a young follower of the Moslem faith, presumably, which frowns on smoking—and about his courage, perhaps his first act of emancipation, involved in writing across the ocean to his parents for permission: "Dear Mom, I have started to smoke cigarettes. Just one or two a day, but I like to, and all the other kids do it, and I wondered..." And then, of course, to speculate on how the parents received this grave request, their conferring about it, and what sort of permission they wrote the school. Did they wonder about the morality at Cranbrook? Often I would see a rookie standing in front of one of those bulletin boards, and when I would pass in the corridor he might half turn and nod weakly, but more likely he would move in closer, working up his own thoughts about those dated and dog-eared announcements. You could keep your mind occupied wondering about such things.

The rookies had a common room down at the end of their wing with paneled walls, one of them decorated with gloomy prints of the cathedrals at Strasbourg and Anvers. A portable television was set up in there on a table, the thin metal ears at an angle, the sound usually turned on as soon as the practice was over, echoing down the corridor, though often when I dropped in, just lazying about, the picture had gone awry with no one at hand to adjust it. Sometimes I'd find a card game going on, but usually the place was deserted. Not much to do in there. College catalogues lay in piles on the tables, and also the Cranbrook catalogue, which began: "Turning boys into men is not done overnight."

There was a small library—an encyclopedia, a collection of O. Henry, Owen Wister's *The Virginian,* an edition of Charles Dickens, a number of books on gardening, Hervey Allen's *Anthony Adverse,* with a note on the title page, "See page 263," which turned out to be the salacious part, very rococo and old-fashioned to reread, Ullman's *The White Tower,* and a book on the cocktail hour by Bernard De Voto. On the flyleaf of the Owen Wister book someone had scrawled, "Look on page 64." I looked, and was instructed to turn back to page 38, and from there was prompted on to page 120, then back to page 40, and I went on faithfully, knowing what was coming, and it finally did with a notation on the last page of the series: "Ha ha sucker!" I looked around for a pencil, going back to my room for one, finally, just ambling along, and when I got back with it I rubbed out the notation and referred the reader to page 263 of the Hervey Allen book. I took my time about it, writing the numbers down carefully and checking with the *Anthony Adverse* page to make sure it was right—doing this without any sense of wile or prank, somberly and lethargically, and when I'd done I put the books back on their shelf, and stood looking at the print of the Anvers cathedral, done in sepia-brown sunlight.

Then, perhaps, a yawn would begin to collect—arching up along the throat muscles, working at the nostril wings, flaring them, and the mouth would go ajar, enormously, and the yawn would arrive *audibly*— I don't ever remember yawning as much, or *hearing* yawns as noisily delivered as one heard along the corridors of Cranbrook, particularly in the rookie wing. The veterans did a lot of belching over in their quarters—smartly delivered exhalations which seemed to indicate contentedness, and comfort, a good meal down, and not much to worry about. The yawns and the strange lethargy on the other side had nothing to do with boredom or fatigue, but were from the nerves, and the newness and uncertainty of the situation.

In the evening after classes it helped to walk in the school grounds — alone invariably, just moseying around, down by the swimming lake, which had a string of round colored floats across it, and pine trees along the shore, dark and still under them, with the smell of pine tar worked out by the day's sun. I went down there and stared into the brown water, trying to remember the Harvard football song so I could sing it properly when called on in the dining hall.

Through the blue obscurity

Was that it? Something on that order?

Dum-dum-dum-dum-de-de-de-dum

I sang to myself by the lake border, straining to remember, walking stiff-legged, eyes squinted half shut as if effort itself might bring the lyrics to mind. Curious bits of other college songs I had not thought of in a long time suddenly offered themselves — just snatches of them. One of them was a Yale song which came abruptly to mind — just a line or two of it, remembered, I suppose, because it was so odd:

Oh Yale was begun back in sev'nteen one
By a gift of books weighing nigh a ton.

There were other places than the lake to wander in the school grounds — perhaps up to the art museum and the gaunt Carl Milles statues, tall, stick-like women standing around a fountain that was cool to walk around, a faint mist coming off it, and under the surface ripple you could see the glint of coins visitors had tossed in. There were the basement windows of the biology laboratories to look through — an airplane model hung from the ceiling, high stools around the benches, the Bunsen burners, a miniature skeletal model of a dinosaur off in a corner, and big beakers, quite unarranged, as if the students at the last bell of the spring session had rushed out leaving everything as it was. One window in that same building, which was too high above the ground to look into, faced out from a one-room apartment where a school superintendent had lived. Friday Macklem told me about him. He was from Scotland originally, and he drank, and when the school dismissed him he let himself into the swimming lake and floated up, drowned, among the colored floats. His face appeared at the window (the youngest Cranbrook students were told) from time to time, and at night he was supposed to sail across the lawns, down past the pines, and settle in the lake, where he sat on the bottom, in the weeds, looking up toward the surface. The lawns were suitable for phantoms, being very broad, with nighthawks tilting busily above them, and they were artfully decorated with occasional heavy boulders, Stonehenge-sized, trucked in and set about with great care—so that certain aspects of the grounds, with the night coming on, seemed parts of ancient ruins sinking into the groomed lawns. The Episcopal bishops wandered about, some wearing cassocks, always in pairs, conversing very earnestly, heads down, so they seemed to be watching their feet move them aimlessly across the grass. The dormitory lights came on, and we would start in, the bishops in pairs, the rookies singly.

When night came it was the worst. There was nothing much to do except try to sleep. From their beds the rookies could hear a guitar going over in the veterans' wing, an occasional laugh, the hum from some distant room where players lounged around telling stories—sounds drifting down the corridors bringing the lonesomeness to them as they stared into the close darkness of those cubicle-sized rooms, turning then, restless, the springs of the boys' beds complaining under their weight. I wasn't in their wing, but they told me about it. Lucien Reeberg, who before had slept easily, was having his troubles sleeping, and he said that his roommate, Jake Greer, the spindly end, tumbled around in his sleep, talking a fit, a long leg flopping off the bed, and when his toes fetched up against the hard linoleum of the floor he started up with a little yell, and a moan, and Reeberg would call out, "Hey, cool it, man!" Reeberg said that at times Greer sounded like a couple of people moving around on a haystack, stamping in it, but then he reckoned he thrashed himself around some too, and weighing over three hundred pounds he probably outdid his roommate. I asked Greer one morning, and he shifted his toothpick slightly, revolving it, and then he giggled slightly, shy as he was about any question, and suddenly, with a rush of words, he said it wasn't Reeberg so much as his *bed* and its springs. "Ma', he got a bed...well, ma', you throwed a comic? a shoe? you drop anything, much less three hundred po', on that bed and ma' she stand up an' *scream*."

Much later, with the guitars stopped and the veterans turned in, many of the rookies were still awake. For Frank Imperiale, in the daylight hours trying for a defensive end position, it was often two or three o'clock before he could get to sleep. He'd lie and listen to the hands of big clocks in the corridors click forward every minute, audibly, which I'd noticed too, like post-office boxes clicking shut, and he'd count from one click to the next, trying to match them to the count of sixty. He got expert at it, murmuring his numbers in the darkness. There were variations he could switch to. His room was next to the latrine, which had a row of urinals which flushed automatically, every fifty-three or eighty-three seconds, I forget which, and Imperiale would count the seconds off to whichever it was, and when he got there a low moan of machinery would rise from next door and culminate in a harsh flush of water, the machinery would shudder slightly, and sigh, and things would quiet down in there.

Mainly Imperiale kept at his numbers to keep his mind off football and worrying whether he'd made the team, and to bore himself to sleep, but every once in a while his mind's eye would fill with a vision, always the same—an enormous phantom lineman opposite him on the line of scrimmage, down in his crouch, the hard eyes staring out from the cage of his helmet, the heavy coil of his body behind. When Imperiale launched himself at the figure he did so with such an effort to establish contact, muscles straining, that in his bed he suddenly felt pounds lighter, not far from levitating himself completely, sailing up off the bed stiff as an ironing board, and then with a gasp he'd collapse back, the sweat beginning to work out and prickle his skin. He'd blink his eyes open and shut to remove the image. His phantasmal opponent in these mental illusions, despite his tough appearance, was always decimated, run through, but launching all that power without the actual shock of physical contact was so frustrating that Imperiale far preferred concentrating on the groaning of water pipes and the sounds of clock mechanisms. But sooner or later the lineman would appear, the outlines of him gathering in the darkness. The nights were hard for the new men.

CHAPTER 12

For the veterans the evenings were easier. Many of them had cars and went into town, or to their homes around Detroit, particularly if the evening classes were canceled or curtailed, though all of the players, married or not, were supposed to be back in camp by eleven. At eleven there was a chance of a bed check by one of the coaches. He would come around with a clipboard and if a player was missing from his room or the dormitory floor he was presumed absent and subject to fines or punitive action—such as extra wind sprints on the practice field the next day.

At Detroit the bed checks were rare. The coaches treated the men as professionals, unlike some of the other training camps where there was a more procrustean attitude. John Gonzaga, who played briefly for the Dallas Cowboys, said that Tom Landry, their head coach, pulled a main switch himself at 10:30 to darken the training-camp dormitories there, and that the players would bring out big deer-hunting lamps, the bright beams crisscrossing up and down the dormitory corridors. Gonzaga did a crossword puzzle each night, and when he was with Dallas he fashioned a flashlight holder for the headboard of his bed so he could see to do it.

At Cranbrook, there always being the threat of a bed check, most of the players, if they went out after the evening classes, were back in before the eleven-o'clock deadline. But others stayed out, taking the risk, and at two or three in the morning they'd coast their cars into the parking lot, with the motors low or off, and walk slowly across the school grounds, keeping to the shadows of the buildings, with an eye out for a coach, and when they got in the dormitory they'd shake their roommate awake and ask if a check had been made.

"No, for Chrissake," the roommate would murmur.

I went out with them a few times. They'd come around to my room and they'd ask if I wanted to come into town. They had begun to accept me as one of them. I'd bounce up off the bed and get ready. One favorite place was a big dance hall in Dearborn, about a half hour down the main pike, called the Gay Haven. The sound in the place was concussive—big rock 'n' roll bands—and out in front of the bandstand the place packed, and here and there girls in mohair sweaters, despite the heat, sitting at small tables waiting for dance partners. They would get up without looking to see who had offered them a dance, walking quickly to the dance floor, which was raised, with three or four steps to get up to it, and they'd run up the stairs to get themselves going in the steps of the monkey and the mess around and the others, the variations of the twist—not a word out of them, but it was enough to jog up and down opposite and watch them move their bodies. Some of them were terrific dancers.

One could tell from the condition of the dormitory washroom after the evening class how many players were skipping out for a long night. Sometimes, if communal plans were afoot, it took on the aspect of a college weekend coming up—the place lively with players grooming, and heavy with the scents of cologne. But as the practices became more severe and the evening classes longer, with the training moving into full schedule, the night exodus was cut down considerably. It was too risky, with as much competition as there was at each position, and the possibility of a bed check, to go out on the town and try to get by with four or five hours' sleep before undergoing the rigors of training under that hot August sun.

Usually, after the evening classes, the veterans started up with their card games—pinochle, and bridge, and gin rummy. Often, the music would begin, mildly cacophonous since it would drift out into the corridor from different rooms, and meld—LeBeau and Maher on their guitars, and perhaps Night Train Lane, dressed in his siren suit—lying on his belly listening to his wife Dinah Washington's records plopping down, one after the other, on his record machine on the floor next to his bed.

Then, too, some of the players would collect in someone's room—very often John Gonzaga's, who would lie in bed working on his crossword puzzle book—and the storytelling would begin. Six or seven or more would collect in those small rooms, those who couldn't find a chair or a place on the beds sitting on the floor with their backs up against the wall so their legs stuck out straight into the room.

Often I was reminded of the fine, droning stories that one heard in the Army—lying on the top of one's bed in the barracks on the summer weekends with the faint scent of wood and tar being worked out of the tar-paper roof by the afternoon sun, and down the line one of the regular Army soldiers telling about a trip somewhere, to Baton Rouge, or about a night brawl in some neon-lit bar, or about the arguments in the cheap motel rooms, the glass empty, with the low beds flush on the floor like mattresses—joyless sagas long and sonorous like the sound of summer bees, and yet transfixing. The outside world hardly touched the military: they lashed out at it on the weekends or on furloughs, darting out at it, taking what they wanted, and then they came back inside, skipping through the camp gate, to the security of the barracks, where they talked about their ventures, retelling the stories a little differently each time, until they were just right, set pieces to be installed in their repertoire of misanthropy. The experiences were cruel and heartless, invariably angry and obscene, and there was always scorn and, if one was lucky, humor—and from the best of the storytellers one could hardly get enough: "Jake, tell about the time at Mother's Bar in Shreveport," and everybody would cork up, and Jake would clear his throat and begin.

The football players' world was more sophisticated and not as insular as the military's. Their stories did not have the venom and the suspicion of the outside that one remembered from the Army chronicles. But there were similarities: their view of the outside, a trip to a foreign country, Mexico, say, was usually essentially provincial and chauvinistic — the drama that of struggling with unknown and suspicious foods, and customs, and languages, leading up to a tortured and bizarre nighttime frenzy of corrupt guides, bars, fights, tiny girls perched on stilt heels with black hair stiff with lacquer, perverts, jails, police courts, monumental hangovers, and then finally the security of their car, moving them on to the next adventure. The stories were long and rich — and like the great Army stories they had been told often enough, or thought about, so that they slipped into the form of the epic and one never tired of them. They began properly: the car trip, the town they started from, coming across the border, and where the car broke down in the mountains, and why, and how they got it going again, and coming down into the desert town with the long dusty main street with the bars on either side in the bright sunlight, and inside where the strippers worked in relays for twenty-four hours, a girl picking away at a button on her white glove for ten minutes — that was the pace of the strip tease — and how they started on the cool *cerveza* that had a red rooster on the label. Then one of them felt that the drummer nodding over his drums should quicken the tempo for the girl so she could get those gloves off, and start working at the zipper along the side of her dress, and he went over to the drummer to see what could be done, and behind that bar the big men in the white shirts took their arms off the counter and stood up.

The players knew that I had lived abroad, and sometimes they would say, "Tell us about the Riviera, the chicks there..." but I demurred. I could not sort out an epic about it. There were generalizations to be made, I would stir and think about the Carleton Hotel, and the terrace bar with the producers standing about with their starlets, and the tables with the beach parasols up through the middle, and the girl with the black panther crossing the Croisette, and the quiet of the quais at night, and the little stony beach with the dark sea sifting at it, and the distant high bulk of the carriers of the U.S. Sixth Fleet like apartment houses moored on the sea. But I could produce neither an attitude about these images nor a straightforward narrative. One should arrive in an old Peugeot at film festival time, with the steam coming out of the radiator, and coast into a garage where a Frenchman with a striped shirt, a horrible garlic breath coming out past a thick down-drooped cigarette, and a beret down over one ear, comes to the window of the car and says: "I am Jacques—your guide if you pleez." That was the way the story should have started, and the players would have arranged themselves comfortably for something like that. I would have too, if someone else could have told it.

Not all the stories were about traveling away from home. Sooner or later, the conversation would move around to football—reminiscences of past games and training camps, gossip about coaches and ex-players and other teams, and what were good football towns, and the places in them to eat, and often they told stories about each other.

One evening before classes I looked in a room down the hall and saw the legs sticking out from where the players had their backs up against the wall, and the chairs occupied, and the beds, and I knew they were sitting in there conversing, whiling away a half hour or so before it was time to head for class. Everyone had his blue loose-leaf notebook with him. I dropped in a corner to listen. They were telling stories about their teammate Night Train Lane. Dick LeBeau, who apparently collected Night Train stories—a self-appointed archivist—was describing Night Train as a theorist and tactician. He was saying that often Train had come close to taking over the classroom from Don Shula, who the previous year had been the Detroit defensive backfield coach before moving to Baltimore as the Colt head coach.

"Of course," LeBeau was saying, "Shula was a great theorist himself, and he liked to work on the blackboard. He'd say: 'All right, here's what we're going to do,' and he'd start diagramming. You'd hear this creaking in a chair behind you, and it'd be Train itching there, and maybe he'd slide out of that chair and into one closer to the board, until he was right up there in the front row finally, mumbling and shaking his head, and he'd say co'ah, which meant coach, I guess, and pretty soon he couldn't take it no longer and he'd be standing up there with Shula, the chalk going at the board, talking away to beat the band."

"What does he say?" someone asked.

"Well, that's it," said LeBeau. "You don't know *what* he's saying. He has these theories he goes on about, but it's like stepping into another world to listen to them. He's all the time talking about 'angles'—angles between him and the pass receivers, and also between him and his defensive teammates, Gary Lowe, and Mather, and me, and the rest of the secondary. I remember a couple of years ago in the first five games of the season they began hitting passes on Train deep, and it made him pretty sour. He'd stay long after practice, and you'd see him there in the evening, a loner, practicing his footwork down there on the field, talking to himself—cussing, I thought, because they were getting to him—and then afterwards, for the rest of the season, they don't catch a cold on Train. So I went up to him and I said: 'Train, you made a hell of a comeback.'

" 'Dickie-bird,' he says. 'I figure out what happens.'

" 'What's that, Train?' I ask. 'You find a false step in your moves?'

" 'It ain't *me*,' he says, grieved-like. My, he looks at me like I struck him. 'It's Gary Lowe,' he says. 'He's been comin' in at a bad angle on me.' "

The players whooped and rocked back and forth. They never could get enough Night Train stories.

"Maher," one of them said. "Tell the time Train fessed up and allowed he was wrong."

The others had heard it before, so Bruce Maher, who played corner-back on the defense with Train, looked at me as he told it: "Well, this one time George Wilson sent me in at left safety to play for Gary Lowe. Train's up in front of me, and when I get set to my position he looks over his shoulder at me and calls out a lot of things but of course I don't understand a word of it. He calls me 'Bru'!' So I hear 'Bru'!' and then a whole mess of jabber. On the very first play Train gambles and it goes wrong. He goes for the quarterback. They get a pass out to a man in his zone, and he's off. I lit out for him, but he's going across the goal line as I get to him, and when I give a big last jump at him I get nothing but the breath knocked out of me and a long slide into the end zone. So I get up, and who should I see running down the field toward me but Train. When he gets to me he says, 'Don' worry, Bru'! That was *my man*' — the only words I understood from him all that year. But as he says this what he's doing is jabbing his finger at me like he was lecturing. Up in the stands the people — oh, sixty thousand of them — can't hear what he's saying, so to them it looks like *I* was the one who let the man score — after all, I was the closest to him when he crossed the line — and here's the great Night Train coming on down to tell me what I did wrong. So I say, 'Clear out, you fink!' and he says, 'But Bru', don' you worry none. That was *my man!*' — his finger jabbing at my chest. I tell him to quit poking at me, but by that time it's too late. My stock had dropped to nothing in that place, and running back to the bench I could hear them beginning to let loose with the boos. Train was trotting right along behind me, and I was pretty sure he was still pointing. 'Bru'...don' you worry.' I could hear him saying that." Maher shook his head, and began to laugh.

"That's beautiful," someone said.

"Is the jabber absolutely unintelligible?" I asked, fascinated. "What does he say in the defensive huddle?"

"One time," LeBeau said, "he came into the huddle and he said, clear as a bell, very formal, 'Good evening, gen'l'men,' don't ask me why, and when he got back out to his position he said it again, like he had it on his mind to say. When the offense comes out of *its* huddle and takes up a formation, often Train calls out, 'What sort of setup we got heah?' reflecting on it, like he had something spread out on a newspaper to look at. Then his mind begins to go to work, and that's when you can get into trouble if you listen. One time he calls across to me: 'Dickie-bird, on this play fuss with a zone defense over theah and over heah I'll play a man-to-man.' I yell at him he's crazy, plumb crazy, and he calls back: 'Mix 'em up, Dickie-bird, con*fuse* 'em!' "

Gary Lowe, leaning up against the door with his playbook, broke in, speaking in a rush of clipped sentences: "Shula? He used to make these horrible faces at what Train'd do. He'd say, 'That crap'd never better backfire.' Of course it did—like what happened to Bru'. But then damn if it don't work. In the Playoff Bowl? Against Cleveland last year? He calls at me, 'Gary!'—he says it *Gow-ay*—'you covah fo' me,' and he sprints in and *red dogs* the passer. Now what sort of crap is that for a cornerman? I stand there and my jaw drops. He gets to him too, knocks the ball loose, and their quarterback, that kid Ryan? When he gets up he looks at Train like he seen a ghost."

"How does he get away with it?" I asked. "Can't the offense take advantage of this sort of thing? It sounds like what you might find in a touch football game."

Jim Gibbons said, "He gambles, but then he recovers if it's going wrong. That's what separates him from most cornermen—his natural reflexes. You can't learn to play like him because he gambles so much. There's no one like him."

It was getting close to eight o'clock. The players collected their playbooks, and we idled out to the quadrangle. The shadows were sharp across the lawns and walks, and the summer evening so quiet that we were silent ourselves, strolling for the evening classes through the vague murmur of the school's fountains. One of the largest fountains was just outside the classroom door, its pool surrounded by a wide cement rim on which some of the players sat, their backs to the water, waiting for the Hawk to call them to class. The players seemed subdued then, with little of the chatter and fooling around, many of them affected by a curious self-absorption. Perhaps those lovely surroundings touched them, I thought, though afterward I found out that squad cuts took place during these evening sessions. Night Train was sitting on the rim, drumming his heels, and looking up and grinning as the players passed him. The mood did not affect him. "Hey!" he called out happily when our group approached.

Inside the classroom, George Wilson was in a foul temper. He waited at the blackboard until we had all filed in and settled, and then he wheeled on us and said, "I'm fed to the eyes," sweeping a hard stare at us. We all stared back. Outside the fountains splashed loudly in the evening. It was not football Wilson had on his mind, it turned out, but a school regulation about parking cars which the players had been ignoring—a housekeeping problem that Wilson felt so beneath his dignity to bring up that having to do so turned him nearly apoplectic. "Cranbrook keeps getting on my tail about your cars," he shouted at us. "They tell me their campus looks like a used-car lot. I've warned you about this before. You're supposed to keep your cars in the parking lot. Is that so damn difficult?" He lowered his voice and leaned toward us. "Three cars are out behind the dormitory where they don't belong. I'm fining the players responsible." He looked at a list in his hand. "Whose is a Ford station wagon, whitewall tires, and a black top?"

Max Messner, a big linebacker, put up his hand.

"All right, Max," Wilson said, "that'll be a one-hundred-dollar fine."

There was a quick involuntary hiss of reaction throughout the room and Lucien Reeberg, who didn't own a car, gave a little whoop and flapped his fingers as if they had been singed.

"Cut the noise," Wilson said. "Now whose is a Ford Falcon, two-tone black and white?"

Tom Watkins put up his hand.

"Tommy, that'll be a one-hundred-dollar fine. Now the last one"—one could tell from Wilson's haste how distasteful the matter was to him—"is a Chevrolet Corvair, bright maroon in color, with wire-spoked wheels. Whose is it?"

No one spoke up.

"I said it was *maroon*. Damn thing looks like a circus wagon," Wilson said. "If that isn't enough there's a license plate number." He looked down at his list. "It's a Michigan plate, number M 6 9524."

No one stirred.

Wilson said quietly, "I'll read this information over again, and when

I've done there'll be a hundred dollars added to the fine for every minute we have to wait for an answer."

He read the specifications off his list, and we all waited, some of us with our mouths half open in suspense. Then a chair creaked loudly, a voice was cleared in the silence, and Night Train put up his hand. He cleared his throat again, and then he said—in that high distinctive voice of his—"Jawge, was that Chevy you talkin' about a two do'ah or a fo' do'ah?"

A storm of laughter erupted. Wilson could not keep a straight face, though he tried. You could see his shoulders shaking, and that made everybody laugh harder. When he had composed himself, Wilson had a few announcements to make that were pertinent to football, and then he turned the session over to his subordinates. Later on, I turned in my chair and Wilson was standing in the back of the room. He still had a big grin on his face. The matter was not mentioned again. Messner, Watkins, and Lane all looked relieved, though perhaps the happiest of us was Dick LeBeau, the Night Train archivist, who had another item for his portfolio.

CHAPTER 13

Sometimes, late at night, the "natives would get restless"—as John Gordy would say, and in the dormitory the hijinks would begin. It was a way of letting off energy not consumed by the day's practice. The mode changed from year to year. It was water pistols one year. My year it was fright masks. And it was rare that the players missed a chance at a practical joke.

I had been warned to expect juvenile behavior. A friend of mine had come to see me before I left for Detroit.

"The jocks—that Army barracks, locker-room mentality, peabrained—the *stupidity* of ballplayers," he had said. "Overgrown brats."

He had played a few years with the Washington Redskins, but it was his Boston College career he kept recalling. There, the athletes were bedded down in their own dormitory, which the students called the Playpen. In the evenings after practice, when the rest of the campus was settling down to its books, a curious ritual went on in the Playpen—done half in jest, though there was something mock serious about it, as if the athletes, being segregated on the campus, felt compelled to play up their reputation of thickheadedness.

What sort of thing went on? I had asked him. Well, this one fellow, every night, ran the hundred-yard dash lying on his back in his bed, everyone sitting around, and then someone would say, "On your mark, get set, *go*," and the fellow would pump his legs, really straining, the bed hopping underneath him, the springs squeaking, and after ten seconds or so of this someone would say "Time!" and he'd stop, chest heaving, and he'd pant, "Did I make it?" The players would shake their heads and make clucking sounds, inspecting their watches, and he'd be told, "Sorry, John, you haven't done it — you haven't broken ten seconds. You did it in twelve point two. Maybe tomorrow," they'd tell him.

Afterward, the spelling bee would begin — except they did not spell words, they spelled *sounds*. Someone would say, "How do you spell *Yeeeaugh!!!*" letting out a piercing scream, and the players would sit on the edge of their cots, nibbling at their thumbnails, and *think* about it. Or someone would say, "How do you spell...?" and he would vibrate his tongue rapidly in a Bronx cheer. Down the line of cots a tackle's brow would furrow. "A toughie," he would say. "W...?"

"Come on, now," I said. "Surely, that was done in fun." I told him that at the Coffee House, a New York club which is a favorite lunching spot for staff writers on *The New Yorker* magazine, often these worthies sit around and play similar games. "Animal sounds in different languages — that's what they're up to," I said. "One of the staff will come rushing in and he'll shut everybody up sitting around the big round table there by announcing that 'bow-wow-wow' in Polish is such and such, or 'cock-a-doodle-doo' in Japanese is such and such. Then someone at the table, very blasé, will cork *him* up by revealing what the Hindus say for 'quack-quack-quack.' There's no fooling around — no easy ones. I mean if you said that the French say *mimi* for 'miaow' or the Germans *wau wau* for 'bow-wow-wow,' you'd get short shrift."

"Well, there you are," my friend said. "What those staffers are doing is something quite special — I mean that requires *erudition*."

"Seems to me even a *New Yorker* writer might stumble trying to spell a Bronx cheer," I said lamely.

"You know the joke, don't you?"

"What joke?"

"The coach says: 'Shape up. That guy in the line is outhitting you.'

So the player says: 'Don't worry, coach. After I hit him a few more shots, he'll be as stupid as I am.'"

"Oh, *that* one," I said.

My friend kept at it—assuring me that the general mental equipment of a professional football player was pea-sized, that I'd find no erudition around a training camp. He could not have been treated well at Washington. He kept pressing the point, and he called me when I got back from Detroit.

"Whatja think?"

"About what?"

He told me, and I remembered. It was his first question, even before an inquiry as to the state of my health, whether or not I'd survived without breaking something.

"Well, you were wrong," I said.

"A bunch of Einsteins? Come ahn!"

"The four years of college rub off. The average intelligence has got to be higher—certainly higher than in baseball. It's a crazy question anyway. You can't general..."

"So what do they do in the evening. Read books?"

"No," I said truthfully.

I hadn't seen any books around the camp, and I never saw anyone writing a letter, nor, afterward, did I ever receive a letter from one of the Lions just wanting to stay in touch. Communication was done by phone.

"It's an aural society—no different from the rest of the country," I said. "It has nothing to do with intelligence."

"So what do they do?"

"Cards. Music. Talk. Damn good talk. Better talk than I've heard in places where it's *supposed* to be good."

"And there was no infantilism?"

"What the hell happened to you in Washington?" I asked.

I didn't tell him about the big men scampering down the corridors with water pistols and fright masks...off on pranks. Nor did I disclose my own involvement, that I'd look out into the corridor in the evening at Cranbrook and see the task forces going by. "What's up?" I'd call. "Want any help?"

They'd motion me to be quiet, and they'd fix me up with a fright mask and we'd tiptoe down the hall.

Detroit, as might be expected, had long had a reputation for the prank and the excessive gesture. Jim Hardy, who backed up Bobby Layne at quarterback, once told me that to announce his arrival for the training season (the management had persuaded him to come out of retirement and he was arriving a week late) he not only hired a small private plane and buzzed the practice field, but he dumped a couple of hundred jockstraps, dyed kelly green, out on the players below.

He told me, "The pilot looked over and saw me cramming these things out the window. He said, 'Hey, what's going on?' I was having a devil of a time stuffing those things out. You couldn't get the window open much. 'Jockstraps,' I told him. 'Green jockstraps.'

"We had to make about twenty runs on the field to get them all out. The pilot was fractured by it. He kept saying, 'Well, if you gotta, you gotta,' and he saw it through until we didn't have a green jock left in the plane. They were all over the landscape, let me tell you, up in trees, on roofs, and they turned up for months—you know, a guy'd be walking his date along the lane, and he'd see this thing hanging on a bush, and he'd say, y'know, very sudden-like, 'For Chrissake, there's a green...' The *wives,* that year the wives of the Lions wore those jockstraps to the game on Sunday, no, not wearing 'em like *men,* for Chrissakes, but as headdresses, armlets, scarves, crap like that, like wearing *favors* it was— I mean those girls used such imagination you couldn't tell looking that what they was wearing was green *jock*straps, for Chrissakes...."

When I was at Detroit, the pranks were on a lesser scale. The most elaborate practical-joke apparatus belonged to Friday Macklem. He kept it in his equipment room. It was a wire enclosure with a wooden box at one end which had a round entrance, like a woodpecker's hole, and Friday called it his "mongoose box." He'd tell you that there was a mongoose in there, back in his house, and sometimes at the round entrance just his nose would appear, because he was shy. Friday would tell you all this, tapping at the cage to get the mongoose to show himself, and when you got right down, face right up to the wire mesh, trying to peer in the round hole to see the mongoose's nose, Friday would press a spring, the top of the box would fly off, and a pelt of fur would leap up, unleashed by some sort of catapult, extraordinarily lifelike. The victim would beat around the room for a while, starting and leaping, until he could see he had been duped by a weighted piece of mangy foxtail.

Friday worked the thing very satisfactorily on me, a group of players standing around watching, trying to keep their faces solemn as I got my face up close to the enclosure.

Friday had made the whole contraption himself and he had a good time with it, even making money with it, renting it to the trainer of the Detroit Tiger baseball organization. It gave him pleasure to recall the reactions of some of his victims. Joe Schmidt had been his prize. Somehow the fake mongoose had sprung up and attached itself to Schmidt, caught on him somehow, as if it had sunk its teeth into his suit, and Schmidt spun around, whacking at the pelt, and yelling. "For a big man," Friday said, "he had great moves in here that day."

Roger Brown had been another fine victim. He had crashed around after the mongoose sailed at him, and he swept the equipment off the length of a workbench. Jokes of this sort were always dangerous, since a sizable victim, which all the Lions were, properly terrorized, could decimate a room, particularly a dormitory cubicle, simply by thrashing around.

Most of the props used for enjoyments of this sort were far less elaborate than Friday's mongoose box—someone might have a whoopee cushion, or a fright mask, or a rubber snake to coil and put on a bed, or perhaps there would be a sudden spate of cap pistols. There was always improvising with what was at hand—such as the pleasure that a frog found hopping around the quadrangle fountain could afford. One of these was put under an ashtray in front of Roger Brown at an eight-o'clock meeting in the classroom one night, and it moved when Roger did not have his eye on it, but he heard the scraping sound of something across the tabletop just in front of him, and he stared, until finally the ashtray moved again, convulsively, and he let out a great yell just as Aldo Forte was asking if there were any questions or comments about a play he had diagrammed on the blackboard.

"Any questions?"

"Man, what's going *on?*" Brown called out, his voice high and alarmed, as he scraped back his chair.

Forte was just as startled, assuming that Brown's anguished shout was directed at his diagram, and he gave a quick glance back at the blackboard to see what he had done wrong.

The year before, Alex Karras had a frog set under *his* ashtray at an eight-o'clock meeting, and when it moved his eyes grew very nearly as large as his spectacles—it was recounted—his chair went over behind him, and with a yell he bolted from the room, playacting probably, being a great clown with a fine sense of timing, his yell coming just at the moment when Forte, as might be expected, was turning from a diagram, waving his dead cigar, quite as usual, and asking for questions or comments.

"Any questions?"

Karras's shout went up, making everyone jump and turn in time to see him rip out past the fountain, career around a corner, his legs pumping hard, and disappear.

"What's going on?" Aldo called out. "What's wrong with Alex?" He looked out at his players.

"Maybe he had to go to the can," someone said.

Karras was the favorite victim of practical jokes that year, because his reaction was invariably very pronounced, playacting or not, which gave great satisfaction to the perpetrators. Dick LeBeau was another attractive victim, primarily because of an abstracted air which made it possible for the jokesters to work around him, setting up their props, without his being aware. LeBeau was from Ohio, with a pronounced Midwestern twang, nasal and slow, which made the songs he put to his guitar quite incomprehensible, though fetching: gentle songs full of melancholy and poverty, one supposed, and love unrequited. He himself had a lady-killer reputation. Thin-hipped, built like a high-school basketball player, his hair worn longer than most of the others', he was called Ricky, less a diminutive of Richard than derived from a crop of teenage movie stars and singers of the time, all of that name, whose manner and attitude he seemed to cultivate. At the Gay Haven he was a great dancer with the twist variations of that summer—the frog, the bird, the slop. He danced with an aloofness close to disdain, which made the girl moving opposite him, invariably pretty, work very hard, though in the manner of those dances he never looked at her, staring out to one side, then the other, then over the girl's head, self-absorbed, the motion of his body stiff yet graceful, and always controlled.

In the evening in the dormitory he would murmur at his guitar, or lie in his bed like someone sunbathing on a beach, eyes half shut, humming, and in his mind's eye—one always assumed—an acreage of girls. At such times, with his concentration elsewhere, the pranksters would work close to him, like a matador to the controlled bull, and a hotfoot would be bestowed, or perhaps his shoelaces tied together, or a rubber snake coiled up on the floor beside his bed. The favorite prank was to terrify him with a fright mask—suddenly jumping at him, or leering over his bed, which made him squawk and rise off the bed as if doing a levitation stunt. Often the fright mask would be used very late at night, the wearer carrying a candle and making moaning sounds as he crept into LeBeau's room, and though it was done to him a number of times it was not something one could get used to easily, and his yell would reverberate in the corridors.

The fright masks were made of thin, pliable rubber, grotesquely featured, which fitted entirely over the wearer's head down to the neck, with small slits to see out of—vampire heads, some of them, Frankenstein's monster, and others, and chilling to see suddenly from around a corner. The most effective one I saw belonged to Joe Schmidt, which was a dark gray mummy's face, creased like an elephant's foot, with a long white tooth that hung out from the lower lip and flapped. He kept it on the shelf in his clothing alcove. John Gordy borrowed it one night to "fright" LeBeau. His idea was to slide into LeBeau's clothing alcove among his suits, and wait there until LeBeau finally bestirred himself to prepare for bed—coming to the clothing alcove for his toilet kit, which he kept up on a wooden shelf there, at which point the mummy's face would jut out from between his jackets, and from within Gordy would deliver his patented "mummy's scream"—which he demonstrated to me once, and which I heard with respect.

Outside LeBeau's room he slipped on the mask, and when he peered in he saw LeBeau on his back, looking up at the ceiling above his head. The light was on. The clothing alcove was just next to the door, and Gordy took two soft steps into the room and began to back into the alcove, working his way back among the clothes, crouched, so as not to jostle the coat hangers. Suddenly, *behind* him, deep in the alcove, he heard the sounds of someone breathing; he felt a hand brush against his neck, then he heard a muffled shout, and Gordy let out a yowl which was not his patented "mummy's scream," but one of his own bona fide terror, and he bolted from the alcove with a houndstooth jacket of Le-Beau's caught across his shoulders.

I have forgotten who was in the alcove behind him—Pat Studstill, I think, who had crept in there earlier with the same intent as Gordy (they had talked about such a caper a few nights earlier in the dining room), wearing a U-Fright Mask Company Special, which was a pale vampire mask with two red fangs hanging down from either side of the mouth. He had slipped this on, and got himself into the alcove without LeBeau's being aware, and he waited in back of the clothing, listening to LeBeau's humming. His plan was to fly out when LeBeau came to the alcove, calling, "Hi, Ricky, baby!" like a moonstruck teenage girl, and fling his arms around him. It was hot under the mask, and he was getting impatient, when the dim light in the alcove suddenly faded, cut by the dark bulk of something moving stealthily in to join him, which was, of course, though he didn't know, Gordy backing up. He took a look to see, assuming it was LeBeau, and there was just enough light to see the back of Gordy's fright mask, which was very nearly as awful a thing to see as the front, a fearful expanse of wrinkles, a bas-relief map of mountain country in the shape of a head, an old woman's knee moving toward him, and Studstill took a startled whack at it, sucking in his breath involuntarily as he did so, which brought the rubber of his own mask back into his mouth and made him strangle and cough. That was the muffled shout Gordy heard—at which he had bolted.

As for LeBeau, he heard the wild commotion, and he started up in bed to see a first figure erupt from his alcove, just a glimpse of a mummy's face floating by above his houndstooth jacket, then a second figure emerge, arms flailing, bent almost double, with a white face mask severely puckered in at the center, the whole mask, as it happened, flowing into Studstill's mouth—it looked like a decomposing skull—and some clothes went out with him too, a few pairs of slacks, and these LeBeau recovered from the corridor, which was deserted when he looked out, except for his jacket and a few other articles of clothing lying in discarded heaps.

All of this came out later. It took a long time to piece together what had happened.

The night before the Pontiac scrimmage, they tried to work the fright mask on me. It was late, but I was wide-awake, staring up through the darkness, thinking about the game the next night, and I heard the giggling and the whispering outside my door. I watched the door open and the candle come in, with the fright mask looming above it—it was Joe Schmidt's mummy face at work again, with him inside it—and I could look past and see Terry Barr and the others behind, all grinning, peering forward to see what would happen. It did not work at all. From inside his mask Schmidt could see me grinning at him, and he swore lustily.

"Poor moves out there," I said, using football terminology. "You sounded like a herd of cattle."

It was very often like that—the perpetrators giving themselves away by breaking down and giggling behind their masks. But there was thought to be one player on the Detroit team who was very serious about such activity—a near-pathological case. He was called the Mad Creeper.

No one was quite sure who the Mad Creeper was, but he was talked about, and it was thought to be only a matter of time before he went on the prowl. His habit was to creep along the corridors late at night, three or four in the morning, sneak into someone's room, lean over his bed, and throttle him hard and briefly, just closing his hands around the fellow's throat and then skittering off down the corridor, listening to the gasping behind him. He always worked alone. No one had ever seen him, and he probably did not wear a mask. Almost everyone thought Brettschneider, "the Badger," was the Mad Creeper, and, though he denied it, there was strong evidence to support the theory: the Badger had originally played for the Cardinal football organization, where the Mad Creeper had first appeared, so famous for his night forays there that every team in the National Football League had heard of him. When the Badger was traded to Detroit, the throttlings ceased in St. Louis. True, there had not been a Mad Creeper attack at Cranbrook, but the feeling was that it would come—that the Badger had simply been intimidated by the heavy traffic of fright-mask people in the corridors at night. The experience of Gordy in LeBeau's clothing alcove was not lost on him.

One evening, sitting around in someone's room—talking about the Mad Creeper—someone said to me, wondering what my attitude was toward these hijinks, "You must take us for a bunch of nuts...that we've gone...well, *ape*."

"Well, no," I said honestly. "I was studying for a while at Cambridge, in England, where this sort of thing went on all the time—and that place is one of the great...er...seats of learning."

They wanted to hear about it.

"Well, the sport of frightening people at night there, at least at my college—King's College—was called 'Hoovering,'" I began, "after the Hoover vacuum cleaner, which was the essential piece of equipment. These vacuum cleaners were stored in broom closets. Very late, at three in the morning, an expedition of students, great scholars among them, mind you, future Parliamentarians, barristers, would set out and swipe one of them—preferably with a big circular floor polisher attached. The thing to do was hustle this thing back to the room, stand it up, and maybe test it out, just to be sure it worked. The Hoover gives off a fine groan, the way cleaners do, and if it had the floor polisher attached, this would turn and move the cleaner across the floor—eerily."

I demonstrated, moving my hands around vaguely, and they all nodded.

"Well, the idea of Hoovering was that you'd sneak this thing into someone's room, in the dark, and…well…set it going…scare the hell out of the fellow in bed"—the effect sounded miserably tame—"but the fun of it," I continued gamely, "was in the *preparation*—deciding whom to Hoover, and getting the equipment, and testing it, and then the reconnaissance into the fellow's room, because you had to turn the lightbulbs loose in their sockets so when you plugged in the Hoover's extension cord and threw the main light switch the lights would stay out. Sometimes, when you reached for a lamp in the dark, doing everything by touch, hearing the fellow breathing in his bed, you'd find the bulb still warm—which meant that he'd only just turned it out. After that, the Hoover'd be carried in, very quietly, plugged in, and everyone would back out of the room, the last one out throwing the light switch and shutting the door. Inside, the lights wouldn't go on, being disconnected, but the Hoover *would*, starting up with that eerie moan and all, the black bag puffing out, and the circular polishing brush would revolve, hauling the machine around after it, you see, so that the poor fellow in bed'd wake up and hear the moan and see the bulk of the thing moving, knocking against the furniture, and he'd reach frantically for the lights, which wouldn't go on, of course, and very often he'd leap up and bolt for the door. Peering around a corner, you'd see him stumble out into the corridor wild-haired—which was, well, that was the *ultimate* in Hoovering, to see the fellow stumble out into the corridor wild-haired like that. Most of the time, of course, that wouldn't happen. You'd hear the Hoover going, then it would stop, the door would open, and the Hoover'd be tossed out, landing with a crash on the stone flagging, the black bag collapsed, and the handle off at some crazy angle.

"Sometimes the fellow inside'd lean out into the corridor and shout: 'Christopher Cory, for God's sake act your years!' Cory was a very large fellow who'd been to Eton and he thought about Hoovering a lot of the time—he had a special outfit he wore, all black, even black gym shoes so he couldn't be spotted in the dark of a victim's room. He came to my room one night, very excited, and he said a small group of choirboys had arrived for tryouts with the King's College Choir, one of the best in the country, and they were bedded down in college somewhere. Well, we went up there that night with the others and did it, and I remember that particular expedition because we set this Hoover going in one room—occupied; you could see the shape of the choirboy under the blanket—but this time it was different: the Hoover kept on groaning away, it wasn't turned *off*, and you could hear the polishing disc fetch it up against things, and the crash of a glass ashtray, and the clank of a big wastepaper basket going over. We waited out in the corridor, nervously, because we couldn't reckon what was going on in there, and finally Cory went in and got the machine out. He said that as best he could tell the choirboy had pulled the bedclothes up over his head, and Cory, telling the story later, used to say that when the boy appeared for his audition the next morning and opened up his mouth to sing, nothing came out of his throat at all."

"Perhaps the sound of a Hoover," said one of the players. They had listened respectfully.

One of them said, "I like the idea of feeling for the lightbulbs and finding them still warm."

I felt, though, they were of the opinion that sneaking vacuum cleaners around was pretty small potatoes—that is compared to the Mad Creeper on the prowl, or Joe Schmidt in his fright mask—and of course they would be right.

Talking about this got everybody restless, and later two or three of us went to Joe Schmidt's room to borrow his mask. He was eager to use it himself. He had been reading a paper, but he put it aside and got the mask off his shelf and put it on. "Let's give it to Friday Macklem," he said.

The face really looked awful on him.

"Quick and simple," he said.

"That could kill him," I said.

"Friday is indestructible," he said.

We went up the stairs to the second floor and down the dormitory hall toward an end room. I had been in there earlier that day. Friday had a bottle of Scotch in the back of his bureau drawer, and he had taken it out and offered me a drink. I did not feel very comfortable standing outside his door watching Schmidt set his mask and turn the doorknob. He was gone quite a while. Then we heard a yelp, and Schmidt came out, walking quite slowly, as if he were sure whoever was in there would not be coming after him.

We went down the corridor.

"Friday wasn't in," Schmidt told us. "But his assistant, that kid Jerry Collins, was in the next room. So I gave it to him. It was beautiful."

CHAPTER 14

One afternoon I was driving back with Don Doll and Aldo Forte from the coaches' hideaway bar after a turn at liars' poker. The two coaches were commenting on a magazine story which speculated that there were very few superstars in the National Football League. The Green Bay Packers had a plethora of them, perhaps as many as five, but many of the teams, of their complements of nearly forty players each, according to the article, had not one player of great stature. Both coaches were inclined to agree, though when I asked them about the superstars on the Lions, pridefully and with dispatch they eclipsed the number of Packers with their own list. Well, there was Joe Schmidt, of course, and Roger Brown, Terry Barr, Alex Karras (if one could assume his being active), John Gordy, certainly, and Gail Cogdill and Night Train Lane, and possibly a few more could be added, Wayne Walker and Yale Lary, for example, though certainly those first seven would have to lead off such a list.

"The championship's in the bag," I said.

There are weaknesses, they said, pointing out that a pro team has twenty-two positions; a strong bench and specialists are essential. They did not discuss the soft spots; they preferred to talk about their superstars, going over their list with relish. The last two, Cogdill and Lane, were the easiest to talk about, they said, because their skills were so markedly evident. Cogdill was an astonishing athlete, fast, with extraordinary coordination, the natural athlete of the club, for whom everything was almost too easy. He was an attack by himself. You could always rate a player by imagining how much trouble he'd be playing against you; the thought of Cogdill with a good quarterback to throw to him running out of an opposing formation and floating around in the secondary was enough to bring on the fits.

"And Night Train?"

"I tell you I wouldn't like to play against him," Aldo said. "He's the roughest cornerback in the league. He's got pipes for legs, all bone, with just strings of muscle holding him together, but when he comes up, there's no fooling around: he's a ferocious tackler." He shook his head thinking back on some of the tackles. He recalled Y. A. Tittle, the New York Giant quarterback, describing being hit by Night Train (it happened on a freezing afternoon in 1962) — so hard that the Giant plays simply popped out of his head. He got off the ground and reeled back to his huddle, and his teammates all leaned in toward him to pick up the next call, the faint puffs of steam at the cages of their helmets, and hearing only their own heavy breathing, and then Tittle saying, "Christ, I don't...I can't think of any plays."

They hurried him back to the bench. Dr. Sweeney, the team physician, stood in front of him and said, "What's your name?"

"Y. A. Tittle."

He knew all those things—his name, the doctor's name, the day, that the Giants were playing the Lions, but the Giant plays and formations had gone. He had some old high-school plays he could offer, and a few San Francisco formations (he had played with the 49ers before coming to New York), but nothing else, until the halftime intermission when the plays suddenly flared back into his consciousness and he was all right.

Don Doll suddenly said to me: "Tomorrow, why don't you take a try at Night Train's position, cornerback, the toughest there is — see how much tougher it is than playing the offense." He grinned at Forte, who coached the offensive line. There was always rivalry between the two units.

Forte shook his head and grunted. "We can't lose our quarterback," he said. "The *big* Pontiac scrimmage coming up next week."

"Is there a scrimmage tomorrow?" I asked, haltingly.

"The offense will be running plays against the defense," Doll said. "We'll slip a red shirt on you, and send you in for a couple of plays."

"Well," I said. "I guess so."

Doll suggested I talk with Night Train that evening and pick up a few pointers. I saw Night Train in the dining room when we came in together, and I got my tray and sat with him, asking him if he had some time to confer that evening.

"Certain," he said.

We met in his room before evening classes. The Dinah Washington records were turning on the record machine when I got there. Train turned the volume down but not off. The records turned, and slapped down on their predecessors, the arm would grope and set, and the voice of Train's wife would come on, just barely audible. At the camp, conversations always seemed to be carried on over a background of transistors or record machines.

"It must be fine to have that voice around," I said.

Train grinned and said it was. Set up on his dresser were big glossy photo prints of her, some showing her flanked by two youngsters from a previous marriage. Night Train was her eighth husband. All of her photographs were autographed and inscribed in a flowing script. One was signed "Mommy," and the inscription read: "I keep my eye on all trains."

Train was easy if occasionally puzzling to listen to—his voice high and friendly; if something serious was on his mind the tone became gentle and curiously poignant. He had an odd habit of lengthening one-syllable words into three—"but" into "but-ter-ah"—he used involved rather than simple words, and he was likely to slap suffixes on the ends of words, such as "captainship," so that his sentences were rich, and a certain strain was necessary to get the gist of them absolutely straight. He motioned me to a chair, and he sat relaxing on the bed. He had on his siren suit; I noticed a small monogram on the handkerchief pocket.

He began by talking about the changes that he had seen since his start in the professional leagues, what he called his "commencemanship."

"Ballplayers are not made up of that old vigor," he said. "These days when Sunday rolls aroun', there's like to be too much kibitzing going on, which ought to be left in the bedroom, or somewhere, so that you don' find it lyin' aroun' on the day of the game."

"Kibitzing...?" I asked.

"Not being serious enough. Not being able to get up for a game—that's what I mean. We're only here for a little while, so this bereaves me. Sacrifice ought to be made. I know what happens when you don' make it: the last eleven years I look to play on a championship team, and *six* years, think on that, I play with Chicago where we have this kibitzing and win maybe two games a year. There's not so much time left now. Every year it's a challenge to see if I have the ninety percent I had the year befo'. Maybe not. I don' look forward to it. To finding out. It seem like it come too fast—that old express train."

I asked Train if he would start at the beginning—if he would go back to his "commencemanship."

Train settled himself comfortably.

"I was an adopted kid," he began, "and I had a lot of harsh days. I grew up in Austin, Texas—that was the basis for my playing then, football, and a little basketball, but I was always getting the gigglings 'cause I weighed 135 pounds. What broadened me out was the services. That was a break. After thirteen weeks of that apprenticeship training I felt like a man. After, they get me into the Army Language School in Monterey to study intelligence. They give me a sort of runaround there, and a break too, because they send me across the Bay into Special Services at Fort Ord."

Train shifted on his bed. "We become to enjoy each other," he said. "We play badminton there," he went on, "a lot of badminton, and every Wednesday we set up the boxing ring. Weight began to shift onto my bones, not a whole lot, but some. We get along jus' fine with each other. At that time I was playing offensive end for the Fort Ord team—we busted some good records, and played in three bowls. On the weekends we go to see the 49ers play in the Kazoo" (Kezar Stadium), "where I fall in love with football. Settin' there one day I see a player from the old New York Yankees miss a whole mess of tackles. So I went back and I jot me down a little letter to Buck Shaw, the 49er coach. I was in business administration then at Fort Ord, and the colonel's secretary helped me to draft it up. All I done was to tell Shaw that I had a good pair of hands, and why not? Nothing lost, nothing gained. Well, Shaw—who is called the Gray Fox—he jotted me back a letter, but I never did activate on it.

"After," Train went on, "I won a football scholarship to a college, but just as I was packing my bags and getting set to go, why this college *drop* football. So I played basketball for North American. Played against Kirby Shoes. It was not much to my liking, so one day I was out riding around Los Angeles, and I stopped in to see Joe Stydahar, the Ram coach. Gabby Sims, out of Dallas, who had played on the Fort Ord team, was with the Rams, so I thought it'd be all right to drop in at the office. I said, 'If you please I want to see the head coach.' So they sent me in. Stydahar was built solid, a big Polack-looking fellow. Jumbo Joe. A terrific fellow. Red Hickey, his end coach, kept looking at me and saying, 'How much you weigh?' I was at 185 then, light for the pros, so they ask me about the other players on the Fort Ord team, Bernice Carter, John LaGordia, John Hoch, Hellwig, and all of them. So the next day I came in with a scrapbook which I open up to show them about Bernice Carter, John LaGordia, John Hoch, Hellwig, and-er-ah... Well, Hoch, he is the only one to make the ball club."

"And you," I said.

"Joe Stydahar says, 'Lane, how 'bout $4,500?' I say to him, 'Joe, before I sign and waste your time, do I get a fair shake at my position?' He says, 'Yes, if you can beat out Elroy "Crazy Legs" Hirsch and Tom Fears.' Well, that was something. Crazy Legs is going to be in the Hall of Fame, and Fears, he wasn't the slightest slouch neither." Train grinned suddenly. "When the camp start that summer, I was sick. I'd faint on the field, and then hittin' the dummies I faint again, jus' faint, and Jumbo Joe, he'd say, 'Take that body over theah.' So they'd drag me ovah by the heels and lay me down. I wasn't getting much sleep at night neither. It was hard for me to learn the system, to run the patterns, and the terminology. Someone'd yell at me, 'Twenty-seven fake toss,' and man, I didn't know where to go. So after the lights go out at eleven, I'd have a little push-button flashlight, and I'd beam it on those playbooks so as to understand the things in there. Tom Fears, he was helpful. He had a phonograph in his room. One night, when I come along to get his advice, he had Buddy Morrow's 'Night Train' playing. Someone said, 'Here he come, Night Train.' "

"And it stuck," I said, gratuitously.

"Correct," said Night Train. "All that training camp," he continued, "I was catching the devils from Red Hickey. He shout, 'You can get your bags packed, Lane, if you miss another pass.' I *did* miss another, natural', but they don' let me go. He an' Joe must've *seen* something— maybe that I never appeared lazy to them. One night we had a big intra-squad scrimmage, like the Pontiac scrimmage you'll be in, a 'rookie scrimmage' they call it, and there's a big mess of folks there to watch, and the newspaper people, course. 'Play defensive end,' said Red Hickey—me, weighing 185 soaking wet! So I went out there and dug in. Stydahar shouted, 'Don't tackle the quarterback!' On the first play he come right by me—Bob Waterfield, who was a great pilot—and my fingers got all gibbely wanting to fetch him in. But I let him go—like I been told. They had a draw play next, and on the third play, by my being so light and shifty, the tackle got fooled up and I pushed him into the quarterback, ol' Waterfield, who fell over. Red Hickey got angry, 'cause the quarterback fell over, and I got angry too, throwing my helmet, and so Hickey banish me out as a defensive halfback. I didn' know about that 'tall. I didn' know how to 'set'—so I fuss around there and I got settled finally, and in it pretty natural. Later in the game, I came up fast on a fullback end around and I was hit by the flanker back, who I didn't see, and he knocked me over so I somersault and land on my feet right there with Deacon Dan Towler, the fullback, in my arms. Well, Jumbo Joe Stydahar, he come rushing out of nowhere and he says, 'That's the type of ballplayer I want.' I get in on the play so much that night that my eyes and jaw get swollen and sore, so that the nex' mornin' when my roommate, Willie Davis, rustled the newspapers at me and is calling out, 'Say, Star, wake up, hey, Star, read 'bout the star,' I say to him, 'Oh you read it, Willie Davis, I'm too sore to read it.'"

"That was when you knew you were set with the Rams?" I asked.

"Well, we had the Los Angeles–Washington charity game one night, and I got me a spotlight there for the introductions before the game, running through the darkness with that big cone of light, and me in it, and all the noise from that crowd, the biggest crowd they had in the Coliseum in a time. Then was when I knew I belong. Then they turn out all the lights, and this man, he says, 'Now light your matches'—and my! The whole place blaze with thousan' tiny little lights, blazing quick so you see the blades of grass at your feet, and a big shout from everyone it look so pretty, and then they go out, so it look sad, and everybody quiet, and finally just one or two little lights are left, and they seem so far away, like we were in a valley very dark and quiet, with a light across in the hills."

He said this rather slowly, thinking about what he had seen. I told him he had a fine eye for detail.

He brightened. He told me that he had been thinking of "jotting" himself down a "little book," and that he had been considering taking a Palmer correspondence course in what he referred to as "authorship."

"Train," I said, "talking of other professions, I thought I'd take a crack at your position tomorrow."

"Goodness," he said, grinning.

"I mean I'd like to *play* it, not run against it," I said, thinking he might have misunderstood.

He nodded.

"Perhaps you could help me on the field—a tip or two down there tomorrow so's I know what I *ought* to do, even if I can't."

"Certain'," Night Train said seriously. "Now playing my position, course the big thing is not to get beat deep. You must keep your angles correct and keep talking so the others know where you are and what's going on—so's you don't bring the defense down."

I asked, "How do you prepare for a game? How would you get ready for the ends or flankers like Terry Barr or Cogdill?"

"I sit in the motion pictures of the games and watch careful so I pick up the keys. A receiver likes a certain pattern and after I watch for a while I'm able to decipher him, and I'm able to tell what he *like* to do. All of the, even the best men, have moves they *prefer,* an' while you wouldn't call it a habit, still you got a little percentage working for you. Now I go a little further. I think to myself, how would *I* play the play if I was the receiver. Now I'm working on him, I'm setting *him* up. He think he setting me up, but no, I'm setting *him* up."

Train was getting excited as he talked. As he explained who was and who wasn't being "set up" he came half off his bed and jabbed a long finger at me for emphasis. "Now heah is how it work."

He settled back and folded his hands. His voice sank, and became almost conspiratorial: "I set the fellow up by baiting him just a li'l bit," he said, "giving him just a bit too much to the outside on the red coverage maybe, until this fellow goes back to his quarterback and he tells him in the huddle, 'Lawd Almighty, I can beat Night Train to the outside, beat him like a drum,' and he *plead* with the quarterback to throw him the ball out there, he practically get down on his *knees* asking for the ball. The quarterback may have been around a time, and maybe he smell a rat, especially when the talk is about Night Train's zone, but then he figure maybe there's no *harm* in trying a pass out there. So he says OK. He calls the play. I watch my man as he lines up. He's trying to look the same as he always does, but he don't—there's something about him, something I can read, trotting out and standing there at the flanker, maybe by the way he curl his fingers, maybe a bit too casual, maybe something you can't even see, but just feel. Joe Schmidt calls the blue coverage, which is what I hope he does, and where before I don' move, I'm there, and that boy, who runs out there looking to make the touchdown *easy,* why he's like to be in bad trouble. Maybe a Night Train interception. Let's say it is. So when he goes back to the bench, he's in *worse* trouble. That quarterback looks at him kinda hard, and he says to everybody, kind of scornful, 'Well, thank *you,* gentl'm'n, but from heah on we stick to the game plan.'"

Night Train grinned. It was an example he obviously savored giving.

I asked how much difference there was in the style of the flankers and ends Night Train defended against.

"Oh, my," he said. "Some are easy. They come at you and pussyfoot around in the zone, and when they make their move you can tell. Wherever those boys go I can pick them up in a few steps. Others can give you the fits — Jimmy Orr, Lenny Moore, Johnny Morris over there with Chicago, Boyd Dowler, Casey with the 49ers, those big long-legged fellows. They have good combinations, and they don' let on when they goin' to turn on the big step. They get me into trouble. They're goin' to beat me, a good fake is *got* to beat me, but the thing is not to give up. You got to have a sense of recovery — to get back on the fellow to cut down the time he's a free receiver."

"Dick LeBeau was telling me he likes to defend against the guys with the long strides," I said. "Because they have to shorten their steps to cut and fake, and he can read them better."

"Well, that's Dickie-bird for you. He's complex. He confirms and thinks on it about reading the receivers."

"What do you look at when they're coming out for you?" I asked.

I look at the belt buckle, at the waistline, which is always fixed no matter how much sashaying and fakin' is goin' on with the feet and the hands. Very seldom do I catch a look at the head or the eyes, 'cause even the half-good ones can pull you out of your boots with a fake if you do. I try to come at an angle where I can see both the quarterback and the receiver, trying to keep the outside, particularly when I have inside help. The big thing is to try to be in position when the quarterback throws the ball, and to do that you try to work the angle with the receiver so's you can keep half an eye on the quarterback to see where he let the ball go. The exception is when your linebackers are red dogging. Then you can't look at the quarterback. He's goin' to get rid of the ball too fast, with the linebackers grabbeling at him, so you move way up on the receiver and keep your eye fixed on him. If you don', he can make a move on you, and bring the defense down."

"It's complex," I said. "What's the main thing I must keep in mind tomorrow?"

"The big thing is a sense of recovery," Train said. "They're going to beat you tomorrow no matter who you is—a good fake has got to beat the defense, like I say. But you got to recover. You can't give up, ever."

"And an interception?" I asked. "What is the procedure?"

Night Train looked at me, surprised. The possibility apparently had not occurred to him.

"I might as well think positively about this thing," I said.

"Well-er-ah—well, I'd just run," he said. "Run for the touchdown."

"I shouldn't look around for interference to form, or anything?"

"I'd go into high gear and hightail it outta there," Night Train said. "I'd incline to drift down the sidelines and keep away from those big fellows hanging around the line of scrimmage."

"Train," I said, "if you're anywhere near me on this interception, I'll lateral it to you first thing."

"You're *playing*," Night Train said, grinning. "I'll be on the sidelines, watching."

"I'll get it to you. It'll be like a beanbag game," I said. "If you refuse it, it's going to that grandmother standing next to you, the one with the baby carriage."

Night Train rocked back and forth on the bed. "Oh my," he said. "I'll remember tomorrow."

CHAPTER 15

It was hot then, the hottest day of the training period. My skin crawled with sweat under the jersey and at the rim of the shoulder pads, which scratched and rasped as I moved. Friday Macklem brought the station wagon down and parked it in the shade by the side of the practice field. George Wilson ordered water breaks; the players clustered around, spouting the water from plastic bottles against the roofs of their throats, and applying towels dipped in pails of ice across each other's necks. I thought about the pails of lemonade that would be waiting in the training room, the ice cubes floating on top, and the big tin dipper to pour it into the paper cups.

The scrimmage was scheduled for late in the afternoon. The spectators, many of whom had been sitting under the big elms while the units practiced separately, began collecting along the sidelines. Don Doll said, "You're going in for Night Train for the last plays of the afternoon. OK?"

"Right," I said.

"D'you talk to him last night?"

"Sure," I said. "My head's stuffed."

"You got it straight then."

"Well," I said. "I'm not so sure."

Doll said, "You probably got some sort of headache."

The scrimmage was run periodically—with the coaches talking

with their units after every play. The concentration was on the pass attack. I watched Train at his position. Two passes came out his way. One he knocked down, and the other was caught on him, which made him giggle sharply, like a boy about to be tagged in a schoolyard game — an unexpected sound in the rough, noisy rush of other defensive backs coming up to push the receiver out-of-bounds. It occurred to me that Night Train had such confidence that such a mistake could only be treated as ludicrous, and therefore comic.

"OK," Doll said. "In you go."

I wrenched on my helmet, wincing as its edges slid painfully past my ears, and I trotted out to Train.

"Here I am," I said.

He skinned off the red shirt — the light scarlet canvas jersey that the defense wears in a scrimmage — helping me slide it down my upright arms, over the helmet, and across my shoulder pads. It was covered with drawings and graffiti, most of them obscene, doodled on with ballpoint pens.

"Train, I'm carrying around an art gallery," I said.

He gave a last haul to the jersey. "Get on in there," he said. He pointed to the defensive huddle forming behind the line of scrimmage.

"You'll be around, Train?"

"I'll be on the sidelines," he said.

In the defensive huddle they did not seem surprised when I trotted in and joined them. A few helmets turned. Past the helmet bars the eyes looked tired, staring from faces slick with sweat. We leaned toward Schmidt. "The coverage is red, George," he said to me. "That means you stick with the flanker — one-on-one, you just stay with him. I'll have your ass if you don't."

The huddle broke and I trotted back to the cornerman position. I looked over at Night Train, close by, fifteen yards or so away, standing on the sidelines. He offered up an encouraging smile, a shine of teeth in his dark face.

"It's red," I hissed at him.

148

"Stick with the flanker," he called back, cupping his hands to his mouth. "Scramble back when he come, and don' give up."

A knot of spectators had collected around him, looking out. All of them, in Bermuda shorts, seemed to have soft-drink bottles in their hands. I avoided their stares. I felt the heat build up inside my helmet. I jogged in place, working the stiffness out, and watched the offensive huddle break finally with a crack of hands in unison and move up to their positions. Jake Greer was the flanker and he came loping out along the line of scrimmage, split ten yards or so from his nearest lineman. I moved along opposite, watching him.

Plum began to call the signals. At the hike of the ball, Greer started toward me with his high, bouncy steps, slow at first, like the slow-motion advance of a klipspringer, coming head-on. Then his speed picked up.

"Fetch him!" I heard Night Train yell. "Scrabble aroun'!"

I began to backpedal, trying to keep my eye on Greer's belt buckle. He sailed up to me, and then cut to my left for the sidelines, with a little grunt, and I could hear the *shu-shu* of his football trousers as he went by, and the creak of his shoulder pads. I was leaning left to the outside when he cut, just chancing he would move for the sidelines on a down-and-out pattern, and when I reached after him I was not too far behind. He pulled up after two or three strides, and I almost cracked into him. The play was over—a pass to the other side had been knocked down by a lineman rearing up. Greer started trotting back to his huddle. I doubted he noticed that I was opposing him at cornerback. I had not seen the pass thrown—the action there as distant as if it had taken place on another practice field. I had no sense of identification with the play. Greer and I had been alone in my zone. My confrontation with him could have been an inadvertent bumbling into the track of a high hurdler out practicing in the evening.

Night Train came hurrying up to give his précis. The whole action hadn't taken more than four or five seconds. I was left with a sense of anticlimax.

"I didn't feel part of that play," I said.

"Not too much to quibble," he said. "You scare the man so much they throw to the other side." He grinned. "Now," he said, "you mus' keep the angle so you see the quarterback. Look," he said. He showed me how I should have controlled Greer, a fast crablike scuttle that allowed him to keep facing downfield to watch the play, both the flanker and the quarterback in his field of vision.

I began to see what he meant by the angle of the receiver.

"Get on up there," he said. The defensive huddle was forming. I trotted up in time to hear Joe Schmidt call out a red coverage — man-to-man again.

Back in my position, Night Train called to me from the sidelines: "Jawge, this time, recall to shout out there ... talk it up."

The spectators, their soft-drink bottles poised, leaned in behind Train, listening.

It was awkward, their being there, but I called to Train nonetheless: "What ... what sort of thing do I say?"

"*Disclose* what your man doing," he called out. "If they float your zone with people, disclose that. Disclose the defense what is goin' on."

The offense was alternating flankers, so Terry Barr appeared opposite me on the next play. Staring downfield, being sure not to give away a move by a flick of the eyes, he stood upright, with hands on hips, his right leg slightly bent to push off. At the hike signal, he was immediately in high gear, quite unlike Greer's klipspringer bounce; with his sprinter's run, his head steady as he came, he was nearly up to me before I had a chance to plan what to do. "Barr! Barr!" I called out as he came — an identification being all I could think of to divulge. Having to announce his maneuvers nearly rooted me to the ground. It was difficult to react physically and keep up a shouted commentary at the same time, particularly as I was unsure of the appropriate vocabulary. So Barr went by me very fast, straight downfield, as I stood announcing his name, calling those loonlike wails, "Barr! Barr! Barr!" before I turned and lit out after him, with one arm outstretched in the classic pose of hopeless pursuit.

Once again, the play itself was to the opposite sideline, but as Barr came by on his way back he looked at me, perhaps puzzled to have heard the demonic repetition of his name, and he said, "Well, now, look who's here."

"For God's sake, keep it to yourself," I said, breathing hard from the run.

I could see him grinning behind the cage of his helmet, before he turned and began trotting back to his team. Train was at my elbow as I stared after him.

"I think he's got something to disclose," I said. "Things may get a little warmer."

"It's possible. Interception time," Train said hopefully. "You got to scatter them feet around some, and *move*. Yo' look a little stiff las' time."

As I walked in toward Schmidt I watched the offense's huddle form, keeping a nervous eye out for helmets turned in my direction. Most were turned toward Scooter McLean, just on the periphery of the huddle, still criticizing the last play; Aldo Forte was with him, talking to his offensive linemen. A play would run, and the coaches talk about it for five minutes, the players shifting their weight from foot to foot, getting their assignments straight.

Finally, the coaches backed away. "OK, the last play of the day," George Wilson called out. Schmidt had given the same coverage, and I was back at my position. I saw the helmets duck down in the huddle, then one of them, Plum's I supposed, rise and face in my direction, just briefly, the egg-smooth surface of the helmet, its cage pointed at me, adding to the sense of that impersonal scrutiny, like a robot monster's, and I thought, "I'm for it. Barr's told Plum."

"Train, I'm a goner," I called out.

"Get yo' angle right," Night Train replied through cupped hands. He offered a last odd flurry of instructions: "Scrabble 'roun'! Don' regard the jukin'! Recovah! Disclose! In*form!*"

The huddle broke. The flanker coming out opposite me was Barr again — being rewarded, the thought crossed my mind, for suggesting that there was a flaw, a serious one, in the defense. His face was no longer expressionless. I suspected a big grin behind the helmet bar.

The strength was lined up to his side. Bent over his center, Plum began the signals, his the only helmet turning as he surveyed the defense in that cataleptic instant, around him the whole frieze of his teammates' helmets motionless, and then he unleashed them as the ball slapped back into his palm, yielding them to the quick imperative of action.

Since the two preceding plays the concentration of the play had been elsewhere, I had felt alone with the flanker. Now, the whole heave of the play was toward me, flooding the zone not only with confused motion but noise—the quick stomp of feet, the creak of football gear, the strained grunts of effort, the faint *ah-ah-ah* of piston-stroke regularity, and the stiff calls of instruction, like exhalations. "Inside, inside! Take him inside!" someone shouted, tearing by me, his cleats thumping in the grass. A call—a parrot squawk—may have erupted from me. My feet splayed in hopeless confusion as Barr came directly toward me, feinting in one direction, and then stopping suddenly, drawing me toward him for the possibility of a buttonhook pass, and as I leaned almost off balance toward him, he turned and came on again, downfield, moving past me at high speed, leaving me poised on one leg, reaching for him, trying to grab at him despite the illegality, anything to keep him from getting by. But he was gone, and by the time I had turned to set out after him, he had ten yards on me, drawing away fast with his sprinter's run, his legs pinwheeling, the row of cleats flicking up a faint wake of dust behind.

"Ball! Ball! Ball!" I could hear Night Train yelling.

I looked up as I ran, and straight above, against the sky, I could see the football heading downfield, as high as a punt it seemed—the bomb!—and I put up a hand instinctively though the ball must have been twenty feet over my head. It was astonishingly distinct—I suppose because my eyes were concentrated on it with such longing—the white laces turning, a faint wobble to its nose, even the literature on it discernible, the trade name "Duke" turning, DUKE, DUKE, DUKE. It sailed downfield, then seemed to drift down, and there was Barr running under it, barely having to reach up for it as he collected it to him.

He kept on sprinting with the football, across the goal line, never looking back, finally slowing to a trot as he headed for the gym.

I stopped and waited for Train to come up. The other players walked by, all of them grinning.

"Well, that's that," I said dispiritedly.

"The referee'd blown the whistle on that play," Night Train said cheerfully. "The whole lef' side of their line was offside. They'd blown it back for a penalty."

"Sure," I said.

He grinned and set off to do some laps around the field, always working, even in that heat.

Bruce Maher trotted in beside me and we started the walk across the fields.

"Well, I sure got beat," I said. "I got beat like a drum," I said, slipping into the jargon.

"It's not easy," said Maher. "And what's worse is what happens *after* a guy catches one on you and goes for the score. You run towards the bench and you know you're going to get hell there. You can see the coaches, with their clipboards, watching you come. Then, as you run in, you've got to pass all these big linemen going down to kick the extra point—your own linemen, looking at you like you're a worm, and then the other team's line, and they have sort of a half grin on their faces, conspiratorial-like, like you *conspired* to fall down and let their guy score."

"Football's all humiliation, isn't it?" I said. "Gonzaga was telling me that playing opposite Doug Atkins was like having your pants taken down in front of sixty thousand people."

"Someone's got to be humiliated," Maher said. "The other guy sometimes. If you intercept and you get stopped back near their quarterback, you can see, if you can spot him, that he's got that same awful look on his face, like he's falling off a cliff. And you find yourself with that half grin, looking at him as if you wanted to thank him for throwing the ball to you, and that you're sure available any time he wants to do it again. After all, it's probably his mistake that's made you look good."

We went up through the pines toward the gym. It was quiet in the shade, but it was hot, the dust kicked up by the cleats, everybody tired and silent, hearing only the click of cleats against an occasional stone as we moved up the path and the creak of football equipment like harness along a dray horse's back.

"Bruce," I said, "the humiliation isn't so bad if you have something to look forward to. It's that lemonade," I said, "that lemonade sitting waiting in those big pails in the training room, with the ice cubes floating in there, and the big dipper along the side, and the paper cups..."

"Roger Brown makes that lemonade," Maher said. "With his feet."

"Cut it out."

"He stomps on those lemons just before practice," Maher went on.

"Come on, now," I said.

"Big old Rhinofoot. He hops around on them like he was in a wine vat."

"That's terrible," I said.

I was going to aim a sort of fake kick at him, but it was too hot.

"Hell," he said, grinning. "Hot day like today, we'd drink the stuff if we knew it'd been made by a real *honest* rhino."

"Well, you're right," I said.

CHAPTER 16

Always after practice, the crowds moved across the sidelines and grouped around the players as they started across the wide fields for the gym. Some of them wanted autographs; others simply walked along with the players for the enjoyment of proximity. The kids were the most insistent about the autographs. Even when Morrall, and other players who might have stayed down after practice, finally quit, there was always a crowd of young autograph seekers waiting before the pines by the tennis courts. I had refused to sign anything at the beginning, but it was too difficult to explain why my autograph was not one they'd be especially keen to have. So I signed what they offered — their books, scraps of paper, and once the cast on a small girl's arm. The scraps of paper were used for trading. I'd heard someone calling: "I'll give you a Morrall for a Terry Barr." Sometimes a familiar hand, overly grubby, with a Band-Aid on the thumb, would appear among the books and pencils with a notebook sheet identical to one presented a moment or so before. And then, after I'd signed it, the hand would withdraw and I'd hear just within earshot: "I'll give you two of these . . . for one Morrall."

"Never heard of this guy."

"He's a rookie. That tall guy."

"Listen, I can't even *read* this guy's name. What is it?" They were bent over the paper.

"Pumpernickel."

I didn't write my name very distinctly.

"He could make it with Detroit," the first youngster said. "He could make it big with them."

"Well, I'll give you one Plum for three of your guy's."

So the same notebook paper would appear, held under a bandaged thumb, and I'd sign it, pretending I hadn't overheard anything.

I was very conscious of the crowds at first, almost despairing to have to perform in front of them, and I never got used to it. What I hoped they would decide about me was that I was a specialist, that whatever gawkiness or gaucheness of performance I displayed could be dismissed on the assumption that my specialty was drop-kicking, or throwing the ball enormous lengths, or punting, that perhaps I was being groomed to replace Yale Lary.

On the sidelines, both for the morning and afternoon practices, there were always a couple of hundred people watching. If nothing much was going on, they sat up on the knolls under the big elms, and they had thermos bottles standing in the grass beside them, with iced tea probably, and brown paper bags with sandwich lunches. Like English crowds at a county cricket match they came to spend the summer day, and they could lie flat out and feel the sun flicker against their eyelids down through the elm leaves. When the teams scrimmaged, or ran through their offensive patterns, they came down and stood along the sidelines. The majority were men — in Bermuda shorts, some wearing straw beach hats, others in bathing suits, and quite a few smoking pipes, toning down from cigarettes, I suppose, which many people were trying to do that summer, and it was odd to go out on a pass pattern and run into a cloud of pipe tobacco, a whiff of it offering up a sudden association of English manor libraries.

The other players were naturally unconcerned by the crowds. Often, though, there were girls along the sidelines, chatting easily, and the players would notice the prettier ones. Occasionally, during a scrimmage, a player would tell the quarterback that something really interesting had turned up on the sidelines, maybe worth a closer look.

Morrall, if he was quarterbacking—Plum was more likely to tend to business—would squint at the spectators where the player indicated, and he'd say: "Sewell, if I'm looking at what you're looking at, that looks like a bunch of *dawgs*—that is, if you want my opinion."

"I've been *over* there," Harley Sewell said. He was an offensive lineman from Texas.

Morrall would duck his head in the huddle and if it was feasible he would call a play which took the ball laterally across the field—a pitchout, perhaps, and the play would eat up ground toward the girls, the ball carrier sprinting for the sidelines, with his running guards in front of him, running low, and behind them the linemen coming too, so that twenty-two men were converging on them at a fair clip.

The spectators would look at the rush wide-eyed, and scatter back—cameras and handbags would be dropped, and the girls would draw back, fluttering, with their hands up, as if alligators were rearing up at them from a pond.

With the play done, the players would stand near the sidelines and gawk at the girls over their face bars, shifting around, and shuffling. The coaches' whistles would blow them back to action after a while, and when they got back to the huddle a précis would be offered:

"Sewell, you got the taste of a groundhog. That was horrible."

"What? Horrible? The one on the right, the one without the hat, she weren't no dawg. Dawg? My ass!"

"Well, *you* take her, Sewell. You got you'self one big leash and lead that hound dawg from *heah*."

Another lineman puffed up and joined the huddle.

"Morrall, for Chrissake, move the ball for the opposite side. Let's clear out." He looked at Sewell, his nose wrinkled.

Sewell was pained. "Where's you' appreciation? I don't take no 'count of the one under the hat—that one on the left. Why, I got something of a start *myself* looking under that hat. But the one on the right, she wasn't so horrible."

The others jawed at him, and kidded, until the coaches' whistles would interrupt. Scooter McLean would call in his high, pained voice: "Come along, come along—no picnic, no *picnic!*"

The biggest crowds turned up on the day of the team photographs a couple of days before the intra-squad game in Pontiac. Friday Macklem handed out the Honolulu-blue jerseys that morning, with the big silver official numbers that appeared in the game programs and were familiar to everyone who followed football in Detroit—Joe Schmidt 56, Night Train Lane 81, Terry Barr 41, Gail Cogdill 89, and so forth. Friday had two numbers available for me when I came to him for my jersey—a zero which had been worn by Johnny Olszewski—"Johnny O" everyone had called him during his playing years, and a 30, which was Hopalong Cassady's number.

Friday made up my mind for me. "The zero," he said. "It has more distinction." He told me that at Washington there was this player called Steve Bagarus. He wanted a double zero on his jersey so the crowd, when they saw him coming off the bench, could call out, "Oh-oh, look out, here comes Oh-oh."

I took the paraphernalia back to my locker and put it on—the jersey, the silver pants with the blue stripe down the side, the blue-and-white socks, and the silver helmet which Friday had resurfaced with a new blue decal of a leaping lion.

Down on the playing field, the usual throng of onlookers was swollen by a crowd of reporters, photographers, TV cameramen, and radio men. Dozens were carrying portable recording equipment around, the stick microphones ready in their hands. I avoided them. Often they stared—I could see their lips move, "Zero? Zero?"—and I would turn away as they inspected press release handouts for some inkling as to my identity.

The team and individual photographs were taken by an odd character named James F. Laughead—"Loghead" to all the players—a familiar transient throughout the professional football camps and also the colleges. He is the Karsh of Ottawa of football circles. He wore a floppy sourdough hat, a red leather vest over a Hawaiian shirt that some observers said hadn't been off his body in a decade, and faded blue overalls that were overlarge so that from certain angles the photographer appeared to be standing in a sack. His cameras were set low — on a two- or three-inch structure he calls his "ground pad" — so that the player in his photograph seems poised against the sky in the grandiose flying-leap poses familiar to anyone who has looked into a sports magazine or a football program. He called all the players "Mister." When he wanted a player like Yale Lary to run and leap in front of his camera, he would shout: "Show me something, Mister Lary — get up there in the air where the birds fly, Mister Lary." He would illustrate with short chunky steps, and then crouch down to his camera. "Dig-dig-dig-dig," he would shout. Lary, with the ball, would run up to a prescribed spot and sail up into a pose he would never find himself in on the playing field though it looked excellent in the photographs. "Once more, Mister Lary," Laughead called. "Fly for me this time. Fly-fly-fly-fly!"

"Photograph Day" brought out many of the team's most fervent supporters — the superfans, the players called them — whose infatuation was such that they attached themselves to football teams like remoras to a large fish, sustaining themselves by their close relationship to the organization.

They could range from the very wealthy (Jerry Wolman, who bought the Philadelphia Eagles — it was often said — so he could shag footballs on the sidelines with his players) to those men one saw turn up day after day at the practices, who later, when the season started, would stand in their long overcoats outside the locker-room corridors stamping their feet in the cold, waiting for the players, calling out to one they may even have met, "Hey, great game, Joe *baby*," and crowding forward to aim an affectionate blow at his shoulder blades.

The first of the breed I heard much about when I was at training camp was Sam Smart, a businessman from Chattanooga, Tennessee. He was a fervent supporter not only of the Lions, but of anyone involved with football. Kyle Rote, the ex-Giant, once told me: "He was the sort of man who never met a stranger. He was all over the place. He followed every football player there ever was."

Detroit, though, was his favorite team. Smart traveled to every game and he spent as much time as he could with the team itself—during training camp, down on the practice field, and on occasion taking as many as would go to dinner with him at a fancy restaurant, where often his emotions would get the better of him: he would collect the waiters and busboys and organize them into a squad of cheerleaders. "All right, now!" he'd cry out to the startled patrons. "I'm Sam Smart from Chattanooga, Tennessee, and we're all going to roar for the Lions!" He was absolutely irrepressible, his enthusiasm such, and his nature so infectious, that he would get the people doing what he wanted, roaring like lions, and carrying on, people who'd never clapped an eye on him, or thought very much about the Lions, for that matter. One of the players told me that on a plane trip to a game on the coast he so roiled up the passengers with roars and cheers "for the Lions" that the pilots had to come back and plead for order. He was rarely silent. He had a strange war cry he often shouted—which the Lions remembered him for—"L-I-A-H-O," it was, bellowed in airplanes, bus stations, or down on the practice field, an amalgam of the initials of the phrase "Let it all hang out!" a spirited appeal that was used so often he finally shortened it to the initials.

Occasionally he would telephone. He was too ill to come to training camp that summer. There was a public booth in the dormitory corridor which the rookies would answer, then shout for the player wanted. Once, when I answered it, a cheerful voice came across hundreds of miles. "Hey, anybody 'round? This is Sam Smart from Chattanooga, Tennessee" (he always included the appendage of his hometown). "Let me speak to a player, will you?" he'd say. "Anyone'll do." I found someone for him, a veteran groaning as he stretched up off his bed to pad down the corridor for the phone. But the players would always talk to him—whatever else they were doing.

The most impassioned of the superfans came and offered to be water boys and locker-room assistants—not the most edifying or pleasant of jobs, but it kept them close to the team. The Philadelphia Eagles had an ex-millionaire for their water boy, Frank Keegan, nearly seventy years old, whose run was sprightly on the way out to the players on the field with his tray of paper cups. He had been on the job since the mid-forties, paying his way to each Eagle game, where his equipment awaited him in front of the bench.

In Cleveland, they had a successful radio producer, John Wellman, working for *their* equipment manager, and in addition they had a local cigar-store operator, a very successful one, named Abraham Abraham, who was a sort of general handyman. Abraham's specific duty during the game was to try to retrieve the football on field-goal and extra-point attempts. A familiar figure behind the end zone, he dressed in a garish orange suit which he thought lucky and wore to games for nearly twenty years. He stared into the sky for the ball, his arms stretched out stiff as if calling for divine assistance, but the ball invariably eluded him, sailing by him and engulfed by mobs of spectators. He was something of a showman, and in his later years he gave up trying to extricate the ball for the Cleveland management and took to capering around the periphery of the melee calling penalties on the spectators struggling for the ball—throwing his handkerchief down and signaling the infraction with appropriate arm signals to the crowds. Most of them, as might be expected, were personal fouls.

Proximity was the thing, no matter how demanding the superfan's position. Scooter McLean, who was once with the Bears, and who kept up on activities there, told me of one opportunist called Motyka, a window washer who worked a five-foot-wide squeegee across the plate-glass windows out at O'Hare Airport. For some years he had suffered his Sundays at Wrigley Field in a miserable seat under the scoreboard, so poor a location that he finally wrote a plaintive letter to George Halas, the Bear owner-coach. To what must have been his surprise he received a letter back from Halas offering him a better, if somewhat ambulatory, view of the game—cavorting up and down the sidelines outfitted in a bear costume as the team mascot. "He grabbed at it," said McLean. For years, thus costumed, in the vicinity of the fifty-yard line, Motyka watched the Bear games through the eye apertures of a reinforced bear head, his suit, heavily furred, stifling hot in the early part of the season and exuding the odor of melting glue. In the winter, the snowballs thudded up against him; he was a favorite target from the stands, but he paid little heed, since he considered his move from under the scoreboard into the bear suit the greatest thing that had ever happened to him—giving him a fine view of the game, and furthermore a certain rapport with the team. "He used to whack them on the butt with his paw when they came off the field," McLean said.

"Quite a sacrifice," I said. "I suppose he had a locker with the bear suit hanging up in it. Or perhaps he brought it to the game in a special sort of duffel bag."

"Perhaps he *wore* it to the game," McLean said. "Standing in the bus with the thing on. I don't know."

He shook his head. "But you want to know the craziest of them all—the real champ of the camp followers is Jungle Jamey." He looked at me. "You heard of him?"

I said I hadn't.

McLean was the first who described Jungle Jamey (John Baccellei was his real name), though the other players often talked about him. Almost all of them had come in contact with him at some stage. He was an eccentric Californian who was a familiar figure in the NFL training camps, as familiar as Laughead, the photographer. His allegiance was not to any particular team, but to sports figures in general. He got around in an old car covered with hundreds of sports stars' autographs. When the training camps opened up, Jungle Jamey "adopted" a team.

One of the Lions remembered him in the Dallas Cowboys' first training camp in Portland in 1960—the ancient car pulling up and Jungle Jamey stepping out, bearded, wearing a white hunter's hat with a snakeskin band, a ragged pair of short pants, and a pair of shower slippers on his feet. He carried a live rabbit tucked under one arm, and with the other he brandished a hunk of meat he claimed was bear. He was on hand to "help" the team get going, he announced loudly—an offer that dismayed the coaches. The players enjoyed him, though—a valued hedge against the drudgery of training camp. On the practice field he shagged footballs, trotting clumsily, his sandals flapping, his patter of comments odd and arresting, a crowd of children scampering after him—an endearing thing about him; there always seemed to be children around him, worshipful, attracted by his strange outfit, his pets, and his pied-piper disposition. At night he'd get into the dormitory and sit around with the players telling his stories, which were long and funny for a while, and he'd show off voluminous scrapbooks, most of them attesting to his boast that he was the world's greatest gate-crasher— certainly of sports events. One year he crashed the Rose Bowl game by walking through an entrance gate leading two goats. No one stopped him. John Gordy told me that one spring he spotted Jungle Jamey's old car leading a line of racing cars participating in the Indianapolis 500 onto the track, not for long, before the officials shunted it off to the side, though for a fine moment or so it was the leader. Jamey had such stories to tell into the evening, up to the curfew, and then he'd close up his scrapbooks and find a place to sleep. In Portland, with the Cowboys, he slept under a grand piano in the common room.

It was never long before Jungle Jamey's welcome wore thin. General managers were usually his undoing. Their sense of control over the camp, and the nicety of how things should be, was unhinged by Jamey, his ragged outfit, the pet rabbit hopping about, the children everywhere, and the autographed car standing out in the lot. To get Jamey to move on was not easy. When Tex Schramm, the Cowboy general manager, tried it, quietly pointing out that there was no place in the organization for him, Jungle Jamey later stood up in the training-camp dining room to offer a startling accusation. "How about *you*, Schramm?" he shouted. "You're no athlete. What are *you* doing here if you're no athlete? I'll tell you what—you're a *freeloader,* that's what."

From the Dallas team he went to the Giants and moved in with Dick Lynch and Cliff Livingston as a personal valet. Lynch, then a bachelor, who owned a mid-Manhattan apartment, has described

Jungle Jamey as having minimal duties as a valet—he washed the dishes, took clothes to the laundry, and answered the telephone ("the residence of Lynch" was his greeting). Both Lynch and Livingston, who was rooming with him that season, were devoted to Jungle Jamey. He was an amusing companion, and when they went to a cocktail party they dressed Jungle Jamey in one of Lynch's suits—his own were somewhat too "loud," as Lynch put it—and took him along. Later, Lynch became engaged to a girl of practical mind who insisted that Jungle Jamey had to go. Livingston had to go too, but she was adamant about Jungle Jamey. She didn't envision him as part of their married life. When Lynch dutifully reported to Jungle Jamey that his days as a valet were numbered, he received a long lecture on the perils and miseries of married life. The girl, Roz, the present Mrs. Lynch, prevailed, and Jungle Jamey left New York wearing one of Lynch's suits, with more packed away in a Macy's shopping bag. He called up from time to time after that—collect—but Lynch said he was always glad to hear from him.

"I'll tell you," said McLean, "I half expect Jungle Jamey's car to roll out from behind those trees."

A veteran sitting beyond him leaned over and said, "There're some odd characters who follow football. I mean to say..." The three of us were sitting under a tree up on a knoll watching Laughead taking pictures. "Dig-dig-dig-dig, Mister Watkins!" Laughead was calling. "Like a bird-bird-bird-bird, *please!*" "Listen to that," the player said. He shook his head. "You ever hear of Roughhouse Page?" he asked, looking at me sharply.

"No," I said.

"Maybe you might have heard of him. He's a great legend over there with the Dallas Cowboys."

He went on to describe how in Northfield, Minnesota, where the Dallas Cowboys had their training camp in 1962, a cab had drawn up in front of the dormitory and a man in his early forties had stepped out carrying a suitcase. He wore a straw boater, an Ivy League–cut khaki suit, with a tattersall vest, somewhat scuffed white buck shoes, and, what was most noticeable, a black eye — so large and colorful that the players standing out on the dormitory stoop thought he had made himself up with a piece of burnt cork for a costume party.

He announced: "I'm Roughhouse Page! Star halfback. Where's my room?"

The Cowboy players looked at each other. The team had recently been organized in the league — one never knew where talent lay — and they hopped off the stoop and gave him a hand with his bag. They found him a room, and sure enough, when he opened his bag, there, lying on top of bright new athletic gear, was a contract made out to Rufus Page for thirteen thousand dollars and signed by Clint Murchison, who was one of the Cowboy owners.

The coaches came down and stared at the contract. One of them said: "What credentials do you have — other than this?" pointing to the document. They had an idea Murchison was laying a joke on them. He was known to do such things. None of them had been told anything about a player named Page.

"The name's Roughhouse Page," the man said. He put his straw boater up on the shelf in the closet. "I played freshman football at Princeton — if *that's* what you want to know — and that's the extent of it. They never appreciated me at Princeton. I was a great light under a bushel basket."

"Oh," said the coaches, looking at one another. Well, how had he come by the black eye?

He replied that he had fallen into conversation with a stranger in a Chicago bar, and this fellow had asked him — after the usual pleasantries — what his profession was. Page had replied easily that he played halfback for the Dallas Cowboys. The other fellow expressed doubt. Page's signed contract was back in the suitcase in the hotel; he had to convince his drinking companion verbally. It had not worked, and the other fellow was so incensed at Page's insistence that he was an active halfback that a brawl had ensued in which Page had been hit in the eye with a glass peanut dish.

"Oh yes," the coaches said. And where had Rufus Page been signed to a contract? they wanted to know.

"*Roughhouse*. It's Roughhouse Page," the man said. Well, *that* had transpired in a New York bar just a couple of days before. He was a family friend of the Murchisons and the two of them, he and Clint, had got to talking...

"Yes, of course," the coaches said.

They did not quite know what to do with Page. He seemed very intense. They kept him around a few days. Laughead, the photographer, arrived while he was there, and they took some pictures of him swinging from the crossbar of the goalposts in a Cowboy uniform.

Finally, it was determined that Murchison should get back some of his own. The Cowboys found out where the owner was—he was vacationing on Spanish Cay, a small island in the Bahamas—and Roughhouse Page was dispatched there by plane with orders to find out "more specifically" how Murchison felt he could fit into the Cowboy attack. The last part of the trip required a small chartered seaplane, which taxied in to shore, and Murchison, looking out the bay window of his villa, was surprised to see Page step off, carrying his suitcase, the straw boater jaunty on his head; he was carrying his suitcase under one arm, and wearing a Dallas Cowboy sweatshirt with the team name across the front.

Page was indeed, as he had said, a Murchison family friend, an acquaintance of personable eccentricity who had been a New York broker. Murchison went out to greet him with a faintly wan smile. His guest stayed on at Spanish Cay. He stayed for a week. Murchison was not sure what to do with him. Eventually, he put Page aboard his yacht and had him ferried to Nassau, a hundred miles away. He had some excuse to offer—that it was a part of the Bahamas that Roughhouse should see. Quite likely there was football talent there which Roughhouse could scout for the Cowboys. They had these big rangy policemen in Nassau.

Murchison himself happened to put into Nassau a month or so later,

Page quite forgotten, and, sitting in a café called Bluebeard's, he was startled to see Roughhouse Page ride through the place on a bicycle. He was still wearing the Cowboy shirt. "Hi, Clint," he called out, raising a hand from the handlebar in greeting, and rode out of the café through the back door. His balance riding between the café tables was terrific — according to Murchison — who said the sight was one he could never quite forget. Subsequently, when he dropped into the Cowboy training camp, or joined them on a road trip, he would ask when he first arrived: "I don't suppose... ah... Roughhouse isn't around, is he?"

"So you never heard of that character," the Lion player said to me. "I thought maybe you might have heard of that cat."

I squinted at him through the sun, wondering if he had a comparison in mind — sitting as I was next to him in my blue jersey with the big zero.

"No, no," I said quickly. "No, I've never heard of anyone like him... truly."

"I tell you," he said, "in the crowds that follow football there are some beauties."

CHAPTER 17

The Lion player who was most conscious of crowds and who particularly enjoyed "Photograph Day" was Gail Cogdill, the split or weak-side end whom Don Doll had spoken of as the greatest athlete on the club. His affinity for crowds bordered on the psychopathic — an absorption so acute that one was aware, watching him, that with every move he made on the field he was pandering to the crowds shamelessly.

The majority of players during a game were scarcely conscious of the crowd, they told me, concerned as they were with the near-private struggle with the man opposite — the anonymity increased by the number of men involved. What the players referred to as "showboating" was difficult in a team sport which required twenty-two men moving in a relatively restricted area.

Cogdill was an exception. His position, split off from the compression at the line, set him apart from the pack, which was quite suitable to his nature, and so were the darting feints of his flickering moves through the opposing secondary. He was very often the last man back in the huddle, not because he had a longer way to come from running a deep pass pattern, but because by dawdling he had a little more time to keep himself from the anonymity of the huddle. When the offensive men came off the field, Cogdill would flop down on the sidelines to one side of the team bench, and there the trainer's assistants, Collins and Stevenson, would work over his legs, kneading and stretching them. He suffered from cramps and muscle pulls, so he said, though there was a body of thought on the team which suspected that he was more conscious of being in plain sight of the crowd than he was aware of pain in his legs; up in the stands he could appreciate that people were saying, "My God, what's happened to Cogdill?" When the offensive team went back on the field Cogdill would cease his cries of "Twist that leg, pull it!" to his masseurs, straining on him like Swedes, leap up smartly, and without the slightest suggestion of disability run onto the field, usually without his helmet—an oversight sure to get the fans looking at him again and wondering aloud, "My God, there's Cogdill without his helmet!" Often he would nearly reach the huddle before realizing—his teammates shouting at him—and running back to the bench for his headgear. Perhaps it was calculated. No one begrudged him his habits; his skills were so extraordinary that nobody cared what motivated them.

At the end of a game, Cogdill was always the last player off the field, sometimes by as much as twenty or thirty minutes, dawdling as long as someone was still around to whack him on the back or ask him for an autograph.

I had asked the players from time to time what they enjoyed most about their profession. Some had said travel, others the money and the security, some the camaraderie of the club, others the excitement of the sport, and Danny Lewis, the fullback, had said simply that it was just the pleasure of hitting hard into the opposing line. Cogdill, when I asked him, had said that signing autographs was the best, down on the field after a game, especially when the kids came up and called him by his first name. It was what he had always dreamed of.

He had been raised in a small Wyoming town, Worland, with a population of about three thousand. He said that actually he came from a small community just on the edge of a forest that ran north clear to the Arctic Circle. Its population was fourteen. It wasn't officially a town, so he said he came from Worland, which was the county seat. He was enthusiastic about the frontier aspect of his upbringing. There were some cowpokes in his family. "I've got Indian blood in me—one-quarter Cheyenne," he told me. "I've got some madness in me. Can't you tell by my eyes?" He looked at me hopefully. He had very light blue eyes. "I don't know," I said, inspecting them clinically. "I've never looked into a madman's eyes, that I can recall."

He seemed disappointed. He had a scar under one eye, a thin blue line where he had been "clotheslined"—the clubbing, stiff-armed defensive maneuver—the bony part of a linebacker's wrist getting past his helmet's cage from the stiff-arm and slicing him severely. Some of the eye black which protects players in a game against the glare of the sun had been sewn into the cut when it was stitched up so that the scar still showed. He was the youngest-looking of the Lions, with his scrubbed high-school face, and he said whatever came into his mind, his ingenuousness being such that when he began talking about himself the players would groan pointedly and leave the room, or someone would cross the dormitory corridor from a card game going on opposite and close the door against his chatter.

Though he had been four years with the Lions, some of the players still called him "Rookie."

He shook his head. He told me: "I had always hoped that if I had a nickname it would be...well, 'Cougar.' I went to Washington State—the team there was the Cougars, and it was a name I liked. I would like to have taken it with me, I'll tell you, but instead they called me 'Rookie' when I first came up in 1960 to the Lions and some of the older players *still* call me 'Rookie.' Nobody called me 'Cougar.'

"Even my wife doesn't call me 'Cougar,' but at least she doesn't call me 'Rookie'! You know who else calls me 'Rookie'? John Unitas, the Colt quarterback. He threw me a pass, a soft lob pass, in the Pro Bowl one year, 1963, no one around me, just like in the dreams except that the ball went right through my hands. So he says to me whenever I see him—at banquets on the circuit—he says, 'Well, Rook, how are those hands of yours coming along?' I couldn't believe it at the time. I put my hands up, and the ball went right through my arms, like they were a hoop. It was very embarrassing. It's then that you become very conscious of the crowd—when you do something wrong. You can feel them looking at you, and the sound is suddenly tremendous, like you're standing in a tunnel with trains moving around. There's nothing you can do. Maybe kick at the grass. I remember Pat Studstill missing a pass once, and he picked up the ball, which was lying there rocking, and he walked around with these little angry steps, everybody hooting at him, and then he kicked it, getting all that frustration and rage into that punt, and he caught the ball absolutely perfect—well, he's a hell of a kicker anyway, as you know—and *my!* that ball went far up into the stands in a perfect spiral, up into the mezzanine, and it went through an exit opening on the fly—*phloop,* just like that, it went through there and disappeared."

"It's to keep from brooding about it," I said.

"You can't have anything on your mind but positive thoughts," said Cogdill. "All week long I run patterns over in my mind. In each one I beat my man, every time. Sometimes I juke him right out of his shoes and he's lying on the ground in his socks. The ball sails over him and my hands go up for it. Every time, you understand, I beat my man." His pale eyes glinted. "Then the game comes and I'm set for it."

"I think that's called psychokinesis," I said. "The power of mind over matter. That's what Cassius Clay does. He runs the future over in his mind—what he's going to do to his opponent in the ring—like a rehearsal. A good dice player has it—the power to will a number by seeing it in his mind."

"What I dream of most of the time is the long one, the bomb," Cogdill said. "Even during the game I dream about the long one. It was two years before I got thrown one. It came in a game against the Eagles, the last game of my second season. When the quarterback first releases it, it scares you, my God!—to look back and get that first glimpse of it beginning to come and to know that it's got the length and the next time you look, which is straight up, moving like crazy, it's going to be above you against the sky, beginning to settle, and you've got everyone beat...I mean there's *nothing* to compare with it...."

I asked about the physical attributes of the split ends and the flankers.

"Speed is important," he said. "But it's overrated: you've got to be able to handle it. You have to learn how to shift speeds, which is more effective than just being able to travel at a terrific clip like those guys they call the World's Fastest Human who last in the league awhile and then disappear. Then you have to have strength. Part of your job is to hold against the big ends. Then you have to arm-fight your way through the secondary, mainly against the linebackers. So strength is important. Then you have to have great eye-hand coordination—that is, when to go up for the ball. Basketball is the best training for that. And then, of course, there's the catch itself. The ability to catch is not something you're born with. It's self-taught. The fact is, I taught myself *wrong*. I catch the ball goofy. I don't cradle it, like holding water in my palms, which is how any normal person catches it. My right hand is always on top, over the left, to clap down on the ball, no matter where the ball is. Sometimes it looks from the stands like I'm trying to make it difficult for myself. That's kind of goofy, isn't it—sort of nuts?"

"I guess so, sure," I said.

"Then comes the best part. Running once you got it…twisting down the sidelines…it's just inexpressible. I wish you could experience it just once," he said, shaking his head. He could hardly sit still thinking about it.

"Do you wear anything on your fingers?" I asked, to get him settled.

"Sure," he said. "Most all the receivers do. It's pine stickum—some sort of tar. I keep a little supply of it on me during a game—maybe in the ear holes of my helmet, or stuck in my crotch. Pat Studstill carries his over one ankle, in his socks. The stuff is great for cold weather—which seems to shrink up the ball so the oil comes out and it's hard to hold. On a cold day I always try to cradle the ball against my chest."

I asked, "Why do ends and flankers who get beyond their man and catch the ball always seem to get pulled down. Isn't it easier to run away from someone than to catch him?"

"You're much slower carrying the ball," Cogdill said. "Your running style has to compensate, ever so slightly. And usually the safety has an angle on you.

"You know what you have to have," he went on abruptly. "You got to have speed, half-decent moves, the ability to shift speeds, quick reflexes so you can come back if a ball is underthrown, how to go up in the air after a ball, and then that important thing I was talking about—hand-eye coordination, how to catch a ball—and yet what makes it tough is that after you've learned what you can, and you get paid a lot of money for it, and you work for it, there is still no such thing as perfection, no matter how hard you struggle for it. Each time the situation changes when that ball comes through the air at you—so it's not the same as the time before, and there's no way you can prepare for it absolutely. There's all sorts of things that can go wrong. Did you know that the air is different in each town? And that the ball acts different in it? That's not so surprising. The water is slower here than in Tokyo. Did you know that?"

"No, I didn't," I said truthfully. "What does that mean—'the water is slower...'?"

"You thought you knew everything, didn't you? Well, now you know something new."

"Sure," I said.

"Why don't you write it down in your notebook?"

So I did.

I asked, "So what *does* happen when things go wrong? What do you do when a play breaks down and Plum is scampering around?"

"Unless that happens, I very rarely break the pattern I'm supposed to run. But if I see Milt pump his arm in a certain way, or I look back and see that things are going badly and he's out of the pocket running for his life, then I usually *reverse* the pattern I've just run—I go back the way I came. Milt knows that, and so almost instinctively he knows where to throw to find me."

"But there are the bad days?"

"Sometimes you fall down, or you don't feel right, like you're running on a beach in heavy sand. But when you're right nothing goes wrong. The trouble is that you can be going just right, beating your man, just like in the dreams you've had all week long, but you've got to remember you've got a quarterback calling signals who may not have you in his plans. He may not heave it to you." He said reflectively: "It's bad for an end not to get thrown to. It's like Nick Pietrosante, a full-back, having to block all the time. He may be the best blocking back in the business, which maybe Nick is, but it drives him nuts. I used to feel strongly about it, more than I should have. I went to George Wilson, like a kid over spilt milk, and I said: 'George, I want to get the ball thrown to me.' I was down in the dumps. So Wilson says, grinning at me, 'Gail, you know how the politicians work. Why don't you take the quarterbacks out to dinner, a nice lobster dinner, and maybe you can get them to throw it to you a few times.' It took me five years before I appreciated that my value as a decoy was important, and I even began to get a kick out of double-teaming and blocking—even trying to hold those monster defensive ends in the front four."

He looked up. "How about that? You going to get into the line, the offensive line, to see what it's like to face those big ends and tackles close up?" he asked. "You got to do that?"

I said, "Gail, if you can describe it very explicitly, maybe I won't have to."

"I'll try," he said, considering. "Well, playing Pittsburgh, my sopho-more year, on an outside run I was in close and I was supposed to take care of Big Daddy Lipscomb, their monster tackle. When the play started, he stood up to look around and I happened to bump him right. He stumbled. I could hardly believe what I had done. He looked at me and he said: 'Li'l man, you better find a different job.' In all the games I played, looking into that man's face was the most frightening. How's that?"

"That's all right," I said. "That's terrific. You're giving me the feel of it. Won't be any need to do it myself. How do you play those bullers? Doug Atkins of the Bears, those enormous people who rely on strength primarily?"

"You have to set up close," Cogdill said, "as close as you can, so he doesn't pick up the momentum on you, which he can get if you play back. Of course, against the big quick guys like Atkins, and Marchetti of the Colts, I can't do much but be humiliated. I bounce off like a bird run into a windowpane."

"That's fine," I said. "You're getting me off the hook."

"When I miss my block, and get bounced off, and the big guy's past me, his head down and moving for the play like a bull, I shout, 'Look out! Look out!' so the quarterback knows that I've missed my block and a big guy's coming for his blind side going like sixty. When you've thrown a 'look-out block' you don't feel much like going back to the huddle. It's hard to know what sort of a face to put on for the quarterback."

"That's fine," I said. "Tell me more about Marchetti and Atkins. I'm getting the feel of it."

"Blocking Atkins, what I try to do is stick my nose in his belt — just hold him up a bit. What happens is that he jumps over you, either that or he picks you up and throws you away. Once he threw me into Ninowski, our quarterback then, and knocked him down with me like I was a medicine ball. Gino Marchetti, he uses his hands on the big fellows to get by them, but for me, he just runs over me, his cleat marks up my belly...."

"Grand," I said.

"Will that do?" Cogdill asked.

"You got me off the hook," I said.

"It was all right?"

"Very descriptive," I said.

CHAPTER 18

It had been my intention to play all the positions—to get, as I put it to myself, a more "rounded" perspective of the game. Before leaving for Detroit, I told a friend of mine what I had in mind, and he said: "What a rotten idea. You're just going to get smashed around. There's no suspense in that. Who's interested? It's applied misery. There is something wrong with you."

"No," I said. "I may get knocked around, but I'll be privileged—it's a privileged position. At least for an observer. You'd be absolutely right if I were trying to be a football star."

"Well, I think that's what you've got in mind. I repeat: I think there's something wrong. You'd better look up somebody and get yourself straightened out."

"I'm an observer," I said stubbornly.

"You got some sneaking idea you can make it," he said. "Don't try to kid me."

"Well, what's wrong with *that?*" I said hotly. "After all, I'm going to be trying my best."

Despite him, when I got to Cranbrook I kept to my intentions, though with a certain prudence. I tried Cogdill's position a few times. Nussbaumer, the end coach, let me try, and described the patterns to run. Raymond Berry had said it was the safest position, but as I moved into the defensive secondary, my eyes darted everywhere for a clotheslining linebacker, and I ran, according to the Hawk, in a crouched run like a burglar coming up through the rose gardens in the twilight. The ball was not thrown in my direction.

I asked John Gonzaga if the professionals ever craved to play positions other than their own.

He told me that Leo Nomellini, who was a great tackle from the University of Minnesota and played with the San Francisco 49ers, used to run the ball as a fullback every once in a while. Frankie Albert, the 49er quarterback, knew that Nomellini's idol was the big star fullback Bronko Nagurski. So in the huddle, if things were going all right, he'd call the thirty-one wedge, and he'd say, "Nomo, you run it." Nomellini only got a yard or so, ever, and he always got the stuffing popped out of him.

The easiest positions for me to try were on the special teams—the kickoff and the kickoff return units. No one minded my substitution. The players called them the suicide squads, and there was always a certain amount of moaning on the practice field at the end of the day when George Wilson would call for these special units to drill. Usually the rookies, being expendable, and yet full of élan and willing to rip down the field full-tilt for the ball carrier, were selected for them. The open-field blocking, with players moving at that clip, was brutal, and the coaches always watched nervously, Doc Thompson on one knee right at the sidelines.

I found that there was a curious, terrifying exhilaration about being on these teams, especially on the kickoff unit, lining up with the others, hearing the whistle blow, and then committing oneself to a full-out rush downfield, yelling, in it something of the exhilaration of running down a beach for the water at a speed one no longer controls toward a humped and chill line of high surf.

My own trouble was that the concept, going downfield, was not only to defend one's lane, but also to maintain a constant position relative to the men on either side, so that the downfield rush was straight, like a ruler sweeping crumbs off a table. The defense would move downfield at absolutely top speed, shouting, and a fold would develop at my position on the line since I was unable to keep up, and when the time came to curve my lane in to contain the play like the sweep of a seining net, I was panting heavily, and the business, which was bringing down the runner, would be done with, the downed ball carrier and his tacklers beginning to pick themselves up as I ran up, puffing.

Don Doll would say, "George, never be last," shaking his head. "Get on down there next time, and un*load* on that ball carrier."

On one occasion, going downfield, I was picked up bodily by Roy Williams, a big rookie defensive tackle, and held aloft. He did it as a joke, instead of throwing a block, and he lifted me up in the air over his head, a great humiliation, weighing as I did over two hundred pounds in football gear, and as I revolved over his head I called down, "For Chrissake, Williams, let me down!"

I wanted to try the running back positions, to take a handoff and see how far I could get into the line. But, whenever I practiced with the backs, I found myself absorbed by the quarterbacking, and I watched Plum and Morrall with fierce concentration. I knew so little about quarterbacking that taking on additional assignments, and learning new patterns and procedures, seemed excessive, though often, on the sidelines, with my notebook, or in the dining room, I talked with the backfield personnel to have some concept of their positions.

Nick Pietrosante was the Lion first-string fullback. He had been a great star at Notre Dame, his picture often on national magazines, and if Detroit had a glamour player it was he—with dark, somewhat Valentino-like good looks which one often saw on television in the shaving-soap or hair-lotion commercials in which he starred. On a team which had a sputtering running attack and in a league dominated by such superstar fullbacks as Jim Taylor of Green Bay and Jim Brown of Cleveland, Pietrosante was a controversial figure often booed by Detroit fans who hoped for long-ranging thrusts by their running backs. Pietrosante's great value was as a blocker, and he was very good on quick openers and trap plays into the middle of the line, which are not much to see from the stands — being apparently a moving hillock of players — but which result in steady three-, four-, and five-yard gains that are invaluable if not spectacular. The sweeps and pitchouts which give running room were not Pietrosante's forte. He constantly nagged Plum to call the short trap plays in which he relied on what he considered his chief attribute: anticipation — to get off on the *"hut"* of *"hut*-one" or *"*-two" and pop through a hole wedged open just momentarily.

"It used to be the force and speed with which you hit a hole," he told me one evening in his room. "Power and speed was everything, and all the talk was about big backs who could do the hundred-yard dash in nine point something seconds. But it's vastly overrated. Jim Taylor doesn't get through the line with great speed. He anticipates, and of course he's sharp and quick, and he knows wonderfully what to do with his blockers. There is always a key moment in a run, which is when the blocker commits himself, at which point the back must make his move to take advantage of however the blocker has moved his man. Skill is involved, and instinct, and anticipation — and Taylor and all the good ones have got it."

"What do you think about as the quarterback calls the signals?" I asked. "Do you close your eyes when you run for the middle of the line and it's...ah...piled up against you?"

"When we line up, first I keep reminding myself not to point the play," Pietrosante answered. "Either with my feet, or my eyes. If I flash a glance where I'm going, and make a habit of it, the linebackers will pick it up, and adjust their defense. What I think about mainly is the count, and the hole I'm supposed to head for. I never think about the ball. That's the quarterback's responsibility. You must remember that in Pontiac if you call any of my plays — to get that ball to me. I'm not going to hold up and wait for it. All that's on my mind is the count, getting off on it, and the hole to head for."

He ignored the question about his eyes, whether he closed them. I did not pursue it.

"The pleasure is something, I mean to tell you," he was saying, "to get through that hole, to get past those first big four. Of course, the size of the front four linemen is increasing, and they move faster, and they're smarter. That sweetens the pleasure, if you please." He grinned. If you get past them, it usually means that you're past the linebackers as well—unless they've sucked back to look for a draw play—so you're moving to pick up a few yards. It wasn't like that in college—where the linebackers and deep backs are all up close and you have twenty-two men in a relatively small area. It's hard to run in such a congestion. That's one of the facts of life in college, where there just isn't the talent to mount a pro attack, which is spread out wide to split and disperse the defense, and consequently needs experts and technicians to make it work."

"How about those front four?" I asked. "What was it like to run against Big Daddy Lipscomb?"

"He talked a lot at his position," Pietrosante said, "telling everybody in that confident, oily voice of his just what he was going to do—that someone was going to get flattened, he was going to squeeze the juice out of someone 'personal.' He was capable of it. He was a great show-boat character."

"What about running against Alex Karras?" I asked.

"He's a type of guy you'd never think is ready," Pietrosante said. "But with the ball in the air, he is: he has everything, the Johnny Unitas of his position—instinct, size, ability, the moves of a ballet dancer, *dainty*…" That was the word Pietrosante used, and, seeing that I was surprised, he said: "Well, one of the nicknames for him is 'Tippy-Toes'—hard to believe, I mean the fellow standing still looks like he's sunk in the ground. But then he takes one step and you can spot that he's all springs and coils inside."

"And Roger Brown? How about him?"

A slow grin worked across Pietrosante's face. "Why should I tell you anything about him?" he asked. "You're going to be finding out about Roger firsthand come the game night in Pontiac. He's not going to be sitting on the bench."

"Well, that's a thought," I said.

"He's down the hall," said Pietrosante. "Perhaps you might drop in and make some sort of arrangement—at least make your peace with him."

"Well, that's a thought," I said again.

I never tried playing any of the big interior lineman positions, such as Brown's—either on defense or offense. Down on the field I tried their drills. I tried the blocking sleds, and also tackling the big leather dummy that hung above a sawdust pit from chains and pulleys attached to a steel support like a playground structure. The team stood in line and sprinted off one by one, and the structure would creak and the pulleys shriek as the dummy was hit. The trick was to use the shoulders rather than the arms, and to keep on driving through the pit and let the bag slide off the shoulders and back. If you wrapped your arms around the tackling dummy, and hung on and tried to wrestle it down, as I did the first time, the bag turned over and one sagged ignominiously to the sawdust pit, the bag on top, somewhat the way one is turned by a rubber sea horse in a swimming pool. Aldo Forte would yell, "Keep your head up, keep to your feet, drive, drive, drive—when your head is down, you *fall* down, head up, up, up!"

The blocking sleds, off in a far corner of the field, had curved padded supports to contain the simultaneous rush of seven linemen, their shoulders to the pads, their legs driving, and the sled, with Bingaman standing on it, would sweep across the grass. It seemed simple enough to try, like pushing a car, except that I found it difficult to spring off the three-point stance with the astonishing drive and timing of the regular linemen. Bingaman would announce the hike number, and then call the quarterback's cadence. "*Hut*-one *hut*-two *hut*-three," and the line would push off at the "*hut*" of whatever the hike number was, getting that fraction of a second's advantage, and the sled would spring away without my getting a shoulder to it—and I would lunge forward after it, almost toppling forward, like trying to catch an animal running low to the ground, until my shoulder would fetch up against the pads. Sometimes on the blocking sleds the players would gag around, and at the hike number I would be the only one to drive forward at the sled, the others holding up on some secret signal, and without the others to help, and with Bingaman's weight, it was like jarring a shoulder into a wall. The players all stood up, grinning, and Forte yelled, "Keep to your feet, drive, drive, drive, head up, up, up."

I never tried the "nutcracker drills," in which an offensive lineman and a defensive lineman are pitted against each other. One could watch these drills, the linemen bucking at each other, hearing the crack of gear, and the infinitely melancholy gasps of violent effort, and one learned enough about prudence. Fights often broke out, I was told, during contact work of this sort. It was hard to keep one's equanimity banging into someone else, and being banged into — and finally the tempers could not be contained, and the flailing would begin. The year before, Karras and Gordy had a fight which required four or five men on each player's back to separate them. Yet the two were roommates. The violence never lasted for more than a few minutes. Wilson occasionally talked about fighting. There was a pair of boxing gloves in Friday's training room, which he said were to be used if an argument was to be settled. There'd be none of it on the field. The gloves collected dust. The eruptions of temper died as quickly as they came.

One's impressions that the positions in the interior line required solely heft were faulty. Guile was as much a part of the tackles' equipment as the feints and fakes were of the flanker backs' and ends'. Both Roger Brown and Alex Karras thought all the time about removing weight, not to the point where they were weakened, but just enough to be able to couple their weight with speed so that their attack was both massive and agile. I found this out talking to Brown. I followed Pietrosante's advice and dropped in on him. He delighted in talking about his position, but it was always the technical aspects he talked about rather than the physical demands — so he seemed to deprecate his enormous bulk, half out of a little armchair, as he talked in favor of the other factors which made a play successful against the offense.

His "keys" for example — which he talked about at length — were essential: "keys" meant hints he could pick up from the actions of the players opposite to help him diagnose the play. He keys (the word is both noun and verb) on the guard in front of him, then the center just to his left, then the off guard, and finally the backs within view—seeing their moves almost simultaneously with the snap of the ball; as he moves to the attack he must decide from what he has seen what the opposition is up to. It is not simple. If the guard in front of him pulls left, toward the center, an end run toward the opposite side might be indicated, but then again the offense may be trying to fool him: the guard can take a step or two to the left and then return, and if Brown has committed himself to defending against an end run, and acted accordingly, the offense may have succeeded in removing him from the play's actual line of direction. Offensive moves are planned to make the defense commit itself, particularly the enormous interior linemen, and then take advantage of that commitment, and the offense can do this, if a guard's feint is successful, without ever having to lay a block to those cat-quick three-hundred-pound defensemen. Thus, for the defense, if only to save embarrassment, reading the keys is an essential adjunct to strength and speed, and success at it comes with experience. For example, when the guard opposite pulls left, Brown has additional keys he knows to look for: the blur of moving backfield men will tell him something, and if from the corner of his eye he spots the center falling back to block to hold down the pursuit, then a power play to the opposite side is almost surely indicated. Reading this key fast Brown bolts left for the center himself, hightailing along the line of scrimmage for the spot players call the "cutoff," where the halfback with the ball will run out of playing field and must cut downfield, often to find Brown reaching for him as he does.

Even in straight-ahead blocking, which to an onlooker seems a simple test of strength, there are infinite subtleties. If Brown, in the first few seconds of contact with the guard opposite, feels the exhilaration of out-bulling him, pushing him back, he must worry immediately that perhaps he's being led on, being suckered out of position for a takeoff or a trap play, and accordingly he must contain his rush. Equivalently, on a pass play, with the quarterback in his sights, Brown must hold his final commitment until he is sure that the quarterback is no longer in position to initiate a draw play; he must wait a half second as he controls the blockers with his hands until the quarterback is out of the "roll zone," and is himself committed, and then Brown goes for him.

That provides the highest satisfaction—to break down the protection and reach the quarterback, to loom over him, seeing the last quick frantic turns of the passer's helmet before it ducks in resignation, and the quarterback's body begins to jackknife over the ball tucked in the belly for protection as Brown enfolds and drops him. Brown does not feel he has had a good game unless he has been able to do this once or twice during the afternoon.

"Well, what sort of pleasure is it?" I asked him. The Dinah Washington records were going and Night Train Lane was lying on his belly on the next bed, watching them turn.

Brown shrugged.

"Well, what about rage?" I asked.

He blinked behind his spectacles. It was strange to think that his vision was poor. I remembered him one night trying to slap a big moth that was hammering around the overhead light. He shouted, "Fly *still*," flailing at the moth with a big towel so wildly that he drove Night Train out of the room.

"No," he said. "I don't go around growling. But the feeling's there. You know what I feel, Train," he said to Lane. "I think back on all the guys I know who have been injured, and I say to myself those guys across the line are trying to do it to me. Well, they aren't *going* to do it," he said.

Night Train nodded. "You got...er...a great communion to get to the Hall of Fame," he said.

Brown stared briefly at him, and continued: "It's not hatred. You feel deep you want to win. It feels good to get to the quarterback, but you never want to dis*joint* him. Mind, you want to let him know you're there. For sure. So I get plenty worked up. Home with the wife and then on the field, I'm two different people—like Mr. Hyde and Dr. Jekyll. On the field—" he began laughing—"I don't know that I'd like to meet myself on the field...I mean I can think of other folks around that I'd *prefer* meeting."

He turned his palms up. He had a large ring with an embossed RB set in diamonds, and it flashed with the movement of his hands.

Night Train looked at me and began giggling. "Jawge, you set to find if Roger's goin' to dis*join* you? I mean in Pontiac you are goin' to have expectation in this whole question—he's goin' be at you shufflin' and breathin' right *hard*."

"Perhaps the time has come for me to make some sort of donation to his favorite charity," I said.

Brown was grinning from his chair. His jaw was very wide, his teeth strong and set apart from each other so the gaps between them showed. He seemed benign enough; he leaned out of his chair to fetch a black porkpie hat, which he set on his head. It seemed small and rode high.

"Smart?"

"What about after a game?" I asked.

"I lie in a hot tub," he said, "with the water up to my chin, and just ease. My wife stands around and pours in the Epsom salts and tells me what happened and what she would have done if she was the quarterback. She's a big fan, and she can talk longer about a game I been in than I can."

I asked him how much he thought he was going to miss Alex Karras at the other tackle. He shook his head and said that while he admired what he had seen of Floyd Peters, the tackle that Detroit had traded for to fill Karras's spot, he expected to spend his autumns with two men always working on him, the offensive guard and tackle, and also the fullback in reserve, and even the offensive center dropping back to pick up his rush if his penetration was to the inside. With Karras playing next to him—with his great ability—the offense couldn't afford to concentrate its blocking power against one man in such a manner.

Brown was not particularly effusive about the pleasures of football.

Night Train Lane, on the bed, tried to get him to say something more profound (Train himself got so excited talking about his love of football that he was unintelligible, or at least more than usual), but Brown was insistent: it was the pleasure of winning that pleased him most, and having played a good game, which meant getting to the quarterback and dumping him at least once. And it was the little things too — getting through a game without too many bruises, and lying for hours in that hot tub with the salts in it.

It was pleasant sitting with Brown and Train. It was easy talking. They found some soft drinks, and some Nabisco crackers. We listened for a while to the Dinah Washington records. The two of them were especially curious about my view of the team. I told them how impressed I was with its apparent solidity — that it was knit strongly, at least to my eyes. Of course, I had no idea what happened when things went badly.

"Well," said Train, "people stand whispering in rooms. You can always tell. Look in the locker room of a team that's slumping and just lost another game, and oh my: the owners set around in one corner, whispering, the coaches in another, and the players all huddled, with the talk low down." He turned on the bed. "There's no misery like that."

I wondered, talking about the strength of a team, if racial questions were ever a problem. Brown was as reluctant to talk about the racial problems in professional football as I was to ask him about them. He said that once in North Carolina, during the exhibition season, a black girl had refused him a date because he was too *light*. "So you get it both ways," he said.

Night Train said from the bed: "Yo' don' think maybe yo' three hunnert *pounds* had somethin' to do with this girl bein' bawky?"

"She didn't say nothing about the poundage," Brown said, "only the *color* of the poundage."

Nor did the white players talk much about racial problems. Dismissing the subject, they often said that in professional football it was performance that counted, that was all, that football was a business in which a player was rated by his ability to help the team. The concept of the team and team play was essential. Nothing else made any difference. All players knew that. If their prejudices got in the way, that was the end of them. You could be prejudiced against a rookie trying for your position—that was a clash of one man's ability against another's—but prejudices in respect to race or color were violations of an unspoken code. The Lions were quick to rise to any slight that involved a black teammate—there had been some difficulty registering in a hotel on one occasion during an exhibition swing through the South and the team had formed a bloc to force the management to back down.

Still, the situation was paradoxical—which was why, I suppose, the subject so rarely was mentioned despite the civil rights headlines in the daily papers. While the relationships among the players seemed easy enough in the communal living of the training camp—except in the rigors of competition—the players felt about the world outside with prejudices intact. The Southerners on the team, who made up almost a third of the players, continued to have their firm and expected views on school and social integration. In the off-season, the social communication between black and white, however close the rapport seemed in training camp, was almost nonexistent.

Even in the strict business of football, despite what was said, if one probed it was easy enough to find the taint of prejudice. One of the coaches told me that as a matter of principle he would never want to have more than six black players on a team: cliques formed if you had that many—that was his idea—and the whole all-important concept of the team went awry.

Once, when I was traveling on the West Coast with the team, I dropped into a bar after the game with some of the Lions, and in the bar was the opposing quarterback. The Lions, who had won the game, had handled him roughly, though he grinned at them when we came through the door. He was drinking champagne out of a mug. He had consumed a lot by the time our group arrived. He began criticizing the black on his own team, and then he extended his criticism to the rest of the league. His idea was that the black backed away from contact, that he hadn't the nerves for the game. The people along the bar began shouting at him.

"Look at this," he said, weaving. "*Listen!* Take the linebackers. The search-and-destroy guys are the linebackers. How many black linebackers you got in the NFL? Maybe one or two. They haven't got it, I tell ya. They flinch. It's the same with the running backs. My guys do, they flinch, I tell ya, and I'd rather hand off to a gimpy fullback who's white druther than my guy, the guy they make me hand off to, who's got mush for guts. You know why I got to hand the ball to a colored back? Because the NAACP says so, that's why, and they're calling the tune these days, not the coaches."

Around the bar he was listened to with some embarrassment. Someone said, "That's balls, fellow, real balls." I asked John Gordy about it on the drive back to the hotel. He is a Southerner, from Nashville, Tennessee.

"He got beat bad in the game," Gordy said, "and he's drowning it with champagne — what d'ya think of *that?* — and he hasn't got himself a good fullback or halfbacks. You give him Jim Brown for a fullback and Lenny Moore and you wouldn't hear that stuff from him, and maybe he wouldn't put such a run on the grape."

"But the prejudices would remain — bigotry in that fellow's case?"

"That quarterback has a good head. He's under pressure. He's losing, and he's not as sensible as he could be."

"Well, all right, call them prejudices," I said. "These would remain."

"Sure," Gordy said. "Why not? You come to the leagues with your prejudices already set for you — from your home, your school — and not much happens to change them. What is increased is understanding. After all, you're living together, playing together, and you learn it's easy enough. Perhaps that undermines the prejudice. But not too much. We get along."

CHAPTER 19

George Wilson addressed us one evening at the start of the eight p.m. class. "Next Saturday night," he said, "that's only four days away—we've got the big intra-squad game coming up in Pontiac. That's about half an hour down the main road. We'll dress in game uniforms here and drive down there by bus. They've got a fine stadium, good lights, and there'll be a big crowd there. They make quite a ceremony of it—a Queen of the Day on hand, fireworks, bands, and all of it. Before the game there'll be some contests—punting, sprints, field-goal kicking, passing accuracy—there'll be a number of them, cash prizes, and those of you who want to enter, sign up with the Hawk."

One of the players wanted to know how the scoring for the intra-squad game worked.

Wilson explained that for the offensive unit, the scoring was regular. The defensive unit would get one point for stopping the offense from making a first down in a series; it would get two points for a fumble recovery, an interception, or a blocked field goal.

"The game's the big chance for you rookies," he said. "We want to see how you do. We're going to take a look at the third-string quarterback"—my heart jumped—"to see what sort of reserve strength we got." He looked to where I was sitting.

"Whitlow," he said to the big center. "How's the kid coming along receiving the snap from center?"

"Well," said Whitlow. "He's...ah...coming along."

"Whitlow," he said, "you'd better stay down after practice a little longer and work with him on his plays. And you too, ends—Gibbons and Cogdill—and Pietrosante and Lewis. Right?"

The big men nodded.

Terry Barr leaned across from his seat. "Learn everything you can," he said. "One of those crazy rookie linemen is going to try to make his reputation off you." He nodded gravely. "If one of them snaps you in two—I mean, *literally*—the club's not going to think about letting him go. He'll fill Tiger Stadium with people in to see the killer."

"I've got four days to beat those rookies to it," I said. "To develop some crippling ache or other."

As if reading my mind, Wilson said, "Now you guys, don't go and get yourself hurt before the game. We want to see what you can do—and if you're sitting on the bench with a muscle pull, you're not worth anything to us. You can think about packing your suitcase."

A prime topic with the Lions—not of conversation but of concern—was the question of physical condition. George Wilson mentioned it almost every evening at the team meetings. "Don't drink nil," he said. "Don't let food run you out of the league. Don't go swimming too much. If you think a muscle is going to pull, take it easy and pull up, particularly you receivers and halfbacks."

The training room at one end of the gym was the most popular of the hangouts. Millard Kelly was the trainer in charge—"Mallard" or "the Duck" the players called him—with two assistants who did such chores as taping the players' ankles and running the various machines which stood around the training room: the two big tanks of the whirlpool baths, then a large black box in a corner with four or five dials called a Paerst muscle stimulator, which had pad attachments to put on the arm or leg which made the muscles jump involuntarily; also there was a large dental-like piece of equipment called a "modality machine" which produced—I was told—100,000 ultrasonic waves per second, or it may have been a million, which probed down to stimulate deep-lying muscles. Almost all the machines were designed in one way or another—through the rush of water or by electrical impulse—to increase blood circulation and thus speed healing in an afflicted area. The training room and its procedures and machines had come far since the days of John Heisman—after whom the trophy which is the highest award in collegiate football is named—who felt that soap and hot water were debilitating, and in his coaching days urged his teams to refrain from their use.

The training room began to fill at eight-thirty in the morning, just after breakfast. The rookies were the first to arrive, hopping up one after the other on one of the two rubbing tables to get their ankles taped. The veterans, by reason of their status, had an extra fifteen or twenty minutes in which to loll around in their rooms.

After practice, the place crowded up again. There were two galvanized pails with iced lemonade; the players after a hot day stood around them as if at a trough, spooning up the drink with ladles or with little paper cups which gave them a swallow or two, and then they'd scoop among the ice cubes again. The atmosphere was very lively in the training room—a place for talk, where the players congregated rather than in the dark aisles between the lockers or back in the small dormitory rooms, so that at times it sounded like a coffeehouse. Sometimes, Bruce Maher, sitting up on the edge of the whirlpool bath with one leg in the swirling water, would strum his guitar and sing. Other players sat in rows on the rubbing tables and joked back and forth. There was a lot of coming and going. In an alcove just off the training room some exercise barbells were often in use, and when I glanced in there I usually saw players straining at the wall doing isometrics.

There are some odd places that appeal to ballplayers. The Chicago Bears had a big tackle named Fred Davis who had an intense feeling about the ambiance of the locker room. He was always the last one out, not because he was a slow dresser, but because he enjoyed hanging around the place. It gave him a sense of security; he had probably spent his easiest and happiest days there amid those familiar props—the long worn wooden benches, and the metal lockers with the light metal doors that clanged and had perforations through which the toes of white wool socks could be pulled so they hung properly inside and dried; the liniment odor, and the faint chlorine smell, and the rubbing alcohol, and the sweat, and the piles of towels, and the dripping from the loose taps in the showers — all of it was balm to Davis, and when the Chicago equipment manager, who understood it, locked up for the night long after practice, he would call, "Hey, Davis!" and sometimes it would be quiet, but more often a call would come from the locker rows: "Hold on, I'll be along." And then he'd come out. "They hid my damn shoelaces on me," he would say.

The training room was obviously a more congenial place than an empty locker room. And yet for all its conviviality, the training room, with its odor of disinfectants, and the sight of the porcelain cabinets with the rows of bandages and syringes, and the squat bottles in rows on the shelves, always made me feel uncomfortable and apprehensive. I felt about the training room as I did about any doctor's office — and I stayed away as much as I could. I got my ankles taped and grabbled the salt and vitamin tablets from their boxes by the door (which was required), and then later, after practice, I came back for the lemonade.

The others were not as sensitive as I was, though it was apparent that the players reacted to the concept of injury by trying to ignore it completely. When a player was hurt in a scrimmage, the others seemed to turn their backs pointedly, and they moved away as if an injury were communicable, like mumps. Sometimes, if the injury did not appear serious, and the player was just having difficulty getting to his feet, they would call to him, "Forget it — it's nothing — get up!" almost nagging him, as if the pain were a state of mind and could be dismissed by will. If the player remained in trouble, with Kelly running out to him, or Doc Thompson, they would turn away as if nothing had happened, snubbing him.

Injury is the most nightmarish aspect of football because its threat is impossible to handle — its nature unpredictable, even quixotic. In 1960, fourteen major injuries had occurred in an insignificant preseason exhibition in Texas against the Chicago Bears. Detroit's chances for the season were destroyed. The game had not been noticeably hard fought. By comparison, in one of the roughest games that the Lions played back in the forties, there had only been one injury: Lloyd Cardwell injured himself, and quite badly, getting himself a drink between the halves. He leaned over to press a plunger on the water fountain, jammed two vertebrae, and was carried away on a stretcher.

So much—even a championship—depends on the health of a team, and often on the condition of one star player. When I was with Detroit, Terry Barr was having trouble with his knee following a ligament operation. There were two long new scars alongside his kneecap. It was difficult for him to move on the knee with full efficiency. He told me once: "I look at it—my knee—every night, and I damn near cry." His concern was matched by that of a whole complex of people—fellow players, coaches, owners, fans, and then reporters, who wrote columns about what was going on under Terry Barr's kneecap—all of them wondering if the intricate surgical patchwork job, the areas involved being the size of tiny transistor tubes, could withstand the extreme stress.

Sometimes an injury is kept from the press. One year Alex Karras had a groin injury which cut down his agility in lateral moves, and the quick side bounds that so often got his opposite number off balance so he could proceed past him into the enemy backfield at the angry bustling speed that was almost comic to watch, like a speeded-up film clip of a running washerwoman, but which was one of the most destructive rushes in football. The injury was kept secret so that the Green Bay Packers, their opponents the following weekend, would not take advantage of Karras's comparative immobility. Karras was strong enough so that despite being restricted he was able to put up a competent rush straight forward. But the offensive guard opposite, a rookie who had been told he was in for an awful afternoon, had much less trouble than he expected. He made the mistake of saying so in print. A reporter asked him a week or so before the two clubs were scheduled to play again how he expected to fare against Karras. "Well," the Green Bay rookie said, "I didn't have too much trouble with him in the last game. He's overrated. He hasn't got that many moves—at least none that I can't handle."

The substance of the rookie's comments appeared in a Michigan paper, which was passed on to Karras. The Lions knew that he would be interested. The groin injury had cleared up. He was in perfect condition. His teammates watched him stare at the clipping, and they shook their heads and thought about the rookie when Karras said, "Hee-hee-hee," cracking his knuckles; they noted that his skits and monologues, which he performed in the dining room, began, in somewhat tight-lipped fashion, to include the rookie's name.

The Lions told me that the afternoon of the game had been high comedy for them—all of them coming off the bench and standing on the sidelines grinning when Karras ran on with the defensive team. They stood up to watch what he was doing to the rookie, and when the game films were shown the following week they rocked their chairs back and forth, guffawing, as if a Mack Sennett comedy were on the screen. "There's no word for it," Pietrosante told me. "That poor kid, he was raped, keel-hauled, he was just *destroyed*. Finally, Lombardi took the rookie out, he *had* to, Karras having jumped over him, around him, under him, and then motherin' around in that Green Bay backfield. And as the kid went off the field, his mouth hanging open, Alex said to him, hardly breathing, like it had been hardly no exercise at all, 'Well, ass face, how you like *those* moves?'"

Pietrosante himself had an odd physical ailment. One evening after leaving the training room he told me.

"I'll let you in on something," he said. "I've got gout."

"Come on," I snorted.

"God's truth," he said. "I've got gout in my big toe. You ask Mallard or Doc Thompson." I did, afterward, and it was true, unless they were joshing me.

Back in his room after supper one evening I asked Pietrosante about the causes of most injuries, and he picked out two particularly crippling maneuvers, both of which were legal, namely the "clothesline" and the "crackback." The former is a defensive stiff-arm tactic used by the linebackers primarily, and the other, the "crackback," is a blocking technique that the flankers and split ends use *against* the linebackers.

Nick Pietrosante told me he thought the crackback might eventually be outlawed. "It's too dangerous," he said. "What happens is that the split end or the flanker takes two or three steps across the line and then cuts [cracks back] in towards the middle, barreling towards the linebacker, who isn't likely to see him since he's facing the play. The block delivered is almost a clip, and it's delivered to the side of the leg with speed. The flankers and ends aren't big men, but they're fast, and they launch themselves going full out at the linebacker's knee, and if it's a good blind shot, it'll just cave him in and is like to finish him for good."

"Doesn't the linebacker get some warning from the cornermen and the safeties?" I asked. "They must see the flanker cutting in."

"It's hard to tell what the flanker may have in mind. He could be moving into the middle on a pass pattern. Of course, the cornermen *do* yell, damn near scream, if they think the flanker's moving for a block. They yell, 'Crackback! Crackback!' and the linebackers, hearing that, half turn and their hands come down to fend off a block at their knees. If you want to test how linebackers feel about the crackback, drop into a linebacker's room down the corridor, the Badger's or Schmidt's or the King's, and call out, 'Crackback!' and he'll leap and look alongside his leg like there was a sidewinder coiled there."

"I'll take your word for it," I said.

"It wouldn't be a safe thing to yell," Pietrosante agreed. "Not unless you had a lot of running room, and maybe a Ferrari outside with the motor turning over…"

I asked Pietrosante about the "clothesline." I'd seen it demonstrated down on the practice field. The maneuver is simple: the linebacker sticks out his arm, stiff and straight, usually when the receiver coming into his area is looking back over his shoulder at the quarterback, so that he runs into it, his feet churning ahead very briefly, his head motionless against the clotheslining arm, and then he hits very hard on his back with the sound of a bladder being whacked at the ground.

Pietrosante told me a story about clotheslining. In a 1959 game against the St. Louis Cardinals he caught a divide, which is a pass pattern, and began to move downfield. He'd gone a way when he ran into a Cardinal who had a clear shot at him, but instead of tackling, the Cardinal swung his arm stiff and clotheslined him, smacking him down and slicing him past the helmet bar so that three stitches were required to patch up his lip.

Pietrosante felt his mouth where he had been hit. "I never thought much about who did it," he said. "I got hurt in the knee that game and I had other things to think about. Then later that year, Brettschneider was traded to us from the Cardinals, my roommate it turned out, and if it hadn't slipped from my mind I could have asked him who did it. I didn't bother. Well, 1961, two years after, and two years rooming with the guy, he finally brings himself one day to say, looking at his feet, "Uh...Nick," and he tells me *he's* the one responsible.

"Well, I was over it by then. Besides, if you think about it, the linebackers have an awful tough position to play: they've got to slow down the backs, anything to keep them from getting behind them, and the clothesline is a big weapon."

"I'd be nervous running against them, knowing they have it to use," I said.

"It's like when they speak of a quarterback 'hearing footsteps,'" Pietrosante said. "When the quarterback thinks he hears someone coming up on his blind side, and he cringes, or throws hurriedly, his nerve's gone...that's usually the end of him. The linebackers, if they worry too much about crackbacks, they hear footsteps too. And it's the same with the ends and backs with the clothesline. They've got the problem as soon as they come into the defensive secondary. As soon as they turn back to look over their shoulders for the quarterback, that's when they begin worrying and wondering if there's a clothesline hanging around somewhere. That's why often a back or end doesn't turn quickly enough for his pass—because instinctively he's looking for the outstretched arm that's going to deck him. He's fair game until the ball's in the air, which is why you hear the linebackers and the safeties shout 'Ball! Ball! Ball!' when the quarterback gets off his pass. Sometimes, the linebacker will say 'Ball!' anyway, before the passer's got his arm cocked, and the flanker will turn his head over his shoulder to watch for the pass and *bop!* he's got himself clotheslined."

Just then, by chance, Joe Schmidt and Wayne Walker came by and looked in. Involuntarily I hopped to my feet. They looked at me curiously and Walker asked, "You standing up out of respect or fear?"

"A bit of both, maybe," I said. "I've been learning something from Nick about your positions—some of the weapons."

"He jumped up like he was bit," said Schmidt.

"The fact is I always stand up when somebody comes into a room," I said.

"Maybe he got so nervous he was running off to take a quick shower," said Walker.

"Well, that's where I'm going," said Pietrosante. He looped a towel over one shoulder. "You entertain the rookie. Tell him about Jim Hill and Pellington and some of the other murdering linebackers and cornerbacks you call brothers." He sauntered out down the hall.

The linebackers settled themselves. They talked a little about Jim Hill, the All-Pro cornerman from the St. Louis Cardinals, that he worked his area when receivers were running through it like a small but angry tornado with a whole mess of things in it—crowbars, eggbeaters, auto fenders—that whirled out and whacked anyone approaching the funnel. Very often, after a play you'd see a helmet rolling around near Hill, lifted off with a sidearm blow or a thrust off the flanker's head as he came through the area. Hill relied more on defensive contact of this sort than he did on trying to match speed and agility against opposing receivers.

Schmidt said, "It's a question of adapting a style to your potential. Some players have to be dirtier than others. Some teams are too. Green

Bay plays the game the way it should be played. Lombardi's a purist and with his teams you don't have to worry too much about redneck tactics. The Packers learn a few plays—a simple offense, a comparatively simple defense, and they tune them both up to perfection."

"Does it seem rougher now than it was?" I asked.

"Everything seemed wilder and tougher back then," Schmidt said. "And when I came up there seemed to be more desire. A lot of it had to do with Bobby Layne, of course. Very often he was a more important man on the field than the coach. He'd go to the coach in the middle of a game and tell him to pull a guy because he wasn't delivering. 'Get that son of a bitch out of there, or I'll throw him off the field myself,' he'd shout. And he meant it too, and the coach knew it. Out the punk would come. Layne was really the team. He was the whole works. He used to have these goddamn champagne parties after the game. I remember Brettschneider turning up this one time wearing tennis shoes and a trench coat—nothing on underneath. Don't ask me where he had been or what he had in mind."

"How about the technical stuff?" I asked. "Has the linebackers' job changed much?"

"It's changed a lot," Walker said. "Not too long ago, defensive backs were primarily concerned with the run. What were needed were big fast driving men who moved with the play and piled it up. Diagnosis was a matter of instinct and common sense. Now, with the prominence of the pass, it's changed. Pass coverage makes it unbelievably complicated. The easiest defense, one-on-one—the defender sticking to one man and trying to cover him—that can't be done: the receivers are too good. So what's essential now is coordination between the defensemen. It's no longer an individual effort. Basically, there are three separate teams: the middle linebacker and the two defensive tackles, that's one, and then the two teams on opposite ends of the line—each with an end, an outside linebacker, and the cornerman. Each of these teams works not only within their group, but with the other teams—communication between them absolutely essential."

"That's the talking that Night Train insists on," I said.

Both linebackers laughed. Walker said, "The big thing is knowing the guy's with you — so that even if he does something separate you can compensate, and cover for him. We've been five years together. We've worked so long together that we hardly have to talk to each other. You've got to have the knowledge. It's possible to come out of college and be a good linebacker, but three years later you look back and remember how bad you were. Every year, twenty men come out of college that are bigger, faster, meaner, and they move like great cats, but what you got over them is knowledge, developed knowledge — and that keeps you rather than them hanging on to the paycheck."

I asked, "What is it you're thinking about when you see their quarterback break his huddle and move up for the line?"

"I take a mild guess at what he's told them — a calculated guess. After all, I know a lot about the quarterback himself — that's part of the knowledge — about his mind, and then I know what *he* knows: the down, the position of the ball, the number of yards to go for the first down. By eliminating what he can't do, or shouldn't do, in a given circumstance I can narrow down the possible plays he can call. When the backfield gets itself lined up, the choice is narrowed down further: I know what he *can't* run off that formation. So we're getting to it. Then I key on the three men opposite. I don't watch the ball or the quarterback. Just those three men. Perhaps they tip the play before the quarterback gets the snap. Even if they don't, with the first few steps they take I can see the pattern, and this gives me the play for sure; even if my guess isn't quite right, I can make the proper adjustments."

"You don't get fooled?"

"You don't get fooled very often," Walker said. "If you do, you're finished up here. The only time you get fooled is when they pull something on you that you've never seen before. The A formation the Giants used one year. Or the shotgun formation that Red Hickey out in San Francisco sprung on us. Right, Joe?" He looked at Schmidt, who nodded. "That hurt us bad when it was first used. We all felt like rookies — we'd never seen anything like it."

"Why isn't it a good tactic to devise new formations or new...well, razzle-dazzle plays for each game?" I asked.

"It's not as easy as that," Walker said. "Even if you do, it's likely the keys are still the same, and adjustments can be made quickly. The shotgun was an exception. And fortunate too, since if you could produce a new formation as effective as that one week after week the defense'd be run out of the parks. It's tough enough as it is."

While Walker was talking, I had my mind turned idly to what might work against him in Pontiac, considering what he had said.

"What about the...ah...pitchout?" I asked. "What do you do if that is...ah...run to your side?"

Walker caught it immediately. "You thirsting to send that out my way in Pontiac?" he said. "Gulp, holy cow..." He whacked the side of his head with his palm. "Don't, pul-lease!"

"No, no," I said. "I'm just curious."

"If you call for a run out my way," said Walker, "my function would be to delay the play, turn it inside so that the pursuit can catch up and take care of it—"

Schmidt stopped him. "That's fine, professor. Now let's talk about red dogging the quarterback. Let's tell him how we do it. Wayne, tell him how I say 'Jumbo' in the huddle. Tell him how my voice throbs."

"Well, Joe's voice—"

"Tell him about my hands, Wayne. How are my hands, Wayne?"

"Like claws," Walker said quickly.

"Now tell him about Brettschneider. Tell him how this little spot of spit turns up in the corner of the Badger's mouth when he hears that word 'Jumbo.'"

"Well, there's this little—"

"Tell him about the big a-a-aagh sound that Roger Brown makes in the huddle—like he's finished a big beer."

"Roger—"

I interrupted. "Come on. Cut it out. Seriously. How do you get to the passer?"

When the two of them had quieted down, Walker explained. "Red dogging, blitzing—a lot of names for it—means committing the linebackers to a rush on the passer, means for me that I got to run over the halfback opposite who's trying to block. There are two ways of getting by him. You can come at him and give him a juke—a fake—and dodge by him. Or, because he's sure to be smaller, you can run right over him, *jump* over him."

"Come on," I said.

"If he's set up right for it—that is, he's crouched down trying to block low—then it's a great move...You sail over him. It gives you a great feeling and it's a great photograph too. I've got one of myself clearing Jon Arnett of the Rams."

"When you come down," said Schmidt, looking at me, the grin beginning again, "and you're moving right lively, guess who's there, just getting to throw the ball...oh, maybe just three feet away from you, your arms reaching for him? Three guesses."

"I dunno. The official timekeeper?"

"Boom!" said Schmidt. "Pow!" He drove his fist into his hand.

"Zap," said Walker. "Bwang!"

"Biff!" said Schmidt.

"Gentlemen," I said. I rose from my chair. "There are holes, exploitable holes, in the defense. You have unwittingly talked too much."

I tried staring at them somberly, but it didn't work too well.

CHAPTER 20

The closer the Pontiac scrimmage, the more the Lions became interested, day by day, in my reactions—how my amateur's eyes were taking in what they knew so well.

"Whatja think today?" they'd ask, dropping by the locker after practice. I would sort out a few observations and tell them, though it was difficult. Even with a couple of weeks behind me, the experience was so new that I was left each day with a jumble of impressions. Wayne Walker said he wasn't surprised. General observations were difficult for someone just starting out. He had an idea, thinking back on his first days as a professional, that for the dozen or so first plays one's concentration is such that the *light* seems to dim.

"You'll notice in the scrimmage. Everything gets dark," he told me, "like seeing everything from a dark tunnel."

"You mean the peripheral vision goes?" I had asked mournfully. "That's about the only physical attribute that...well, that I *might* possess."

The night before the game I dropped in on Milt Plum and Earl Morrall, hoping for some last-minute instruction.

"Wayne Walker tells me everything's going to go black," I said.

They grinned and looked at each other. "Well, he's blunt enough about it," Morrall said.

"He didn't mean I was going to get *hit*." I explained what he had said about the field of vision seeming to diminish. The two quarterbacks said that was new to them, but they both spoke of the advantages of peripheral vision — "a type of split vision," Morrall described it. "Tomorrow night," he said to me, "let's say you run the pass play ninety-three. Once you're back in the pocket here's what you *should* see: you see your short receiver, the number three man, and you see how he is going, then you pick up the long man to see if the defensive safety's got him covered, then back to the three man, and you *go* to him" — Morrall slapped his fist into his palm — "unless the linebackers are in his zone, in which case you throw out into the right flat to your swing man, the safety valve. Then you have the man going down from the eight hole ten yards to the left and buttonhooking, so that actually you have four possible receivers in an arc of 180 degrees, and since you've only got two, maybe three, seconds to pick one of those people out you can see how helpful a wide angle of vision can be."

"The angle seems to widen with experience," Plum said. "When you start out and don't know quite where to look, it's as thin as a flashlight beam, which is what Wayne is saying."

"Pass patterns are set up to help you see your receivers fast," said Morrall. "Your primary receivers are usually on a direct line of sight from you. For example, tomorrow night" — every time he said "tomorrow" I could feel my stomach tighten — "if your short man is covered, all you got to do is raise your eyes, like clicking the sight up on a rifle, and there's the long man on the same line of angle."

The two quarterbacks began talking about the other mandatory attributes of their position.

Morrall said, "If you could put a quarterback together with all the skills he *ought* to have, you'd give him, first, speed — speed going back those seven yards into the pocket, which a quarterback like Van Brocklin had, which gave him time to see the action and the pass patterns develop. Then you'd give him the ability to fake well, which Y. A. Tittle and Eddie LeBaron have: good dramatics and action, good enough to make the defense *lean* the wrong way. And then, of course, an arm, a good arm, and strong."

"I'd put that first," Plum said. "The coaches look for someone who can throw the ball fifty yards, and almost on a line. In college, there's not much emphasis on pass defense. It takes too long to develop a good one. With your receivers getting ten yards clear of the defense, you can loft the ball without danger. But any pass which gets up in the air in this league will have four defenders crowding around waiting for it to come down—like an infield pop in baseball."

They could see from my fidgeting that I was uncomfortable as they put together their composite super-quarterback. Down on the training field both of them had seen my passing efforts, which over the length of twenty yards began to develop the high trajectory of a howitzer shell.

"Look," said Morrall. "You don't need to worry tomorrow if you call running plays and get the ball to the running backs. Make those people pick up the yardage for you."

"How about experience?" I asked. "That must be an important attribute."

"Big," said Morrall. "The rookie has to rely on his game plan—what the coaches have told him to do. That's the only weapon, outside his own natural ability, that he's got. As the game goes on, he can't feel or sense what's going on—that, for example, a defensive back has inched up too far, or is moving about in such a way that he's susceptible to such and such a play working on him. That's what the veteran can do—he seems to have the field fixed in his mind like a chart—and that makes him infinitely more valuable than the rookie, even if his throwing arm's about to come unscrewed and fall off."

"What are you going to call for your first play?" Plum asked.

"A surprise call," I said. "Something that'll really jar those people. I think about it a lot—some odd play, one out of the past perhaps. Columbia had a play at the turn of the century in which a guy named Harold Weekes was used in what they called a 'hurdle' play. It was his specialty, poor fellow. He'd get the ball some five yards behind his front line, which was all pinched in tight, and he'd get off to a running start, and using the back of his center—a fellow with the name of 'Bessy'

Bruce—he'd go off like a diver from a springboard, y'know, trying to launch himself into space. His ends would come around and push him if he was in danger of toppling back. It was like trying to scale a mountain sometimes if the opposition bunched up on him."

"Oh yes," said Plum.

"In 1902, in the Princeton game," I went on, "the Princeton people came up with a defense against Weekes: they got a guy named Dana Kafer and they hurdled him the same time Weekes was coming over; they met, and both were carried away."

The quarterbacks looked at me.

"Well, I'll tell you it's true," I said. "I read it in a book. I've done my homework."

Morrall grinned. Plum was solemn.

We sat around and talked some more—Plum, as always, helpful but distant. The thought often crossed my mind that he looked askance at my participation, though it may have been his manner, which was prim, almost stiff, the demeanor of a company executive. He didn't strike one as a football player; it was always surprising to see him appear on the field as carefully groomed as he was, his hair dark, with a careful part, and then incongruous up around his ears the high bulk of the shoulder pads, and then to see his fingers gripped around a football. His voice wasn't a footballer's: it was clear and boyish, with a nervous, acid timbre to it, which made it seem in a higher register than it actually was. Some said that his voice rose under strain, and that he couldn't inspire confidence with it. It wasn't a player who told me that. The players, at least the first-string players, only talked about each other's skills to praise them, unless they were joshing. Otherwise they kept quiet.

Someone told me that about Plum's voice and I remembered the dictum that the French instructors quoted at the military academy at St. Cyr. "Learn to pitch your voice low," they told the young cadets. "An order given in the soprano register, Mister, is not calculated to drive troops to impossible glories."

"That's it," the critic said. "That's it exactly."

"I don't know about that," I said. "Someone say that about Plum?"

He was a newspaperman. "Sure," he said. He was writing a story about Detroit's two-quarterback system.

"You ask around if they'd rather have a big, sincere voice, like a bullfrog's, in the backfield," I said. "Or Plum's arm."

"I'm not taking anything away from the guy's arm," the newspaperman said.

"Well, you ask around," I said.

"Man, don't get so touchy." He was grinning. "I'm not knocking the guy."

"Well, just ask around." It was amazing how protective one got about the Lions.

Earl Morrall was more easygoing, less the technician. His qualities of leadership were those of the squad leader. He was easier to joke with. There had been a lot of joshing about his big toe, which he had lost to a power lawn mower. Since then his passing had improved, and the players had suggested that he get the toe mounted like a rabbit's foot to carry around as a watch charm. They kept an eye on his passing in practice; they quacked happily in derision when his passes fluttered, and reminded him that he still had nine toes left to experiment with; Plum's fluttery passes, which were few assuredly, drew no comment from them. Their admiration for him was high, but he wasn't anyone to kid around with. He was essentially serious.

In a sense Plum reminded me of Hemingway's description of Marcial Lalanda; the bullfighter was described as taking no pleasure in his skill, and deriving no emotion or elation from it—a sad and unemotional performer, although he was technically skillful and completely intelligent. That seemed to me Plum's attitude toward his profession, at least from a distance, whereas Morrall's seemed more gypsylike, emotional, impassioned, yet often haphazard, a trait which marked his play as well—it often seemed scrambled and styleless, the play breaking down all around him, so that in the din from the stands Morrall scampered about like a chicken under pursuit; and yet he would somehow extricate himself—finding his way back to the line of scrimmage, or getting off a successful pass from his shoe tops while being flipped down on his back. He was a very exciting quarterback to watch, though it was difficult to sit comfortably and feel confidence in his attack, which seemed improvised out of turmoil.

"What else?" I asked. "Give me some more advice."

"Well," said Morrall. "You've got to remember the things *not* to do, so that you don't tip the play. Not to wet your fingers, or look to see how your tight end is being defensed. We used to hear that Jim Ninowski— who went to Cleveland in that deal for Milt—had the habit of tipping off his plays: the linebackers could tell what he was going to do by the way he shifted his eyes at the line of scrimmage. Our coaches put the cameras on him to see if they could pick out what it was he was doing. They never found out. It may have been a false rumor to worry us. Still, the defense is always looking for little things that'll help them. A good lineman can tell from seeing how much pressure the man down opposite him has on his fingertips whether he's going to charge or pull. If he's got his weight forward on his fingers, they'll show pale, and that means he's going to charge."

"What are you *really* going to call?" Plum asked. "What's on your ready list?"

"Two pass plays," I said, "the ninety-three you were talking about, and a short slant pass to Jim Gibbons. Then I've got a pitchout to Pietrosante, and also two handoff plays into the line. There are one or two others I know, but I'll stick to those five."

"Audibles?"

"You're kidding," I said.

Plum kept at me. "What are you going to do if the defense is stacked against your play?"

"Run right at it," I said. "Test it. There's nothing else I can do. Besides," I said truthfully, "if the defense *was* stacked against a certain play, I'm not sure I could tell."

There were four main secondary defenses quarterbacks were likely to see as they came out of the huddle up to the line—a 4-3, a 6-1, a 4-2, and what was called an "over defense." When Aldo Forte diagrammed a play on the blackboard such as the 3 left 48 flip (the three back lined up to the left, with the four back receiving the flip pass from the quarterback and heading for the eight hole at his right end), he would say that it would work OK against a 4-3, be an excellent play against a 6-1, but against the 4-2, and the over defense, he preferred a checkoff. So in the case of the latter two, Plum and Morrall would make mental notes, if the situation arose, to call "forty-eight" as the first number in the sequence of three, which checked off the original play, and they knew the players, poised at the line, would be alert for the second number to tell them what they were now supposed to do.

I said, "I don't see how you can keep all this clear in your mind. First of all, you've got to keep the field position in mind—what down it is, and so forth. You've got to remember over seventy-five different offensive plays. True, the coaches, relying on their scouts and the game films, give you fifteen or twenty for the ready list—plays which ought to do well against the club you're playing. But the defense can throw four or five formations against those plays, which means almost one hundred possible situations you have to diagnose to see if you should go ahead with your choice of play. Then, after you call the checkoff, they can jump the defenses around on you, and you may be forced to call another. And the clock is running all this time, just a few seconds available for you to decide what to do, and on top of that, your nose is bleeding, and as you stand up behind your center you have the feeling that your shoelace is untied. And *then,* for God's sake, you've got to give the signal and *execute*—as Casey Stengel says. It's damn breathtaking!"

"You're right," Plum said. "It's got to be almost second nature. There's too much to consider consciously. You don't have a quarterback out there who's saying to himself, 'Now let's see: the forty-two is the four back into the two hole.' There's no time for that. The quarterback's mind's got to be on the subtleties, not the basics."

"I should think you could lose your mind out there," I said. "I mean the stuffing could just leak out under all the pressure, and you'd have this quarterback cackling and carrying on...."

Morrall said, "You find you *do* lose your mind out there sometimes— even if you've been at the game a long time. It's not only the quarterbacks. Joe Schmidt will tell you."

They described it. Apparently, Joe Schmidt once was sent into a preseason exhibition game in the terrible late summer heat of Texas with only a few seconds to go. Detroit was leading. The Philadelphia Eagles had the ball in Detroit territory, but all their time-outs had expired. Schmidt ordered a rush on Van Brocklin, the Eagle quarterback, and dropped him as he was trying to get off a long, last pass. The second hand on the clock swept around and the onlookers stood up to begin filing out of the park. Whereupon Joe Schmidt called: "Time out!"

The referee looked at him blankly for a second or so. His eyebrows then arched up, and he blew his whistle to stop the clock with five seconds to go. The players all stared at Schmidt. Some of them had started off the field, expecting to hear the final gun before they reached the sidelines. Schmidt himself couldn't think then, or ever, why he had shouted for a time-out. He said, "Maybe I just wanted a drink out of one of those little paper cups. The heat was horrible out there." The time-out gave Van Brocklin another chance to throw the football, which he did with success—connecting for a touchdown.

Perhaps the most famous story about the inconstancy of players under stress concerns a rookie quarterback on the Chicago Bears— either Sid Luckman or Bernie Masterson; the story is told about *both* of them, which suggests it may be apocryphal—who was sent into an exhibition game against Cleveland with orders from George Halas, the coach, to "run over guard," "try an end run," and then "punt." Whichever quarterback it was had considerable success with the first two plays, running the ball out of his own territory deep down to the Browns' twenty-five-yard line and a first down. Whereupon, in the third play, Luckman (or Masterson) stepped back into kick formation, just as he had been directed, and *punted* the ball from thirty yards or so out—which sailed the ball out of the high-school stadium where the exhibition was being played. The veterans in the huddle, according to one account, said "Hmmm" when the rookie called for a punt, and Musso, who was the captain at the time, is supposed to have said that the purpose of the training season was to let the rookies "learn for themselves" what it was all about. That was why nothing had been said in the huddle.

"All sorts of things can happen to the quarterback out there," Morrall said. He described how a quarterback, distracted, would sometimes stray off center as he walked up for the line of scrimmage from the huddle, concentrating on the alignment of the defensive backs, perhaps considering the advisability of calling a checkoff play, and he would step up not behind the center, but behind a *guard,* whose eyes would widen inside his helmet to feel the unfamiliar pressure of a hand in under his backside, and more often than not he would bolt across the line and cause an offside penalty. On one occasion Jug Girard, the Cardinal quarterback, stepped up behind a guard by error, but his count was so quick that the play was under way before the guard could demur, and the center in beside him popped the ball back though he didn't feel the usual pressure of the quarterback's hand, swinging his arm, and the ball shot straight up in the air as the two lines came together, as if squeezed up like a peach pit by the pressure.

"That's the damnedest thing I ever heard," I said. "I didn't think I'd have to worry about getting in behind the wrong man. You've shaken me," I told them. "I think I'll go to bed."

Morrall said, "Let me give you some advice if you're going to bed. Clark Shaughnessy, who invented the T formation, used to advise his quarterbacks to lie in bed the night before and play the entire game— to imagine situation after situation and supply the solution. It's a good exercise if you have the right sort of imagination—I mean if you imagined yourself *dropped* every time you wouldn't be in the best frame of mind the next day."

"Put me in a good frame of mind," I said. "Tell me about a quarterback's triumphs."

Plum looked at Morrall. "Tell him about the Baltimore game. Describe the last quarter."

Morrall leaned back in his chair. "This was a couple of years ago down in Baltimore. We were behind eight to three with not much time to go. I threw a pass to Cassady. He got it all right and ran *bam!* into a goalpost, which bounced him back out about four yards, and then he went in the end zone again, rubber-legged, like a guy with the shakes. I ran up to him with my hand out to grab his — it was a great effort of Cassady's — and he wandered right past me, just dazed. He didn't know where he was or what he'd done. It sort of took the pleasure out of it for him. They told him about scoring the touchdown. He was sitting on the bench, and when his head cleared, he'd say, 'Tell me again, tell me how I caught it.'"

"Poor Cassady," I said. "He never had much of a time playing for the Lions."

"Well, after that," Morrall went on, "Jim Martin kicked his field goal and that put us ahead thirteen to eight with just enough time left for Johnny Unitas, their quarterback, to put together a drive and score if he did it quick. There's no one around who can do it like Unitas, and, sure enough, we couldn't hold him. It took him eight plays or so, and the last one was about the best catch I ever saw — Lenny Moore, with those spats of his, making with this crazy big leap and sliding away from Night Train, who had him covered, into the end zone on his belly, his arms out, and he got that ball with what must have been the tips of his fingernails, clawing it to him, and they had the touchdown, which put them ahead fifteen to thirteen. You should have heard the noise that the Baltimore crowd made. Night Train told me later that his heart plumb stopped ticking over when he saw that catch pulled in, and what got it going again was being stepped on and pummeled around by the Baltimore crowd trying to get to Lenny Moore to carry him off on their shoulders. The noise was fantastic — that whole place had gone wild, and they were all over the field. You could hardly blame them — they thought they had the game. Ten seconds to go, that was all, and they were really raising the roof. Of course, those ten seconds gave us a chance — not much, it didn't seem — but we needed only a field goal to win. So while they were trying to clear the field, the whole place this crazy bedlam, we were figuring what to do, over by the sidelines shouting at each other in that mad noise — how to get the ball into Colt territory for the field goal. We had all our time-outs left, and I was going to call one as soon as we got the ball. They kicked off finally — the police cleared about ten thousand of those fans to the sidelines — and Bruce Maher got the ball up to about our thirty-five. Then we got what looked to be a big break. Steve Junker, who was an end with us then, was just getting to his feet after the play, when he was hit from behind. One of the Colts was too excited, or he lost his head, or something, and that should be a fifteen-yard penalty for us, which puts the ball on the fifty-yard line with time for a play, perhaps two, to move it down further for the field-goal try. But what happens? One of our players standing near Steve Junker sees this Colt player hit him. So *he* steps over and whacks the Colt with an elbow, really lets him have it. The referee, who's just about to blow a penalty on Baltimore, sees this because it happens about two feet away from his nose, and he blows so hard the whistle floops out of his mouth, and we have two penalties, offsetting each other, which leaves the ball still on the thirty-five-yard line where Maher took it in the first place."

Morrall looked over at me. "Guess who the guy is — the guy who gives the elbow."

I took a chance. "The Badger," I said. "Brettschneider."

Morrall looked at Plum and shook his head. "The Badger's reputation," he said. "What's to be done?"

"Was it the Badger?" I asked.

"Of course it was the Badger. Who else?" said Morrall.

"Well, what happened then?"

Morrall's mind was still on the Badger's indiscretion. "Considering what was going on, it wasn't surprising what the Badger did," he said. "The whole thing out there was crazy."

"Go on, tell him what happened," Plum said.

"Well, like I said, the idea was to get the ball to their forty—a twenty-yard pass play would do it—so that Jim Martin could take a crack at the field goal. In the huddle I called—well, I had to shout it, the noise around was so crazy—*three left green right eight right*—which sends the strong-side end into the middle. Baltimore had a three-man line rushing, and the rest of them, eight men, were dropped back to defend against the pass they knew I had to throw. They had Lenny Moore in there, very deep, for his speed. They had every defensive back from their bench on the field, sacrificing the weight up in the line they didn't need. They knew it was going to be a pass so they sent in speed. Except for the front three they had men in there averaging 180—and I don't suppose you'd ever find a lighter pound-for-pound team on the defense in the NFL than what the Colts had out there. Coming out of the huddle to look at that defense wasn't much fun, I'll tell you. *Eight* men back there—like trying to drop a plug into a pond packed in solid with lily pads. No hope.

"But they were figuring, I think, for something much longer, and when the play started those eight men got spread thin and deep by the patterns. Gail Cogdill went deep and he took three Colts with him. Cassady went deep on the lookout and two men went with him. Webb, the fullback, moved out, and he took a linebacker. Gibbons, the strong end, went down about seventeen yards, a little deeper than he would ordinarily on that play, and he got a step on his man and was moving good when I got the pass to him. Cogdill threw an amazing block, and the Gibber carried it in for the touchdown. It was hard to believe. I think we all felt a little like Cassady when he was stunned running into the goalpost and didn't know what he'd done. I kept looking around like mad thinking something had to go wrong. An official told me later that the gun ending the game went off when the Gibber was still running downfield—when he was crossing the twenty. Of course, none of us heard the gun. The Baltimore crowd was making all that noise. Then when the Gibber crossed the line—it went absolutely silent, just struck dumb, and you could hear this little sound, and it was our guys yelling. Damnedest thing. All this crazy yelling from the crowd and when the Gibber went across the line it stopped all at once, like they'd been gagged, like a cord went tight around all those throats—I thought I'd gone deaf—and then you could hear this little sound that our guys were making. The other thing that was crazy was that the whole stadium was empty in a couple of seconds, it seemed—that big crowd just melting away like it flowed down a big drain, and you looked around where they'd been so many people you could hardly move, and there were only our guys there, with these big grins, some of them still leaping up and down."

"Well, that's something," I said truthfully. "It really is."

Plum said, "You go through something like that and it makes up for an awful lot of bad times, and the knocks, and the hours of training, and running the plays over, and the defeats, and all, and the crap."

"I'll say," I said. "The whole crowd just shut up absolutely tight?" I asked. I couldn't get that out of my mind.

"It was like a tomb in that place," said Morrall. "Just sudden-like—you could hear echoes if you shouted, I swear."

"That must have been something," I said again.

"That's the best of it," said Morrall, looking at Plum. "Just about the best."

Plum said, "You pull off something like that, and there doesn't need to be anything else, ever."

CHAPTER 21

Friday was waiting by my locker. He handed me my game jersey of tear-away silk material, in the deep Honolulu blue of Detroit, with my number in silver, the zero, on both the back and front, and on the sleeves.

"You feel all right?" he asked.

"Oh sure," I said. I sat down on the bench and took off my street shoes, setting them carefully in the locker. The plan was to dress at the training camp in the early evening and ride in game uniform to Pontiac, a half-hour ride by bus, rather than change in the stadium there.

"You better jump to it," Friday said. "Most everyone's dressed."

Sam Williams, the first-string defensive end came by, and looked down my aisle of lockers. "Nerves, kid?" he asked. "How are the nerves?"

"Well, I've got them, Sam," I said. "I feel them in the stomach."

He was in his sixth year of professional football, and I asked him if nerves still affected him.

"Sure," he said. "In the feet and hands... heavy feet, heavy hands so's I can barely move around."

"Heavy feet!" I said. "Think of that. My nerves seem to stick to the stomach." I took a breath, a deep one, to relieve the tension, and went back to dressing, putting on the paraphernalia of the uniform slowly, item after item, overfastidious to get them set right—the tape, the supporter, the wraparound girdle, the thigh pads, the arm pads, the shoulder pads, the sweatshirt. Williams's locker was in the next aisle, and when I was ready I went around and he pulled the blue jersey down over my shoulder pads, which was difficult to do alone, and then cuffed the pads into place.

"That's a good number you're wearing," Williams said. "Johnny Olszewski's — Johnny O's."

"It indicates my talent," I said.

I went back to my locker. My football shoes were up on top, next to the big silver helmet with the blue Lion decal, and when I took the shoes down they seemed astonishingly heavy to the hand.

I spotted Friday coming by again.

"Hey, Friday, what's happened to my shoes?"

He came over. He looked busy. "What's the trouble?" he asked briskly. "Boy, you'd better hop to it. You're going to miss the bus."

"Well," I said, "these shoes seem, well, sort of heavy, that's what they seem."

"Your shoes seem *heavy?*" said Friday, quite loudly, so I moved toward him and I said softly, so as not to be overheard in the locker room, "Well, look here, Friday, heft them for yourself."

He did so, and looked surprised. "There's nothing wrong with these shoes."

"Somebody's put something in them," I said stubbornly.

Friday called out loudly, "Hey, the rookie thinks somebody's weighted his shoes. What'd anyone want to do that for?" he asked. I looked carefully at the corners of his mouth for a turn that would suggest that a joke was being played. Sam Williams came around the lockers, and so did Joe Schmidt.

"Feet seem heavy?" Williams asked.

"Hell no, Sam," I said. "It's the shoes themselves. Someone's stuck some weights in them."

"Who'd want to do that?" asked Schmidt. He leaned over and hefted the shoes. "They seem all right to me."

I took them back and hefted them myself, but I was beginning to lose my sense of proportion, so that they no longer seemed as heavy as they had.

A number of players were standing around by then, dressed for the bus ride, holding their helmets by the chin straps.

"Try them on," Schmidt suggested.

I slipped the shoes on, laced them up, and clomped around the locker-room floor in front of my bench.

"What do you think?" Friday asked.

"Well, I don't know," I said frankly. "I mean I can walk and all, but they still seem all-fired heavy."

"That's not surprising," said Sam Williams. "Look, you got a big night coming up, quarterbacking your first game, and you got a real example of heavy feet, that's all. Perfectly natural. Nothing to be blamed for."

He had a big grin on his face, but I began to wonder if it wasn't one of sympathy. Around the circle of faces there wasn't a glimmer, even on Night Train Lane's, whose manner was so easy he was always laughing, to suggest that they weren't all being perfectly serious.

"Aw, come on now," I said. "I haven't got heavy feet, for Chrissake!" I watched them, particularly Night Train's eyes, waiting for the laughter to dissolve them and give them away. They all remained solemn. At the edge of the circle players just arriving, who couldn't see past the big phalanx of shoulder pads, wanted to know what was going on.

"Someone fainted?" I heard a voice ask.

"You'll get over them," someone else called out, "soon as you get on the field."

Friday suddenly said, "I'll tell you something about those shoes. The *cleats* are worn thin. Hand 'em over and I'll get one of the boys to screw in a new set for you."

I sat down on the bench and took the shoes off, hefting them once more, and shaking my head. Friday disappeared with them.

"Friday's probably going to work a *nail* or two up through the soles, for Chrissakes," I said.

Someone said, "D'ja ever see such a case of nerves?"

The players began drifting away—those who were dressed heading for the buses out in the parking lot, their cleats crashing against the locker-room floor. Someone came by as I waited and said I was wanted—and quick—for the quarterback meeting.

Earl Morrall and Milt Plum were waiting with Scooter McLean. Over the faucets of the whirlpool baths a message on a paper towel had been stuck up which read RESERVED FOR PLIMPTON.

"Look at that thing," I said involuntarily.

The notice was signed with a device—a dagger dripping blood. It was from Brettschneider, the last in a series of messages which I had been receiving at staggered hours that day; I found the first stuck in the mirror of my room when I awoke. It read: *George—you are going to get your butt knocked off* [s] *The Badger and his friends.* The next announced: *We have made arrangements for you to order anything you want for the pre-game meal* [s] *The Badger and his friends.* Another message had appeared in the mirror just before I left for the gym—this one informing me that I had only two hours to go, signed with the bloody dagger and the signature of the Badger and his "gang," not "friends" this time, but "gang."

Scooter McLean was sitting up on a rubbing table; in front of him on wood-slatted chairs sat the two quarterbacks, tilting back as the Scooter ran down the play list, deciding with them what plays would be used that night against the defensive unit.

McLean looked at me when I came in. "OK," he said. "You're going to run the first five plays of the night."

"The *first* five plays!" I said. "You sure?" I swallowed hard. "The *first* five plays." Time seemed to be going too quickly, and the temptation was to try to slow things down.

McLean looked at his play list.

"Start off with the three left twenty-six near oh pinch," he said.

That was a play I had tried a few times in the scrimmages—clumsily and with little effect—a running play, in which the quarterback receives the ball from center, turns, takes a couple of steps straight back and hands the ball to the number two back coming across laterally from right to left, who then cuts sharply into the number six hole between left tackle and end.

"God, Scooter," I said. "I'm not so hot on that play. Can't I...start with ninety-three, the pass play that I hit Pietrosante with, cutting across ten yards downfield? It's my best play and it'll rile them, starting with a pass play—shake them up."

Scooter shook his head. "This is the first-line defense you're playing against. You're not going to rile them up with any ninety-three pass play. Stick on the ground. Let the blockers and the running backs do the work for you. Sure, you can do that twenty-six near oh pinch." He hopped off the rubbing table and demonstrated—the spin, the two steps back, and the handoff to the two back cutting across. "Simple," he said.

"It's a good choice," said Morrall from his chair. "You got more chance moving on the ground because once you get the handoff to the running back he'll be responsible for picking up the yardage."

"OK," I said weakly. "If I can *get* the ball to him."

Scooter went back to his clipboard. "Then the twenty-six roll," he said.

"Look," I said. "I'm not so hot on the twenty-six roll. Why can't I try the ninety-three next? My two best plays are the forty-eight flip" (this was a long lateral from the quarterback out to the number four back running parallel to the line and then cutting for the eight hole, at left end) "and the ninety-three pass. I think about those plays, and I have a certain amount of confidence about them. Scooter, I have a terrible time with those handoff plays like the twenty-six roll."

"OK," said Scooter. "Run the ninety-three next. That's two plays. Then how about the forty-two?"

"OK, that's the third play," I said. The 42 was supposed to be simple, the quarterback spinning as soon as the ball slapped into his palm, a full spin, and then shoving the ball into the stomach of the four back churning straight past into the two hole just left of the center — but still it was a play that filled me with gloom. The times I had tried it in practice, the fullback, with that jackrabbit speed at which a professional backfield moves, would be past me and into the line before I could complete my spin and hand the ball to him. The procedure then, having missed him, the ball held out to his rump going by, was to haul the ball back in and follow him into the line, which I would do, grimacing, eyes squinted almost shut, waiting for the impact, which was invariably very quick.

"Then what?" asked Scooter.

"I'd like to try the slant pass into the Badger's territory at left linebacker. That'd give me great pleasure to complete that one — he's been giving me such a time with the messages." I motioned toward the whirlpool bath. "Besides, I've been working on it after practice with the tight ends, particularly Jim Gibbons. Then I suppose I could end with the forty-eight flip."

Scooter agreed to the list, and he marked the plays down on his clipboard.

Joe Schmidt came in to have something done to the tape on his ankle. He saw us grouped around Scooter, and he called out, grinning, "Hey, Scooter, be sure to let him try the Fake II."

For a week Schmidt had been tempting me to try the Fake II for the Pontiac scrimmage. It was a play in which the quarterback took the ball from his center, dropped back a few yards, pumping his arm to fake the linebackers into moving back, or laterally, to protect against a pass, and then suddenly taking the ball into the line himself — a quarterback draw play, it was, and it meant the quarterback was accepting the horror that came when the linebackers recovered from the fake and picked him up as he came through. There weren't many quarterbacks around who called the play.

Schmidt did a little pantomime there in the training room of a nervous quarterback working the Fake II, poised behind his center, then dancing back in his stocking feet, pumping his arm hard, then running hard in place, head down, emulating the dash for the line, then looking up and screaming as the imaginary linebackers converged, followed by a concussive sound he made by exploding his palms together, and he gave the expiring, anguished cry of a broken quarterback.

"Oh yes," he called out. "You got to get him to try that one."

It was a funny imitation, and we stood laughing at it—except for the Scooter, who said testily, "They're going to make you yo-yos on defense look silly tonight, mind you!" He would take no such kidding from the defense people, simply as a matter of principle, having spent his years, from the first, running against defenses, and afterward, as a coach, attacking them with personnel he trained endlessly, trying to imbue them with his skills and perhaps his antipathy, which was such that when a member of the defense, even from his own team, twitted him, it raised his temper.

Everybody knew this—and admired it—though it did not keep Schmidt and the others from joshing him, knowing just how far they could go. The Scooter turned his back and inspected his clipboard, his quarterbacks grouped around him.

He had no further use for me, so I hurried off to the equipment manager's room to retrieve my football shoes. Friday's assistant was still screwing cleats into them.

"Friday!" I said. "These cleats look awfully long to me. Those aren't *mud* cleats you're sticking in there?"

Friday came over. "What'd I want to stick mud cleats in there for?" he said. "The day's fine outside. Going to be a lovely night. What do you want mud cleats for?"

"*I* don't want mud cleats, damn it, Friday, but those things being screwed in there are long enough to bring up...well, *oil,* and as for the shoes themselves, Friday, they *got* to have weights in them."

Friday began hefting them again, but then suddenly he grinned and broke—with a thin wheeze that left him struggling for breath. "OK, OK," he said. "Look at this." He tugged at the inside sole of the shoe, straining against the glue that had hardened fast, and he skinned out a thin, shaped metal strip. It weighed at least a pound.

"What do you think of that?" he asked. "They were put in this morning."

"Look at those things," I said.

Friday explained that players who wanted to strengthen their leg muscles often wore them in their shoes in the early part of training. You could tell when they came in from running with them—"sort of like gimpy hens."

"Great," I said. "You mean to say they would have let me play the game tonight wearing those damn things?"

"Probably not," said Friday. "They'd all like to see you do well, but it's hard for them not to kid around. Besides," he said, "you could have gotten around all right wearing those shoes, and they would have had a good laugh afterward, and if you didn't do well you would have had a good excuse. Now, you haven't got an excuse."

"Well, I've still got these mud cleats—look at the length of them—to fall back on for an excuse," I said.

I laced up the shoes and hurried out to the parking lot where the bus was waiting. The first bus, with the rookies in it, had gone. I was the last into the veterans' bus, and we started for Pontiac as soon as the door had sighed shut behind me. It was a strange busload—all of us in uniform, the offense in blue jerseys, as I was, and the defensive players in white with blue numbers, the big shoulder pads filling the seats out into the aisle when the players sat two abreast, and swaying almost across to the seat opposite when the bus rocked around a corner.

It was relatively quiet, conversation low, the players staring out the windows, their minds on what they would be doing in an hour or so. In the rookie bus, one of them told me later, they rode in absolute silence for the half-hour ride to Pontiac. Occasionally, in our bus, someone would call out, "Get it up, get it up! Offense!" and a few players would stamp on the bus floor with their cleated shoes—the tension beginning to rise; once in a while the crack of palm against palm would sound, and that tight call, "Get it up!" would come again, sometimes delivered for the offense's benefit, sometimes for the defense.

Earl Morrall, in his seat across the aisle, recalled that the year before, the Pontiac game had been played in a torrential downpour — the worst conditions he could remember for a game, worse than the ten-degree temperatures that swept in off Lake Erie in Cleveland — the players ankle-deep in warm summer rain. Then near the end of the game the rain came down unbelievably hard and lightning hit one of the light standards and popped the row of lights far up, smoke rose from each distant bulb and sparks trailed down, like a country-club fireworks display, and then the other light standards flickered and failed. In one of the lightning flashes Morrall saw Night Train bolting for cover, stretching out in a crazy stride like a man being pursued across tide-covered mudflats, almost obscured by the spray kicked up in his haste.

Across from Morrall, I sat alone trying to clear my mind and get my plays straight, visualizing what I had to do with each — the 26 near oh pinch, the 93 pass play, the 42 (which made me wince, thinking about it), the 9 slant out to embarrass the Badger, and finally the 48 flip play. I was tempted to scribble the numbers down on my wrist with a ballpoint pen, which some quarterbacks do, particularly checkoff plays, so that when they arrive at the line of scrimmage and find the defense set up against the play called in the huddle they can glance down — they have very little time — and spot the play scrawled in blue ink on their wrist.

Jim Gibbons, the tight end, came down the aisle and sat with me for a while. We went over the plays together, keeping our voices down so the defensive players would not overhear. In front of us Paul Ward, a big 250-pound defensive lineman, knew what we were whispering about, and he turned and leered over the back of his seat. He was a big, blond, friendly ex-Marine who had a degree in physical education, and he was writing a postgraduate thesis on isometric exercises, which he practiced, straining against immovable objects. At the training camp I would come around a corner and find him in a doorway pressing out against the sides with his palms, his face flushed with effort. He was always trying to get me to do the exercises, which I did, to humor him, grunting in doorways, and he would say, "Great, great! But you must do it every chance you get—*look* for places to stand up and practice it."

"Hey!" he said over his seat. "Which of the two plays you know are you going to run against us?"

Gibbons said, "Two? This guy knows the whole book—secret sessions after practice—plays you haven't even heard of, and you'll be seeing them from flat on your kisser—you better believe it—now that he's got the weight out of his shoes."

"Yeah, yeah, yeah," said Ward.

Schmidt, sitting a few seats away, who had overheard, said, "I'll tell you the play that's going to bust the whole game wide open—it's the Fake II, *that's* the play," and down the aisle we heard the Badger, Brettschneider, say, "The Fake II! Well, that'll sure'n hell bust the third-string *quarterback* wide open," and the guffawing began. Someone asked if anyone could think of a better play to offer the rookie than the Fake II, and behind me somewhere I heard John Gordy say, "Yes, a club."

The joking did not last long. We were in the outskirts of Pontiac—the traffic heavy, much of it moving toward the stadium. It was dusk outside, and the blue antiglare tint in the windows darkened the bus. The driver kept the inside lights off. Gibbons, beside me, chatted for a while, and then he too was silent. The bus turned, and we maneuvered slowly through streams of pedestrians, ticket holders, who would look up, annoyed at the bus in their midst, expecting to see a fan club from Ypsilanti, perhaps, with colored plastic hats, and saw instead the Lions themselves, the big shoulder pads flush up against the windows—gaping then, and pointing.

The players were on edge now—a few tight comments were leveled at the bus driver, who made a wrong turn and got us blocked in the crowds of ticket holders a few hundred yards from the stadium. He lifted his hands off the steering wheel finally with a hopeless shrug of his shoulders, and opened the door. We clambered down and trotted the short distance to the stadium, the crowd, hearing the sounds of the spikes on the macadam coming up on them, turning and dividing to let us by—always the stares, the mouths half open as if something was to be said, some verbal accord to be reached—though we ran between walls of silence, only an occasional call to someone recognized. Whoever was in the lead, Joe Schmidt I think it was, ran us up under the overhang of the outside of the stadium, then down a sloped incline of a corridor which led through to the football field. Someone, an official perhaps, misdirected him in the passageway—through a small side door, the long line of us trotting dutifully after him, into a small locker room, in the center of which a Marine color guard was standing, with its flags, and two Boy Scouts, with highly polished wooden guns, staring wide-eyed as the room began to bulge with football players. Schmidt couldn't file us out again until the last in line had come in—like a tree boa in a birdhouse who has to get his length in with him before he can get out. The place got crowded full, some of us trotting in place, cleats crashing, waiting, no one saying anything, everyone too self-absorbed to remark on the fine lunacy of that room suddenly filling with football players, then emptying, for no apparent reason, and what the color guard and the Boy Scouts, waiting peaceably enough for their call, must have thought when the door opened and the influx of those big men began.

Schmidt finally got us out on the playing field. It was a lovely evening—a cool summer breeze coming across the wire fence at the open end of the field out of the remnants of a sunset splayed above a horizon of flat farmland. The fields close to the stadium were crowded with cars, with more arriving. The stands, which rose up twenty or thirty rows, rapidly filling, ran along the sidelines, and at each corner four steel towers stood into the hazeless sky, their arc lights on full and collecting clouds of moths, hardly visible until the dusk deepened and the light began to catch them, turning them white as they wheeled and hurtled into the glare as if windblown. A band shell for concerts stood at the closed end of the field; beyond it was a junkyard with a gigantic hydraulic press amid pillars of auto hulks, crushed absolutely flat as shingles and piled up, one on another.

I turned away to join the circle for calisthenics being led by Terry Barr, the captain of the Lion offensive unit—the jumping jacks, the stretching exercises, all of us bellowing out the cadences, the push-ups, the grass cool to the touch—all of us grateful to be active. The teams then split up and went to their respective ends of the field, the offensive unit at the junkyard end, those mournful stacks of flattened cars filling my vision every time I turned.

Wilson walked over. "How's my starting quarterback?" he asked.

Instinctively, I reached for my helmet.

I had been in the habit of pulling it on when there was even the slightest chance of entering a scrimmage—rather than face the awkward possibility of being called suddenly by Wilson and either not having a helmet at all (players were supposed to keep their helmets at hand, but it was easy enough to leave them lying in the grass while you tossed a ball back and forth), or having difficulty getting *into* it—the strain, and getting the ears straightened out, all that procedure—while running out to take over the offensive huddle.

I said, "How much time before..."

"Oh, about ten minutes," Wilson said. "There'll be an award ceremony after the contests and then the game will start."

I turned away from him, got my thumbs into the helmet ear holes, and ducking my head I got the helmet on, and when I'd got my ears straight I clicked the chin strap fast to a little punch-on snap which sounds sharply in the helmet—*pop*—and I wandered over to the bench and sat down.

One of the troubles with wearing the helmet was that it closed off the outside world, the noise of the crowd, the cheering as the contests went on—all of this just a murmur—leaving my mind to work away busily inside the amphitheater of the helmet. Voices, my own, spoke quite clearly—my lips moving in the security of the helmet—offering consolation, encouragement, and paternal advice of a particularly gall-

Fastening his helmet, the author steels himself to enter the action. *(Walter Iooss Jr.)*

ing sort: "The thing to be is *calm,* son, and remember not to *snatch* back from the ball until you get it set in your palm"—this in reference to one of my common faults, which was darting back from the center before I had hold of the ball, too anxious to get back and develop the play; the ball would fall and bounce behind the center's heels—Bob Whitlow, or Jim Martin, whoever the center was—his spikes furrowing the grass as he plowed forward, and I would stop in mid-flight back and dive forward to recover the ball, flailing for it like a man swimming frantic strokes underwater, hearing around me the cracking of shoulder pads and the thick heave of linemen like stress in an ice floe.

"I must hang on to the ball," I murmured.

"But"—the portentous voice came again—"you must not dally, son...On the handoffs you must get the ball to the halfbacks with *dispatch....*"

When I played baseball in Yankee Stadium, my inner voice was Southern in inflection, until it finally broke into hysteria at my difficulties as a pitcher—a pleasant, comforting voice, originally, that said, "*Gol-ding* it" and "Chile's play, this is."

In Pontiac, the voice was not Southern; it might have been New England—severe, patronizing, that of a cleric, or a schoolteacher, perhaps, seated on a high stool, a blackboard behind him, and, out a small square window to one side, a barren field with some cornstalks in it and a scarecrow, and a low stone fence around—it was the sort of voice which fitted such surroundings. It said, "Son, no daydreaming—tend to your knitting."

These instructions were accompanied by short, visual vignettes, subliminal, but which seemed to flash inside the helmet with the clarity of a television screen in a dark room—tumultuous scenes of big tackles and ends in what seemed a landslide, a cliff of them toppling toward me, like slow-moving objects in a dream, as I lay in some sort of depression, a pit perhaps, the pit that Raymond Berry had described, gaping up in resigned dismay. As the avalanche of linemen came down, they were calling out the red-dog cry "Jumbo! Jumbo! Jumbo!" almost loud enough to drown out the schoolmaster's pawky voice whispering close at hand, "Son, do this, son, do that"—all of this a manifestation of insecurity so discomfiting that to cease being a captive audience to it I ripped off my helmet, despite my participation minutes away, and let the outside noise of the crowd, huge by now, wash over me.

A band was playing somewhere in the stands. The wind coming up off the parking fields was cool. The public-address system was announcing the contest winners. There had been footraces, a passing-accuracy contest, a longest-pass contest, and a punting competition for both accuracy and length. A pretty girl wearing a white evening dress and long white gloves was standing at midfield. She wore a diadem—the Queen of Something-or-Other—and she was handing out the awards, to Pat Studstill, the flanker back, as I watched, for the most accurate punt of the evening—it had gone sixty yards on the fly, a yard or so out from the corner flag to upset Yale Lary—and as he stepped forward I pounded my cleats against the ground and called out his name happily, concentrating on what was going on to keep my mind occupied. "Monk, oh you *Monk!*" His face wore a leer, alive with it, as he escorted the girl in the evening dress from the field to conclude the ceremonies, all of us along the bench hooting and braying at him.

George Wilson then called: "All right, teams A and B *out* there!" motioning to me, hard-faced—a door slammed shut on merriment—and the helmets went on.

The officials, in their vertical-striped black-and-white jerseys, were waiting on the thirty-yard line. The kickoff was to be dispensed with, and the scrimmage would start from there.

I came up off the bench slowly, working my fingers up into my helmet to get at my ears. As I crossed the sidelines I was conscious then not only of moving into the massive attention of the crowd, but seeing ahead out of the opening of my helmet the two teams waiting. Some of the defense were already kneeling at the line of scrimmage, their heads turned so that helmeted, silver, with the cages protruding, they were made to seem animal and impersonal—wildlife of some large species disturbed at a water hole—watching me come toward them. Close to, suddenly there was nothing familiar about them. With the arc lights high up on the standards, the interiors of their helmets were shadowed—perhaps with the shine of a cheekbone, the glint of an eye—no one recognizable, nor a word from them. I trotted by the ball. Its trade name "Duke" was face up. The referee was waiting, astride it, a whistle at the end of a black cord dangling from his neck. The offensive team in their blue jerseys, about ten yards back, on their own twenty-yard line, moved and collected in the huddle formation as I came up, and I slowed, and walked toward them, trying to be calm about it, almost lazying up to them to see what could be done.

CHAPTER 22

Jack Benny used to say that when he stood on the stage in white tie and tails for his violin concerts and raised his bow to begin his routine — scraping through "Love in Bloom" — he *felt* like a great violinist. He reasoned that, if he wasn't a great violinist, what was he doing dressed in tails, and about to play before a large audience?

At Pontiac I *felt* myself a football quarterback, not an interloper. My game plan was organized, and I knew what I was supposed to do. My nerves seemed steady, much steadier than they had been as I waited on the bench. I trotted along easily. I was keenly aware of what was going on around me.

I could hear Bud Erickson's voice over the loudspeaker system, a dim murmur, telling the crowd what was going on. He was telling them that number zero, coming out across the sidelines, was not actually a rookie, but an amateur, a writer, who had been training with the team for three weeks and had learned five plays, which he was now going to run against the first-string Detroit defense. It was like a nightmare come true, he told them, as if one of *them,* rocking a beer around in a paper cup, with a pretty girl leaning past him to ask the hot-dog vendor in the aisle for mustard, were suddenly carried down underneath the stands by a sinister clutch of ushers. He would protest, but he would be encased in the accoutrements, the silver helmet, with the two protruding bars of the cage, jammed down over his ears, and sent out to take over the team—that was the substance of Erickson's words, drifting across the field, swayed and shredded by the steady breeze coming up across the open end of Wisner Stadium from the vanished sunset. The crowd was interested, and I was conscious, just vaguely, of a steady roar of encouragement.

The team was waiting for me, grouped in the huddle watching me come. I went in among them. Their heads came down for the signal. I called out, "Twenty-six!" forcefully, to inspire them, and a voice from one of the helmets said, "Down, down, the whole stadium can hear you."

"Twenty-six," I hissed at them. "Twenty-six near oh pinch; on three. *Break!*" Their hands cracked as one, and I wheeled and started for the line behind them.

My confidence was extreme. I ambled slowly behind Whitlow, poised down over the ball, and I had sufficient presence to pause, resting a hand at the base of his spine, as if on a windowsill—a nonchalant gesture I had admired in certain quarterbacks—and I looked out over the length of his back to fix in my mind what I saw.

Everything fine about being a quarterback—the embodiment of his power—was encompassed in those dozen seconds or so: giving the instructions to ten attentive men, breaking out of the huddle, walking for the line, and then pausing behind the center, dawdling amidst men poised and waiting under the trigger of his voice, cataleptic, until the deliverance of himself and them to the future. The pleasure of sport was so often the chance to indulge the cessation of time itself—the pitcher dawdling on the mound, the skier poised at the top of a mountain trail, the basketball player with the rough skin of the ball against his palm preparing for a foul shot, the tennis player at set point over his opponent—all of them savoring a moment before committing themselves to action.

I had the sense of a portcullis down. On the other side of the imaginary bars the linemen were poised, the lights glistening off their helmets, and close in behind them were the linebackers, with Joe Schmidt just opposite me, the big number 56 shining on his white jersey, jump-jacking back and forth with quick choppy steps, his hands poised in front of him, and he was calling out defensive code words in a stream. I could sense the rage in his voice, and the tension in those rows of bodies waiting, as if coils had been wound overtight, which my voice, calling a signal, like a lever would trip to spring them all loose. "Blue! Blue! Blue!" I heard Schmidt shout.

Within my helmet, the schoolmaster's voice murmured at me: "Son, nothing to it, nothing at all..."

I bent over the center. Quickly, I went over what was supposed to happen — I would receive the snap and take two steps straight back, and hand the ball to the number two back coming laterally across from right to left, who would then cut into the number six hole. That was what was designated by 26 — the two back into the six hole. The mysterious code words "near oh pinch" referred to blocking assignments in the line, and I was never sure exactly what was meant by them. The important thing was to hang on to the ball, turn, and get the ball into the grasp of the back coming across laterally.

I cleared my throat. "Set!" I called out — my voice loud and astonishing to hear, as if it belonged to someone shouting into the ear holes of my helmet. "Sixteen, sixty-five, forty-four, *hut*-one, *hut*-two, *hut*-three," and at "three" the ball slapped back into my palm, and Whitlow's rump bucked up hard as he went for the defenseman opposite.

The lines cracked together with a yawp and smack of pads and gear. I had the sense of quick, heavy movement, and as I turned for the backfield, not a second having passed, I was hit hard from the side, and as I gasped the ball was jarred loose. It sailed away, and bounced once, and I stumbled after it, hauling it under me five yards back, hearing the rush of feet, and the heavy jarring and wheezing of the blockers fending off the defense, a great roar up from the crowd, and above it, a relief to hear, the shrilling of the referee's whistle. My first thought was that at the snap of the ball the right side of the line had collapsed just at the second of the handoff, and one of the tacklers, Brown or Floyd Peters, had cracked through to make me fumble. Someone, I assumed, had messed

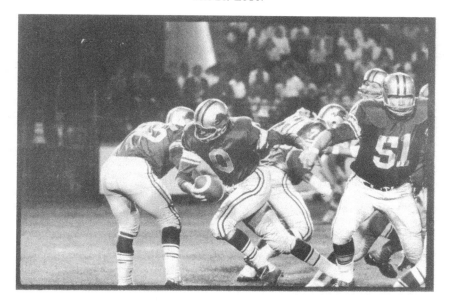

The author, number 0, drops back to hand the ball off in the Pontiac scrimmage. *(Walter Iooss Jr.)*

up on the assignments designated by the mysterious code words "near oh pinch." In fact, as I discovered later, my *own man* bowled me over — John Gordy, whose assignment as offensive guard was to pull from his position and join the interference on the far side of the center. He was required to pull back and travel at a great clip parallel to the line of scrimmage to get out in front of the runner, his route theoretically passing between me and the center. But the extra second it took me to control the ball, and the creaking execution of my turn, put me in his path, a rare sight for Gordy to see, his own quarterback blocking the way, like coming around a corner in a high-speed car to find a moose ambling across the centerline, and he caromed off me, jarring the ball loose.

It was not new for me to be hit down by my own people. At Cranbrook I was knocked down all the time by players on the offense — the play patterns run with such speed along routes so carefully defined that if everything wasn't done right and at the proper speed, the play would

The author, facedown on the turf after a crushing hit from the defense. *(Walter Iooss Jr.)*

break down in its making. I was often reminded of film clips in which the process of a porcelain pitcher, say, being dropped by a butler and smashed, is shown in reverse, so that the pieces pick up off the floor and soar up to the butler's hand, each piece on a predestined route, sudden perfection out of chaos. Often, it did not take more than an inch or so off line to throw a play out of kilter. On one occasion at the training camp, practicing handoff plays to the fullback, I had my chin hanging out just a bit too far, something wrong with my posture, and Pietrosante's shoulder pad caught it like a punch as he went by, and I spun slowly to the ground, grabbing at my jaw. Brettschneider had said that afternoon: "The defense is going to rack you up one of these days, if your own team'd let you *stand* long enough for us defense guys to get *at* you. It's aggravating to bust through and find that you've already been laid flat by your own offense guys."

My confidence had not gone. I stood up. The referee took the ball from me. He had to tug to get it away, a faint look of surprise on his face. My inner voice was assuring me that the fault in the tumble had not been mine. "They let you down," it was saying. "The blocking failed." But the main reason for my confidence was the next play on my list—the 93 pass, a play which I had worked successfully in the Cranbrook scrimmages. I walked into the huddle and I said with considerable enthusiasm, "All right! All *right!* Here we *go!*"

"Keep the voice down," said a voice. "You'll be tipping them the play."

I leaned in on them and said: "Green right" ("Green" designated a pass play, "right" put the flanker to the right side), "three right" (which put the three back to the right), "ninety-three" (indicating the two primary receivers; nine, the right end, and three, the three back) "on *three...* *Break!*"—the clap of the hands again in unison, the team streamed past me up to the line, and I walked briskly up behind Whitlow.

Calling a play in the Pontiac scrimmage. The backfield men are in the back row, the linemen in close. If you look down, you see their feet pointed at you. *(Walter Iooss Jr.)*

Again, I knew exactly how the play was going to develop—back those seven yards into the defensive pocket for the three to four seconds it was supposed to hold, and Pietrosante, the three back, would go down in his pattern, ten yards straight, then cut over the middle, and I would hit him.

"Set!... Sixteen!... eighty-eight... fifty-five... *hut*-one... *hut*-two... *hut*-three..."

The ball slapped into my palm at "three." I turned and started back. I could feel my balance going, and two yards behind the line of scrimmage I *fell down*—absolutely flat, as if my feet had been pinned under a trip wire stretched across the field, not a hand laid on me. I heard a great roar go up from the crowd. Suffused as I had been with confidence, I could scarcely believe what had happened. Mud cleats catching in the grass? Slipped in the dew? I felt my jaw go ajar in my helmet. "Wha'? Wha'?"—the mortification beginning to come fast. I rose hurriedly to my knees at the referee's whistle, and I could see my teammates' big silver helmets with the blue Lion decals turn toward me, some of the players rising from blocks they'd thrown to protect me, their faces masked, automaton, prognathous with the helmet bars protruding toward me, characterless, yet the dismay was in the set of their bodies as they loped back for the huddle. The schoolmaster's voice flailed at me inside my helmet. "Ox!" it cried. "Clumsy oaf."

I joined the huddle. "Sorry, sorry," I said.

"Call the play, man," came a voice from one of the helmets.

"I don't know what happened," I said.

"Call it, man."

The third play on my list was the 42, another running play, one of the simplest in football, in which the quarterback receives the snap, makes a full spin, and shoves the ball into the four back's stomach—the fullback's. He has come straight forward from his position as if off starting blocks, his knees high, and he disappears with the ball into the number two hole just to the left of the center—a straight power play, and one which seen from the stands seems to offer no difficulty.

A slow, agonizing, and inexplicable collapse to the ground during a pass play—without a hand being laid on me. *(Walter Iooss Jr.)*

I got into an awful jam with it. Once again, the jackrabbit speed of the professional backfield was too much for me. The fullback—Danny Lewis—was past me and into the line before I could complete my spin and set the ball in his belly. And so I did what was required: I tucked the ball into my own belly and followed Lewis into the line, hoping that he might have budged open a small hole.

I tried, grimacing, my eyes squinted almost shut, and waiting for the impact, which came before I'd taken two steps—I was grabbed up by Roger Brown.

He tackled me high, and straightened me with his power, so that I churned against his three-hundred-pound girth like a comic bicyclist. He began to shake me. I remained upright to my surprise, flailed back and forth, and I realized that he was struggling for the ball. His arms were around it, trying to tug it free. The bars of our helmets were nearly locked, and I could look through and see him inside—the first helmeted face I recognized that evening—the small, brown eyes surprisingly peaceful, but he was grunting hard, the sweat shining, and I had time to think, "It's Brown, it's *Brown!*" before I lost the ball to him, and flung to one knee on the ground I watched him lumber ten yards into the end zone behind us for a touchdown.

The referee wouldn't allow it. He said he'd blown the ball dead while we were struggling for it. Brown was furious. "You taking that away from *me?*" he said, his voice high and squeaky. "Man, I took that ball in there good."

The referee turned and put the ball on the ten-yard line. I had lost twenty yards in three attempts, and I had yet, in fact, to run off a complete play.

The veterans walked back very slowly to the next huddle.

I stood off to one side, listening to Brown rail at the referee. "I never scored like that befo'. You takin' that away from me?" His voice was peeved. He looked off toward the stands, into the heavy tumult of sound, spreading the big palms of his hands in grief.

I watched him, detached, not even moved by his insistence that I suffer the humiliation of having the ball stolen for a touchdown. If the referee had allowed him his score, I would not have protested. The shock of having the three plays go as badly as they had left me dispirited and numb, the purpose of the exercise forgotten. Even the schoolmaster's voice seemed to have gone—a bleak despair having set in so that as I stood shifting uneasily, watching Brown jawing at the referee, I was perfectly willing to trot in to the bench at that point and be done with it.

Then, by chance, I happened to see Brettschneider standing at his corner linebacker position, watching me, and beyond the bars of his cage I could see a grin working. That set my energies ticking over once again—the notion that some small measure of recompense would be mine if I could complete a pass in the Badger's territory and embarrass him. I had such a play in my series—a slant pass to the strong-side end, Jim Gibbons.

I walked back to the huddle. It was slow in forming. I said, "The Badger's asleep. He's fat and he's asleep."

No one said anything. Everyone stared down. In the silence I became suddenly aware of the feet. There are twenty-two of them in the huddle, after all, most of them very large, in a small area, and while the quarterback ruminates and the others await his instruction, there's nothing else to catch the attention. The sight pricked at my mind, the oval of twenty-two football shoes, and it may have been responsible for my error in announcing the play. I forgot to give the signal on which the ball was to be snapped back by the center. I said: "Green right nine slant *break!*" One or two of the players clapped their hands, and as the huddle broke, some of them automatically heading for the line of scrimmage, someone hissed: "Well, the *signal,* what's the signal, for Chrissake."

I had forgotten to say "on two."

I should have kept my head and formed the huddle again. Instead, I called out "Two!" in a loud stage whisper, directing my call first to one side, then the other, *"Two! Two!"* as we walked up to the line. For those that might have been beyond earshot, who might have missed the signal, I held out two fingers spread like a V, which I showed around furtively, trying to hide it from the defense, and hoping that my people would see.

The pass was incomplete. I took two steps back (the play was a quick pass, thrown without a protective pocket) and I saw Gibbons break from his position, then stop, buttonhooking, his hand, which I used as a target, came up, but I threw the ball over him. A yell came up from the crowd seeing the ball in the air (it was the first play of the evening which hadn't been "blown" — to use the players' expression for a missed play), but then a groan went up when the ball was overshot and bounced across the sidelines.

"Last play," George Wilson was calling. He had walked over with a clipboard in his hand and was standing by the referee. "The ball's on the ten. Let's see you take it all the way," he called out cheerfully.

One of the players asked: "Which end zone is he talking about?"

The last play of the series was a pitchout—called a flip on some teams—a long lateral to the number four back running parallel to the line and cutting for the eight hole at left end. The lateral, though long, was easy for me to do. What I had to remember was to keep on running out after the flight of the ball. The hole behind me as I lateraled was left unguarded by an offensive lineman pulling out from his position and the defensive tackle could bull through and take me from behind in his rush, not knowing I'd got rid of the ball, if I didn't clear out of the area.

I was able to get the lateral off and avoid the tackler behind me, but unfortunately the defense was keyed for the play. They knew my repertoire, which was only five plays or so, and they doubted I'd call the same play twice. One of my linemen told me later that the defensive man opposite him in the line, Floyd Peters, had said, "Well, here comes the forty-eight pitchout," and it *had* come, and they were able to throw the number four back, Pietrosante, who had received the lateral, back on the one-yard line—just a yard away from the mortification of having moved a team backward from the thirty-yard line into one's own end zone for a safety.

As soon as I saw Pietrosante go down, I left for the bench on the sidelines at midfield, a long run from where I'd brought my team, and I felt utterly weary, shuffling along through the grass.

Applause began to sound from the stands, and I looked up, startled, and saw people standing, and the hands going. It made no sense at the time. It was not derisive; it seemed solid and respectful. "Wha'? Wha'?" I thought, and I wondered if the applause wasn't meant for someone else—if the mayor had come into the stadium behind me and was waving from an open-topped car. But as I came up to the bench I could see the people in the stands looking at me, and the hands going.

I thought about the applause afterward. Some of it was, perhaps, in appreciation of the lunacy of my participation, and for the fortitude

The author discussing strategy in the calm moments before the chaos of the game takes over. *(Walter Iooss Jr.)*

it took to do it; but most of it, even if subconscious, I decided was in *relief* that I had done as badly as I had: it verified the assumption that the average fan would have about an amateur blundering into the brutal world of professional football. He would get slaughtered. If by some chance I had uncorked a touchdown pass, there would have been wild acknowledgment—because I heard the groans go up at each successive disaster—but afterward the spectators would have felt uncomfortable. Their concept of things would have been upset. The outsider did not belong, and there was comfort in that being proved.

Some of the applause, as it turned out, came from people who had enjoyed the comic aspects of my stint. More than a few thought that they were being entertained by a professional comic in the tradition of

The author, number 0, watches the action from the bench at the Pontiac Scrim-mage. *(Walter Iooss Jr.)*

baseball's Al Schacht, or the Charlie Chaplins, the clowns, of the bull-fights. Bud Erickson told me that a friend of his had come up to him later. "Bud, that's one of the funniest goddamn...I mean that guy's *got* it," this man said, barely able to control himself.

I did not take my helmet off when I reached the bench. It was tiring to do and there was security in having it on. I was conscious of the big zero on my back facing the crowd when I sat down. Some players came by and tapped me on the top of the helmet. Brettschneider leaned down and said, "Well, you stuck it...that's the big thing."

The scrimmage began. I watched it for a while, but my mind returned to my own performance. The pawky inner voice was at hand again. "You didn't stick it," it said testily. "You funked it."

At halftime Wilson took the players down to the band shell at one

After the coach took me out, I took a few notes. It was always easier to keep the helmet on rather than suffer wrenching it past my ears. Jim Gibbons is on my right. Nick Pietrosante on the left. *(Walter Iooss Jr.)*

end of the stadium. I stayed on the bench. He had his clipboards with him, and I could see him pointing and explaining, a big semicircle of players around him, sitting on the band chairs. Fireworks soared up into the sky from the other end of the field, the shells puffing out clusters of light that lit the upturned faces of the crowd in silver, then red, and then the reports would go off, reverberating sharply, and in the stands across the field I could see the children's hands flap up over their ears. Through the noise I heard someone yelling my name. I turned and saw a girl leaning over the rail of the grandstand behind me. I recognized her from the Gay Haven in Dearborn. She was wearing an Italian mohair sweater, the color of pink spun sugar, and tight pants, and she was holding a thick folding wallet in one hand along with a pair of dark glasses, and in the other a Lion banner, which she waved, her face alive with excitement, very pretty in a perishable, childlike way, and she was calling, "Beautiful; it was beautiful."

The fireworks lit her, and she looked up, her face chalk white in the swift aluminum glare.

I looked at her out of my helmet. Then I lifted a hand, just tentatively.

CHAPTER 23

After the scrimmage, the disappointment stuck, and it was hard to ease. It was quiet in the bus going back; everyone was tired, thinking back on the game. We were a long time blocked in traffic outside Pontiac, but no one complained. It was dark inside. Up ahead, a police car had its revolving beacon going, which illuminated the interior of the bus with quick periodic washes of deep rose. I was sitting alone. George Wilson came down the aisle. He sat down, and looked, and began talking easily. I was feeling low, and he knew it.

"God, George," I said. "I couldn't get unstuck. Those first three plays, I didn't even get to *complete* them. It was like getting into a car and having the motor drop out on the pavement before you even turn the ignition key."

"It's not easy, is it?" he remarked. "You have to be a certain type of person to do it well." He began talking about the character of the football players. He picked Bobby Layne, the Detroit quarterback, whose teams would take anything from him because he *performed* and was tough, the personification of the football player. At the base of it was the urge, if you wanted to play football, to knock someone down, that was what the sport was all about, the will to win closely linked with contact. Wilson told me that his teammate Jumbo Joe Stydahar once shouted at a losing team when he was a coach: "No wonder you guys get kicked around. Every one of you's still got his teeth." Joe himself had none. He was an enormous man, a compulsive eater, and when the Los Angeles

Rams tried to pick him up on their shoulders after he coached them to the '51 championship they dropped him. That was what it was all about: hitting. Wilson himself would be remembered for perhaps the most vicious block in football history, clearing out two Washington Redskins, Chug Justice and Jimmy Johnston, to uncork his fellow Chicago Bear Osmanski for a touchdown on the second play of the championship game that ended in a 73–0 rout. Wilson was a member of one of the greatest teams ever assembled—George Halas's Monsters of the Midway, the Chicago Bears of the early forties: with Wilson were Norm Standlee from Stanford, Sid Luckman, the quarterback from Columbia, Bill Osmanski of Holy Cross, George McAfee of Duke, Ray Nolting of Cincinnati, and Scooter McLean, who was, of course, still with him, as was Aldo Forte. In the line at center was Clyde "Bulldog" Turner, who came to the attention of the pros through a publicity photograph supplied by his Texas college, which showed him carrying four-hundred-pound cows around on his shoulders. According to a story Red Grange used to tell, Turner fell out of a four-story window once, for some reason—it was never explained—with a big, heavy thump, and when a policeman rushed up, shouting, "What's going on around here?" Turner, who was brushing himself off, replied, "Damned if I know, just got here myself." Hampton Pool of Stanford was also on that team, and so were Joe Stydahar, Ken Kavanaugh of LSU, Danny Fortman of Colgate, Ed Kolman of Temple, and then Ed Sprinkle, an extremely rough player who was known as "the Iceman." These players made Chicago a power for over a decade, right up to the war. The year after their 73–0 rout of Washington they beat the New York Giants 37–9 two weeks after Pearl Harbor, with a few more than 13,000 people in the stands, and the winnings to the victorious team only $430 apiece.

Sid Luckman had always said that the one play of all these years that would stay in his mind was Wilson's block. In the car after the game Wilson's wife had innocently asked who it was that had wiped out the two Redskins in the brutal move—her tone implying that one of her husband's teammates was near inhuman.

"Well, I...ah, *I* did that," Wilson told her.

I could hear him laughing in the darkness as he remembered. "Well, now," he said. "I may be wrong. Perhaps you *like* physical contact. After all, you boxed Archie Moore and did some rough things in this series you're doing."

I said, "Well, I have these tear ducts which react quickly to being hit. It's an unconscious reflex. There's nothing I can do about it. I suspect it embarrasses my opponents—to see that tear-streaked puss opposite them; I'm told that it's called a sympathetic response—it means in fact that I *don't* like to be hit. It doesn't mean I run away...."

"Of course not," said Wilson. "But the love of physical contact happens to be a quality that's suited for football, and you can tell it early. When kids, out in the park, choose up sides for tackle rather than touch, the guys that want to be ends and go out for the passes, or even quarterback, because they think subconsciously they can get rid of the ball before being hit, those guys don't end up as football players. They become great tennis players, or skiers, or high jumpers. It doesn't mean they lack courage or competitiveness. But the guys who put up their hands to be tackles and guards, or fullbacks who run not for daylight but for trouble—those are the ones who one day will make it as football players.

"What did you put up your hand for?" he asked.

"Well, end," I said. "I always thought that was because I was tall and spindly, and better suited for that position...."

"Sure," said Wilson. "You probably were."

I said half jokingly, "Do you suppose I can pick up a liking for physical contact before the Cleveland game?"

Wilson laughed. "One interesting thing," he said, "is that you begin to lose your zest for it after a while. Take Bobby Layne. In his great years, when he was knocked over because someone missed a block, he'd shove a friendly elbow into the guy's ribs and tell him to forget it, that he could take it. The fellow'd think, 'What a guy!' and the next time he'd do better—out of sheer respect for a quarterback who *could* take it. He'd block a bull elephant for Layne, or run through a brick wall for him. But then after a while it wasn't so easy to take, and Layne began to say, 'You son of a bitch, you missed your block.' The players said Layne began to flinch. It wasn't that—he just lost his liking for it. So he chewed them out. That was all right if he was infallible, but no quarterback is, or ever could be, and his players began to lose respect for him—and when that was gone, his capability diminished at the same time.

"And when that really happens," Wilson said, looking out the window, "you're done, and you have to go on to something else."

He began talking about coaching then, about its complexities— almost with regret, as if the pleasures of the game with its fundamental simplicity of physical contact were unavailable to him watching from the sidelines—as if it were a frustration and a nuisance to find self-expression in the actions of others. No matter, he said. It was a tough and absorbing job.

And did the coaches change, I asked, under the rigors of it? As Bobby Layne did as a quarterback?

He nodded. "After a while the coach can't take the losses out on himself. So he turns on his players. He forgets that his players are men. And also he forgets that once he was a player. Why, Joe Stydahar, my old teammate on the Bears, when he was the Rams' coach, once crept around a hotel lobby, sneaking around behind the palms—which was hard for him, being as big as he was—and he jotted down a big number of fines for his players coming in late after losing a night game. I heard about that and called him up—I knew he wouldn't mind—to recall to him that he'd been a player once, and, what's more, a 'rounder'—which was what we called a guy who didn't care too much for the rules and regulations."

"The players say that of Vince Lombardi of the Packers," I said. "That he was once a player's coach, and that the pressure in Green Bay changed him into a martinet...removed him from his players."

"It's not easy," Wilson said.

The bus was clear of the Pontiac traffic jam, and we were moving along swiftly through the dark.

Wilson compared his job as a head coach at moments of stress with that of a baseball manager, Casey Stengel, not in scorn, but to make a point—the Met manager coming slowly up out of the dugout to see to his pitcher, hunched forward but moving for the mound as if hauling a small garden roller behind him, getting his short stumpy stride arranged so as not to step on the foul line, all the time his mind turning on what to do, three or four minutes available to decide whether to bring in another pitcher, which was a decision often made easy for him by reference to the "book" of percentages. The football coach in a similar situation of stress had to marshal a host of minutiae within seconds, and, applying knowledge or intuition, make a decision which if it went wrong, since only fourteen games were played a season, could cost him his job. Often something would happen—a fumble, a penalty, or an injury—to remove the reins and make the coach as much of a bystander as the fellow ripping tickets in half at the gate, or the hot-dog vendor in the aisles. Yet the disaster on the field was his doing and responsibility.

All of this made my own disaster seem far less important, which Wilson had calculated, I'm sure, and it was easy to sense why his men had such respect for him—a "player's coach" was how they referred to him.

I was grateful to him, and I felt better as the bus turned off the turnpike and headed down the dark country roads for the school.

The players themselves were also concerned about my well-being. When the bus had pulled up at the gym, and we had showered and changed, a group of them took me along that night—a long tearing night through the Dearborn dance halls, all of them shouting, "Fawty-fowah, fawty-tew," from time to time, mimicking my accent, and slapping me on the back and making me feel as though I had really done something more than play the fool in Pontiac, until I began to say, "No, no... it was nothing at all, really."

Perhaps most concerned about my welfare following the game was Harley Sewell. He had been eleven years in the National Football League. He had pale, thinning hair, a rolling gait like a sailor's; he was small in stature for a lineman (his weight was in the record books as 230, though he looked much lighter), but when he put his mind to something he was insistent, and his determination was obviously a major part of his equipment. He was always the first player in the locker room, the first dressed, and on the field he always *ran* from one place to another, never to impress anyone, but because that was his way—to drive himself at a furious tempo. One of the jokes in camp was to speak of Sewell as "dragging his feet" or "holding things up," and often they shouted at him: "Hey, Harley, can't you never get it up?" and he would keep at what he was doing, not letting on he'd heard. Off the field his manner remained the same. A Texan, born in a place called St. Jo, he kept after me to come down to his part of the world in the off-season and try my hand at riding broncos. He was absolutely determined about it.

He'd say, "Now *when* you coming down to ride them broncos?"

"Well, Harley, I don't know..."

"I'd sure like for you to have that experience."

"Well, Harley..."

"No trouble 'tall to set it up for you."

"Harley..."

"Now *when* you think you can come on down?"

"Sometime in the off-season," I'd say.

He was insistent, for sure. John Gordy told me that in his rookie year Harley liked to hear him sing, and kept after him about it. "All right now, rook, *I'll* play," he'd say, picking up his guitar. "You *sing*."

"God, Harley..."

"Sing."

"I can't sing."

"Sing, rook."

So Gordy did. There was nothing else to do.

After my scrimmage and our return to the dormitory, Sewell came looking for me. I would be downcast after my sorry performance and in need of company. For some reason he thought I would like a pizza pie, so he drove off and got one somewhere, which he put in the backseat of his car. Only two or three players were in the dormitory when he got there, chatting in one of the rooms about the scrimmage, and Harley appeared in the door, holding the big pizza in front of him. "Where's the rook at?" he asked.

They told him they thought I was off at the Gay Haven twist palace with the others. He waited around for a while, and they had some of the pizza, though Harley kept a big piece of it in case I turned up. He left finally.

I didn't get in until six in the morning. I had spent two hours in the Dearborn police station, a gleaming emporium where the police sergeants sit up behind a bright-colored Formica-surfaced desk, to retrieve my car, which I had parked too close to a side crossing. In Dearborn, parking violators, no matter how minor the offense, have their cars towed away. I was not aware of this practice, and when I came out of the Gay Haven, a little dizzy in the head from the smoke and exercise, and walked up a quiet street to find the car gone, I sat on the curb, head in hands, and tried to remember where I'd parked it. A taxi cruised by, and the driver, thinking he had a fare, stopped, and after we'd talked a while about the missing car he drove me to the police station nearly ten miles away. Out in back of the station was a big macadam-surfaced parking lot with the yellow tow trucks and the offending cars parked in rows. Mine, they told me, was among them, and I paid up, furious, with no sense of guilt, and then sat in an absolutely immaculate waiting room, as if in a hospital, until the paperwork on the case was done; when they took me out to the car, I drove off with rattling speed through the parking lot to show the contempt I felt.

The sun was up when I reached Cranbrook. It was going to be a hot day. I knew the heat would begin to build up in my room, but the bed looked inviting. I hadn't been asleep for more than what seemed a minute when I heard a voice sing out, "Up you get there, rook. No time for lying around."

I looked and it was Harley, standing in the door. I had a sudden premonition that he had some broncos ready for me, waiting, outside on the lawn. "Wha'? Wha'?" I said. I sat up in bed. His two children were with him, staring around from behind him.

"Time to be up," Harley said.

"What time is it?" I asked.

"Eight," he said.

"God, Harley, I only just got in. I only had two hours' sleep."

"Time's a-wasting," he said. "We'll go for a drive."

"Harley, I've been in a police station..."

He disappeared with his children, but they were back after a minute or so with coffee and rolls from the dining room. "These'll fix you up," Harley said.

I groaned and got up to dress.

"It's best to keep your mind occupied," Harley said.

"My God, Harley, I was *asleep*."

"You would've *waked up* wrong," Harley said.

We went riding through the country in his station wagon. His children sat quietly in the backseat, flanking a lawn mower that Harley had borrowed and had been meaning to return. When I closed my eyes I could feel sleep rock toward me, so I kept the window down to let the warm air, thick with summer, hit, and I tried to keep my mind on what Harley was saying. He was talking about the tough people he had played against, the enormous defensive tackles and ends he had tried to clear out for the offensive backs, and the humiliations he had been forced to suffer. He was trying to make me feel better about my own humiliations the night before. He talked about Big Daddy Lipscomb. Harley said that he had played against him a number of times and that while he was one of the best, and he'd been humiliated by him for sure, he was not as good as Leroy Smith of the Green Bay Packers, who was faster and trickier and much harder on a good day than Big Daddy on an average day. Occasionally, Big Daddy would put his mind to it, and then he was invincible. He talked a lot on the field, announcing to everybody what he was going to do and whom he was going to rack up. Harley's worst day against him was in the 1962 Pro Bowl game when he just couldn't handle him, so he came out and someone else went in to try, and couldn't, then Forrest Gregg tried and couldn't, so finally they double-teamed on him, two men driving at him, and that helped but not much. He had arrived in the National Football League strong and massive, pupil to Art Donovan of Baltimore, where Lipscomb first played, who taught him just about everything he knew, which was instruction from a powerfully knowledgeable source.

I asked Harley why Baltimore had traded such a valuable property even if he did have a bad day or so, to the Pittsburgh Steelers. Well, they'd had problems with him, Harley told me: he was not an easy man, being prideful and quick-tempered, and on one occasion, the year before he was traded, one of the Colts gave a party to which Big Daddy was not invited, and he prowled around until the *idea* that he was being snubbed got the better of him. He turned up at the party and threw the host through a window. There was a big ruckus, of course, particularly since the host, who was a very fleet scatback, cut a tendon in his ankle going through; after that, they didn't think they could keep Big Daddy around. Harley talked about him as if he were still around. The great tackle had died of an overdose of drugs. I asked Harley about his death, but either he didn't hear me or didn't want to answer. We drove in silence for a while.

"The vision I have of him," I said dreamily, "is him sitting in a dentist's chair."

"What's that?" asked Harley sharply.

"I've read somewhere he couldn't stand pain," I explained. "He wouldn't get in a dentist's chair unless he had his wife with him, sitting on his lap, to calm him down at the slightest twinge. I never can think of him without seeing that dentist trying to get his job done with those two people sitting in his chair, and having to work around the girl to get at Big Daddy wearing one of those little bibs."

"I don't see Big Daddy like that 'tall," said Harley. "Regretfully, I see him down across the line from me, maybe that shirt out and hanging down behind him like a tail, and then trying to *move* that boy—like running up agin a barn. He wore these funny special shoes—high on his ankle and made of soft leather—because he had corns, maybe. He had a habit, moving for you, of cracking his palm over the ear hole of your helmet, so it sounded like the side of your face was caving in." Harley shook his head, as if his ears were still singing.

Lipscomb did have one flaw which Detroit was able to take advantage of, which was that he liked to pursue and tackle in the open field, preferably by the sidelines, where he could knock his man down in full view of the great crowds he reckoned had come to watch him do such things. Then he'd reach down and pick his victim up by the shoulder pads, set him on his feet, and whack his rear with a big hand. The ruse was to get Big Daddy to range off toward the sidelines looking to make such a play, and then run the ball through his vacated position. The play was called 47 crossbuck takeoff, and it required the guard opposite Big Daddy—Harley, say—to pull from his position, indicating that he was leading the interference in a move toward the end, sucking out Big Daddy with him, and then the four back—Pietrosante—would light out through the seven hole with the ball. Of course, if Big Daddy *didn't* fall for it and stayed there in the seven hole, refusing to trail out after the guard, it suddenly became very unpleasant for Pietrosante. But he was a showboat sort, Big Daddy, and the chances were—at least at the beginning of his career—that he'd move off laterally after the guard, the long jersey shirt tail, which always came out toward the end of a game, trailing behind him.

"He had his bad days, I'll tell you," said Harley, looking over at me.

"Like mine?" I said, grinning at him.

"Sure," he said, quite seriously. He thought awhile and then he said, "You know of the guys opposite you play each week there's not an easy one in the bunch, that's what it comes to, which makes my position a rough one to play. I worry, and I'm occupied with what I'm doing. I have to block someone on nearly every play, so I usually wind up on the ground—I *should* be there, except on pass protection, something like that—but I kind of like it anyway." He knocked his hand against the steering wheel. "Whenever you move, you got to move quick and hard, the harder you're going, the less likely it is you're going to be hurt. It's like two cars coming together—the faster comes out cleaner. Can't have weak grillwork, of course, I mean there's got to be substance and heft behind the speed."

"Sure," I said sleepily.

"When you move you have to keep your body and muscles tense, because if you're jogging, you're loose, and if you're clobbered when you're pussyfooting around loose you can get unjointed."

"Yes," I said. "Unjointed. I suppose the same principle holds true in bronco riding."

Harley looked over. "You're coming down to do that, y'know."

"Is the man going' *ride,* Pop?" asked one of the children from the backseat.

"Nothing but..." said Harley.

I looked back at the children, the handle of the lawn mower between them, and their eyes seemed to me grave and speculative.

Harley turned off the road and we drove up a short driveway to a house on a wooded ridge. Friends of his were waiting in a screened-in porch. He hadn't mentioned we were going there, but it was like him not to. I was introduced around. Coffee was brought in. They'd heard about the game the night before and they were eager for details of my participation.

I sat down and took some coffee. I rather looked forward to telling them. "Well, it was a disaster," I said. "Just plumb awful."

Harley was out in the kitchen overseeing something or other, the cutting of coffee cake perhaps, and he came hurrying in. He said, "Well, hold on now, I don't know about *that.*"

"Come on, Harley," I said, grinning at him. "I lost near thirty yards in five plays...fell down without anyone laying a hand on me, then had the ball stolen by Roger Brown, then threw the ball ten feet over Jim Gibbons's head—that's pretty plumb awful...."

Harley said, "You didn't do too bad...*considering*..." He was very serious, really trying, consciously, to keep me from being upset and humiliated.

"Harley," I said, "you're a poor judge of disasters."

The others on the porch kept after me for details, but Harley wouldn't let me discuss the subject. "It don't do any good *dwelling* on such things," he said.

"Aw come on, Harley," they said.

"No sir!" he said.

So we humored him and talked about other things, and eventually I managed to get just enough in about the game to satisfy them, though we waited until Harley was off the porch, out on the lawn with his children.

He drove me back to Cranbrook after a while. It had been a pleasant morning, and I told him so, standing in the driveway, hands on the car-door windowsill, though Harley, inside, behind the wheel, continued to look preoccupied. He was still worried about my state of mind. "The thing is not to *fret* on it," he said. "Your luck wasn't running too good. Just forget about it, and get yourself going again for the Cleveland game—put your mind on *that* bitch...."

"That won't be hard," I said. "Listen, Harley, I really am grateful to you."

"When you wake up, it'll be all right."

"Sure," I said.

CHAPTER 24

Five men were cut the day after the scrimmage. There was a meeting that night, addressed briefly by George Wilson. He was wearing a blue business suit and a tie. He had an engagement afterward, I guess, though his severe attire was appropriate to the occasion. He said he was pleased with the Pontiac scrimmage. He said that now it was time to think about the Cleveland Browns. Only a week to go to prepare. He seemed distracted. He said we would have a rookie show, and would Joe Schmidt and Terry Barr, as co-captains, see to it that the rookies scraped one together. After his remarks, we saw him wander outside and stand by the fountain in the shadows. Aldo Forte took over, his dead cigar in one hand, chalk in the other. The diagramming began, the players hunched over their playbooks. Then Nussbaumer, "the Hawk," began stepping around the rear of the classroom, very softly, and he would move forward quickly to lean over a player, who would jump at that sudden touch, and he would whisper to him to come outside, and bring his playbook with him. Wilson was out there in the darkness. The two would sit on the balustrade that ran around the edge of the fountain, and out there, beyond earshot, Wilson would say that he was sorry, that the position the player was trying for was filled, and that there wasn't a spot open.

That was how it was done in the Detroit organization—one of the ways, at any rate, tapping the unfortunate in class when he had his playbook, the organization symbol, so it could be taken from him right then. It was done as unobtrusively as possible, but after a nudge or two from seat to seat we were all aware what was going on, watching the fountain out through the windows. No one paid attention to Forte—all of us, veterans included, conscious of the Hawk moving around in the rear of the classroom, waiting for Wilson to finish with his man at the fountain before moving quickly among the seats to send him out the next one. Dennis Gaubatz, who had played well in the Pontiac scrimmage, gave such a start when the Hawk touched him on the shoulder that his playbook and pencil went flying, and we all turned and stared at him in awe. He went out with the Hawk, but he returned in a minute or so, pale, and shaking his head. He told us later that the Hawk had simply wanted to tell him that he was to be responsible for bringing the blue sack of footballs down to the practice field for the workouts. Jerry Archer had been responsible for that, but he was being let go.

It struck me as a heartless procedure, but perhaps there was no way to let a man go easily. The coaches hated it, because it was hard to do cleanly. There were procedures elsewhere which were hard to believe. A couple of years back at Buffalo, in the American Football League, when the coach cut a player, he let him know by having the equipment manager clear out his locker. When the player arrived in the gym to dress for afternoon practice, horsing around with the others, he would sit down on the bench to work his shoelaces loose, and suddenly find his locker empty, not ever believing it at first, staring up at the locker number, and then into the lockers on either side, the hope beginning to fade, his teammates, now no longer teammates, but acquaintances, looking away from him, embarrassed, staring down at their socks.

Outside my room, just after the meeting, I saw John Lomakoski, the big 250-pound offensive tackle, who had been cut—the only veteran—come down the corridor already on his way out, carrying a toilet kit and his suitcase, a handsome leather one. I would have ducked into my room if I'd had time, so as not to embarrass him. He put down his suitcase and said, "Hello." It was a warm night, and the sweat stood along his forehead in glistening lines. He had ordered a taxi. He wasn't sure where he was going to go—the bus station perhaps, or a nearby railroad station—he'd ask the driver—but the main thing to do was to clear out. I don't think he lived far away, in fact, somewhere in the state, but listening to him I had the impression he wanted to be many miles from Cranbrook before turning to the leather suitcase, and opening it. He said he was sorry we had not had a chance to talk more.

That evening, in their rooms, the players were reminiscing about "Squeaky Shoes," or "the Turk." Tommy Watkins said that at Cleveland, when Paul Brown was the coach he would wait until the players were all in at night and then he'd send a coach to get the fellow out of his room and bring him down to the office, where he was officially let go. In the evenings of those days when a cut was due, the rookies would collect in one room, and to keep their spirits up they'd put on twist records and practice dance steps—the volume up high, and the feet pounding—until Paul Brown from the floor below complained that there was so much noise he couldn't keep his mind clear to decide *who* to let go. Eventually, the door would open anyway, and Brown's emissary would point at the unfortunates through the crash of music and the players turning in the dance patterns, and after they'd left the music would be turned down, because for that night at least there would be no further worry, and they knew the dance steps quite well by then.

At Chicago George Halas used to reach out and touch a man on his shoulder, and the players seeing him coming, if they were worried about being cut, would tend to sidle away. One day he reached out to touch a quick little scatback, a 170-pounder with speed and fine hands, who saw the hand coming for his shoulder at the last second, and dodging it he dropped to the ground with a groan and began to do a series of quick push-ups. "Look," he said, glancing up at Halas, "I'm strong too. I can do these forever." Halas was supposed to have been so touched by the player's desperation that he turned away as if it hadn't been his intention to tap him at all. He kept the player for an extra week, and then came up swiftly behind him in the locker room when the player was skinning himself out of a sweatshirt and got him on the shoulder before there could be any chance of avoidance.

The reactions of the players cut from the roster were likely to be more consistent than the methods of dismissal—often tearful, then sullen, for the most part, as they thought back on all the wasted effort; then there would be a slow shift to the problems of the future, the wondering what would come next, and after a few phone calls they would make a quick departure, to get the place behind them, as Lomakoski had.

There were exceptions, of course. Some years back, after two Lion rookies had been told they were cut, they went up to their room and got mean on a bottle of rye, and came lazying out looking for trouble. They found a Cranbrook mathematics teacher in the lavatory, brushing his teeth. He wore a green silk kimono bathrobe embroidered with a red dragon. He heard them come in behind him, and he turned, smiling at them pleasantly, his mouth full of toothpaste.

"Hi, fellows," he said. "Nice practice today?"

The two stared at him, rocking slightly.

"Who's that clown?" one of them asked, pointing at him.

After studying him, the other said, "He's a chink. A mad chink. Look at that foam on his mouth."

The mathematics teacher turned back to the sink.

What happened then was unclear—as I was told about it—except that the mathematics teacher was "terrorized," and he had a packed trunk (he was about to leave the school for a late summer vacation) hoisted out of his quarters and thrown down a stairwell. The Detroit management did its best to patch things up, but the Cranbrook School said that football players were no longer welcome. The Lions would not be invited back the following year. The school stuck to it for a while, and the Lions trained for two summers on the facilities of Ypsilanti State

College—spartan surroundings compared to the sylvan aspects of Cranbrook—until the school relented and had them back.

I walked around to the rookie quarters. In their common room a gin-rummy game was going on among those who had escaped the cut—full of hilarity and no one's mind on his cards. Nick Ryder, the rookie fullback from Miami, wore a big grin as he looked at his cards, and so did Jake Greer, who, when he saw me come in, turned and piped out in a thin, high cry: "Ma', Squeaky Shoes she didn' get you none neither," and he gave off a little whoop, tilting far back in his chair so his foot flew up past the table, but then embarrassed by his temerity he quieted down and looked solemnly into his handful of cards. Lucien Reeberg, who'd also survived, was there too, and Don King, the one they called "Honeymoon" because he had been married recently, and so was Ernie Clark, whom Milt Plum for some reason had been ribbing since he'd arrived, calling out, when he saw him, "Well, we've nothing to fear, *Ernie's* here." Clark could barely shuffle the cards. Reeberg tried to pretend nothing important had happened, lifting a hand in stiff acknowledgment when I came in, but his actions were exaggerated. He emitted a piercing giggle, and when he riffled the cards they sprayed out over the table, which got them all hollering with laughter—Greer rocked his chair around on one leg—as if they were all high on hashish. Roger Brown sat with them, the only one interested in the card game, indulging the excitement of the others, and occasionally he would say, "Hey, has no one come here to *play?*"—a look of pain on his big face that got the rest of them going again, whooping and pointing at him, not far from idiocy in their relief at still being able to consider him a teammate. They quieted down only when one of the rookies who had been cut came through the common room, or stood by waiting for the telephone, which was in a booth just off the corridor, the group at the table avoiding him as if his humiliation were infectious.

Gene Frantz was cut, the tall ski ranger whose locker was opposite mine—the one the veterans referred to as "the Mop," and more often "the Rug," for a bowl haircut he wore, a Hamlet cut that left a fringe of hair down over his ears, and nearly to his eyes. Around the school grounds he wore white tennis shorts to set off his tanned legs—which, along with his haircut, earned him the quick enmity of the veterans. In the dining hall he was made to sing more than the others, it seemed to me, a soft Mormon hymn (he was a graduate of Brigham Young) which was lengthy and sung with patience. The veterans would look up at him on his chair in his white tennis outfit, as if standing for the anthem on the center court at Wimbledon, and they would say: "How the shit'd he catch anything with that rug in his face?" At Brigham Young he had been the top pass interceptor in the nation, nine of them caught the year before, and Detroit had signed him as their seventeenth draft choice. He was never confident about making the team, and was more prepared for being cut than some of the others were. Pass defense in the professional league was so highly developed that what had succeeded for him in college—intuition, the flair for committing himself, and the luck, and the inaccuracy of the passers—was secondary to knowledge that came with experience. "I'm just beginning to *learn*," he told me once in front of his locker. "Whether I can make it is a question of learning fast enough."

Well, he hadn't, and he and Ron Schieber, also cut, a speedster who had won the sprint races in Pontiac the night before, both had calls in to the Denver team in the American Football League. If it didn't work there, they were self-sufficient enough, and unencumbered by wives or other responsibilities—athletes sufficiently tuned up and able to make it somewhere with any luck, in the other football league, or in Canada, or with any number of semipro teams if they wanted to continue— and Frantz, at least, would go back into the mountains when the snows came in the fall.

It was not the same for Frank Imperiale, also cut by Wilson out by the fountain. He was a big lineman who had arrived as a free agent, with some previous experience at Buffalo—he was the one who had told me about the locker-cleaning procedures there when they dismissed a player—but he had responsibilities, a wife to support, and children, and as such he had to succeed at the top, where there was good money, or give up football altogether and go into his father's business, which, as I remember, was plumbing. He had called his wife in Long Island to tell her he had been cut. Also, he had a call in for the New York Jets, but he was not hopeful. He sat gloomily in the rookie common room, waiting for the phone to ring. I went over and we talked for a while. He had been looking forward to being the master of ceremonies for the rookie show, which had been talked about for a number of days, and definitely scheduled by Wilson that night. Imperiale had turned around at Wilson's announcement in the classroom and made a sign with his fingers to indicate that the rookies—a group of us were sitting together—were going to "wow" them. Imperiale had had some "practical experience" in nightclubs, he had pointed out, and he had tried out a number of his jokes on some of us a few nights before, which we listened to hopefully, needing someone to run the show. His jokes were delivered without much confidence, his voice somewhat flat, and often we only knew that a joke was complete when he'd pause and then say suddenly: "And then there's the one about the gorilla who comes into the bar?"—questioning us with his eyes, and we would nod hopefully, and he would launch into another. Still, he was the only rookie with "practical experience" in the nightclub world, and—as he kept telling us—he got "warmed up" with an audience in front of him. Then, just five minutes after Wilson's announcement about the rookie show, the Hawk had rapped him on the shoulder and he had gone out to the fountain.

Now his expertise would be unavailable. He kept looking toward the phone booth just off the common room. He said, "You can use any of those jokes you want in—in the rookie show."

I said I was sure the show could use them. I said that we would miss him, and I doubted we would have very much of a show anyway without his practical experience. His mind wasn't on it. "The big thing is to take this in stride," he said. "You have to be cut a few times to know how to handle it."

The phone rang—barely audible over the hilarity of the gin-rummy table—and he went over and pushed himself into the booth. The call was for him, perhaps his wife again, and being a big man, 250 pounds, he had quite a struggle with the booth door before he could close himself in.

Jerry Archer, the fifth man cut that day, could not leave. Tight with anger, he moved from chair to chair in the common room. He talked to anyone who came near. "I came here as a linebacker," he said. "What the hell." He puffed on a cigarette inexpertly. I had never seen him smoke before. "Jesus!" he said. He had been in charge of carrying the blue bag full of footballs down to the field across the wooden bridge between the pines every morning—assigned to do that from the first day—and it gave him substance, having that responsibility, and confidence; you could see it from the way he carried the bag. He had a big, friendly, ruddy face, streaming with sweat always, and chipped front teeth with gold inlays showing when he smiled. I thought of him on the field tossing the blue bag down, and the footballs spilling out, and those long mornings and afternoons, sweat dripping off his chin just forward of the nose of the ball, before he centered it, which he did hundreds of times a day, and the shout at him, "*Pop* it back, Archer, *pop* it back!" He never did get that correct swing of the ball back into the quarterback's palm, not being truly—as he said—a center, but a linebacker. "What did I come here for? I'm not a center. What the hell? Why didn't they give me a crack at quarterback, for Chrissakes?"

I shifted uneasily in my chair.

"I'm awfully sorry," I said.

I went back to my room after a while, cutting across the quadrangle. Behind me, I heard a crash of furniture, yells of laughter, and I wondered if Greer's chair had gone over. Archer would probably stay around there a long time. Too long. There were many evenings at Cranbrook when I felt myself an interloper more than others, *always* being one, of course, but there was a sense of degree. That night, with the hilarity still drifting across the quadrangle grass from the rookie wing, and down my own corridor the phonographs going, and Maher and LeBeau working on their guitars, surely that was one of them.

The next day, Don Doll said, "Well, that was the night of the Squeaky Shoes."

I said, "Yes, I heard them."

CHAPTER 25

The day after the night of the Squeaky Shoes, George Wilson called me over on the practice field and asked me if I would mind overseeing the rookie show. "You can produce it," he said.

"You cut our best man, Imperiale," I said, "a bona fide nightclub performer."

"He played football like one," said Wilson bluntly.

I said that I would do what I could.

"You're expendable," Wilson explained. "The other rookies have got their minds occupied."

"I'm supposed to be worrying about Cleveland," I said.

"Worrying isn't going to help you against Cleveland," Wilson said. He was being very cryptic that morning. "You might as well worry about the rookie show."

He explained the purpose of the show — which was to give the rookies a chance to have fun at the expense of the coaches and veterans. Afterward, the veterans would entertain the rookies at a party. "Anything goes in the show," he said. "There's no rule book. Make it bawdy. That goes down well. There won't be any dames watching. Put together some skits. You can be as rough on the coaches and the veterans as you want. Then there'll be rookies who play kazoos and harmonicas and crap like that. They can play and fill up the time."

"When are you going to schedule it?" I asked.

"You've got two days. We'll have the rookie night the day after tomorrow." He saw my dismay. "You'll get help," he said. "Barr and Gordy and Schmidt will give you a hand. Most all the Lions are goddamn frustrated actors."

That evening at the team meeting Wilson requested that the rookies stay behind and take over the classroom to discuss their show. Barr, Schmidt, and Gordy stayed on as advisers, and so did LeBeau and Maher. It developed that none of the rookies—there were about ten of them left after the previous night's cut—had musical skills. So LeBeau and Maher volunteered to play their guitars. Wilson was right about the veterans. They had many ideas for skits, and they all wanted to act in them. But the only rookie who seemed enthusiastic was Lucien Reeberg. He began to outline a complex skit he had in mind, but the veterans told him to calm down. "You can do a soft-shoe, Loosh," they said.

Later that night, after our session was over, I wandered around the dormitory and talked to the veterans to find out something about rookie shows. Almost all the teams in the league had them, and afterward the veterans entertained the rookies at a party—a type of initiation ceremonial that took place usually a day or so after the last big squad cut. Some of the shows were especially lavish, I was told, particularly those put on by the two teams on the coast. Often there were memorable acts. John Gonzaga told me that when he played for the Washington Redskins a rookie appeared onstage who was a whistler, a great whistler, who came on with a paper bag over his head, his navel outlined in red lipstick, and he had control of the muscles around the navel so he could make it work like a mouth. Gonzaga said it was the damnedest thing he had ever seen, it killed the audience, and they kept at him to keep it up until the guy's lips got dry, his whistle faded (it was hard enough to hear it through the bag), and his stomach muscles got tired, so that he stood there quietly—a paper bag over his head, and a lipsticked navel which wouldn't work anymore—tuckered out, and they finally let him go.

The next day I skipped practice and spent the day in the cellar of Page Hall, where the school dramatic department had a roomful of costumes and props. I picked through the costumes for inspiration. I was not very hopeful.

My experience in the theater was limited, and what little there had been often seemed tainted with disaster. In one memorable early production of *Macbeth,* truncated for schoolboys, I appeared at the last moments of the play in a procession accompanying Macduff, who came onstage bearing Macbeth's head on a spike. The head was artfully done, cut in profile from the side of a cardboard packing box, painted, and attached to a long pole. Macduff stumbled coming onstage, over a cable, I suppose, and the pole got turned in his hand so that what was displayed to the audience was not Macbeth's head but whatever was on the reverse of the cardboard box, the letters BRILLO, I think, or LUX, quite distinguishable—in fact the announcement soared above Macduff's procession as noticeable as an advertising blimp.

The Earl of Northumberland has the line that greets Macduff. He says: *"Here comes newer comfort."* This unbearable line (under the circumstances) was delivered by the earl (an eleven-year-old classmate of mine) in a high soprano which was only slightly muffled by his spirit-gummed beard, and out across the footlights a fitful murmur rose from an audience trying to contain itself. It was unsuccessful. Suddenly, as sharp as a scream, a single high piercing bray burst from someone in the back of the theater, one of the fathers—probably the hardest that man had ever laughed—absolutely uncontrollable it was, catching up the rest of the audience with it so that our mournful procession moved through a storm of laughter so threatening that some of us, in spite of ourselves, looked out nervously across the footlights toward that dark wall of sound. No one knew what had gone wrong. There was a tendency to huddle together, eyes wide over the beards.

Malcolm, hailed as the new king, has the last speech in the play, and, as I recall, he got through it with great speed, his voice high and nervous, so that he seemed terrified to be crowned the king at Scone. On the uncertain note that Scotland has lost its tyrant, Macbeth, to gain a weakling, the curtain came mercifully down.

I did not mention my theatrical career to Barr, Gordy, and Schmidt. We met that evening and put the show together. I showed them the props I had found in the dramatic department, and it took us two or three hours to work out some skits.

The next day after supper Wilson led his coaches and the veterans across the school grounds to the gym. The basketball court had a stage set back from the sidelines. It was well-appointed, with a big curtain and flies and other accoutrements, including a big switchboard with levers which no one was anxious to fool with. We looked out through the part in the curtain and watched the audience seat itself in a big semicircle of fold-up chairs set out on the basketball court. Wilson sat in the middle with his coaches on either side.

Traditionally, throughout the National Football League, the rookie shows open on a chorus of big first-year linemen, wearing only jock-straps, high kicking in a thunderous cancan.

We stayed with tradition in our opening number, though some of our people wore additional props—some women's hats along with the jocks, and Lucien Reeberg, the big three-hundred-pounder, wore a bell-shaped wire hoop used under Victorian ball gowns, and he spun a large beach umbrella above his head. He danced with such abandon to a full-volume record of *Gaîté Parisienne* that he nearly collapsed and brought down the cancan line with him. The others danced perfunctorily and self-consciously in their jockstraps, looking bleakly out over the footlights at the audience, which gaped at them and cat-called.

When the laughter died away, the curtain came down, and LeBeau went out in front with his guitar to hold the audience while the scenery was set up for the first skit. From out front we could hear the thump of strings as he sang his mournful songs.

The first skit was supposed to be a spoof of Commissioner Peter Rozelle's league headquarters and the goings-on there. I played the part of Rozelle. The part fell to me by default, since no one else had time to learn the lines, such as they were. I wore a Napoleon hat, a cloak, a wooden sword, three cap pistols, and a rubber dirk; and I carried a pair of handcuffs, a tack hammer, and a frying pan. These artifacts, collected from the prop room in Page Hall, were supposed to suggest the inquisitorial aspects of Rozelle's office. He was not popular with the Lions because of the heavy fines he had levied on five of them for gambling, and for the excommunication of Alex Karras, and when I clanked toward the footlights and said, "Howdy, I'm Petesy Rozelle," the audience delivered up a stiff barrage of invective.

The most ingenious device in Rozelle's "office" was a truth machine which spoke its answers—a role performed by four rookies seated bunched in close together on fold-up chairs and facing the audience. The "machine" was rigged in Rozelle's favor, toadying to him, and when I put a question to it such as "What's to be said about those who don't think I—Pete Rozelle—am a grand fellow?" the rookie halfback from Iowa, Larry Ferguson, a Negro of dark blue hue, with birthmarks that crossed his face like tribal scars, would tap his foot three times, and at the third beat, he and the other rookies would reply in sharp unison:

"!"

A sharp obscenity, like a bomb going off.

Or I would ask: "What's my feeling about the Detroit Lions?"

"! 'em"

I put a number of questions to the "machine" during the skit, and I wondered afterward—because the volume the four rookies put to their epithets was considerable—what anybody strolling out on the school grounds would have thought, a couple perhaps, one of the Episcopal bishops and his wife, out under the first stars of the dusk, strolling past the fountains, and then, across the lawn, suddenly hearing from the gym,

"!"

"My God, Ellen, did you hear that?"

"What? I didn't hear anything."

"Well, I don't know…a whole congregation shouting…well…in unison…in the gym over there."

"The African delegates, do you think?" she said. "In the gym?" She could see the loom of the building against the evening. "The bishops from Kenya and Ghana and Sierra Leone, and the other places—how *nice*. It makes you think, doesn't it, Geoffrey?"

"Well, I don't know...*listen*."

In the warm jasmine smell of the evening they waited motionless on the gravel walk, high above them the thin whistles of the nighthawks still hunting, and then out of the darkness of the gym, distinct as a trumpet bray, rose a chorus of male voices:

"!"

She clung to him. "Geoffrey. There's something odd going on in the gym."

My imagination was never able to determine what happened then — whether the couple went and reported to some higher authority that "something odd" was going on in the gym. Or whether they continued their stroll undaunted through the school grounds, as if everything, even the crudities from the gym, was natural and to be endured, as if the nighthawks wheeling in the darkness above had abruptly changed their calls to:

"!!!"

and nothing was to be done but accept it.

After the Rozelle takeoff was done, LeBeau filled in with his guitar while the stage was set for the following skit, which was based on the idea that the coaches were letting the veterans go in favor of a youth movement—each veteran being called by turn and dismissed by George Wilson. I played Wilson—still wearing the Napoleon hat, the cap pistols, the wooden sword, and the dirk. I sat at a table with a teacher's school bell in front of me, and when I banged at it, Pat Studstill, playing the Hawk, would bring in a veteran (played by a rookie) and I would deliver a sharp address and order him cut from the squad. Studstill carried out the order quite literally: he was got up in a knight's helmet he'd found somewhere and he carried an executioner's ax made of cardboard on which he had made a suggestive smear of red paint. After my harangue, Studstill led the veteran behind a low curtain and the audience would then see the ax rise and fall above the curtain—a bit of imaginative theater that was Studstill's own contribution — followed by a sharp squawk and the thud of a body hitting the floor. The sound effects varied — the squawks produced by different rookies Studstill had lined up behind the curtain, and the decapitation was usually indicated by the iron clang of a wrench. A folding chair was dropped once or twice back there, by the sound of it, and so was a toolbox.

The sketches gave a chance to divulge the peccadilloes of individual veterans; the players would turn in their seats to grin at the one of their number being lampooned, and he would scrunch down a bit, his chair complaining shrilly under him, and when it was finished he would perk up and twist around to jaw at the victim of the next characterization, loud in the relief that he himself had been done.

I had been supplied with an item or so about each Lion player who was lampooned in the skits. Barr, Schmidt, and Gordy had furnished most of the material, sitting around the previous night. Some of the items made little sense to me at the time, but they were effective enough when presented. For instance, they suggested that I explain to Danny Lewis, the big fullback, that he was being cut from the squad because he spent too much time in the bathroom. That did not seem particularly funny, but I said it anyway when the time came. "Besides, Lewis," I said, finishing up my diatribe against him, "you're getting axed because you spend too much time in the crapper. Take him away, Hawk." It was some legend about him brought to light (I never discovered what it was) and the players brayed with delight to have it recalled.

The lampoons were mild enough. Gail Cogdill was spoofed for his overconcern with his health: "You've let your body go," I remember shouting at the rookie playing the Cogdill role. He was teetering slightly, bent forward awkwardly on a pair of children's crutches. "Cheating your body... You're finished here," I cried. The same phrase turned up in the spoof of Harley Sewell, in which his determination was mocked, and also his weight, which was light for his position. "Harley!" I shouted at the rookie, who was wearing a doll's cowboy hat high on the crown of his head. "We ask you to get your weight up — to eat like an elephant and crap like a bird. Harley, you've been cheating your body!" I yelled. "You been eating like a bird, crapping like an elephant...etc. etc."

Milt Plum's personal appearance was made fun of: he was invariably fastidious, his hair neatly combed, long for a football player's, every strand of it straight, even in the rigor of a scrimmage, as if it were pasted down with an invisible lacquer. It was always a surprise to see him arrive at the sidelines and wrench off his helmet; no matter how hard he had been knocked around in the scrimmage, even if his nose dripped blood, he would display hair groomed smooth as a banister's newel. In the skit about him (he was played by Lucien Reeberg, still wearing his hoop, who in his eagerness to perform played a number of veterans) I cried out to him: "I'm sorry, Plum, but we've got to let you go. Ever since you came here from the Cleveland Browns, the coaches and I have been trying to do something about your personal appearance, you know, to get your hair *cut* and combed neatly. Scooter McLean even showed you how to hold the comb and apply the hair set. We showed you how to work a pair of nail scissors, clip, clip, clip, and we tried to show you that you can't brush your teeth without opening your mouth. Well, you haven't done it, Milt, and you look like a sheepdog out there...etc. etc."

After twenty veterans had been cut, the curtain came down, a piano was wheeled out, and I thumped at it for a while. The show was concluded with a few short skits based on the filming of television commercials. One of them had George Wilson trying to record the line of a television commercial without including an obscenity. I played the part of a harried television producer. John Gordy played Wilson. The line he was trying to get straight was: "I like Marlboro, a man's cigarette."

I would say, "Let's try it again, Mr. Wilson," pointing a shoe box at him and turning an imaginary handle to indicate a camera.

Gordy would furrow his brow and announce, "I like Marlboro, a ! cigarette."

"No, Mr. Wilson," I would say. "We haven't got that quite right. We've let that word creep in there. Let's give it another try."

So Gordy would say: "I like Marlboro, a man's !."

"No, not quite right."

"I like !, a man's cigarette."

"No..."

"!"

There was a merciful blackout at the skit's close, somewhat delayed since Dennis Gaubatz, the big rookie linebacker, who had refused to dance in the cancan line and had been relegated to "lights," was slow at the switch—the actors stood poised like wax figures as the laughter died at their last lines, and Joe Schmidt, standing in the wings, hissed, "*Lights,* Gaubatz, for Chrissake."

The last skit of the evening was a toothpaste commercial. I said, "Crest toothpaste is proud to bring you the results of one of its surveys. We have two schoolchildren here—on the left little Roger Brown, who is one of two hundred children who for the last six years has been using toothpaste with fluoristan. On my right is John Gordy, who is one of two hundred children using Crest toothpaste with hydrochlorophlexiphil. Now, Roger, will you tell the viewing audience the results of the survey of *your* group."

Lucien Reeberg, who was playing Brown, hammed it up, simpering and carrying on and getting as much into his meager line as he could, which was considerable, considering the line, which was brief: "We had twenty percent less cavities."

After Reeberg was done, I asked, "And now, John Gordy, what about your group?" cranking the imaginary wheel on the shoe box.

Gordy was playing himself. He had removed his bridgework—all his front teeth had been knocked out in some past football war—and at my question he opened his mouth in a cavernous grin, not a tooth to be seen in the front of his head, and he reported loudly: *"No cavities at all!"*

He kept his mouth ajar, leaning forward slightly, motionless, as I was, and from the wings we finally heard Joe Schmidt say, "Lights, Gaubatz, for Chrissakes, *lights.*"

They were doused, the curtain was drawn, and when the lights went up again Gordy slipped his teeth back in, and we all went out in front and took awkward bows.

The veterans and coaches came up and crowded around. John Gonzaga said there were things about the show to be remembered, which was high praise considering the number of rookie shows he had seen, and the acts he remembered, such as the player who wore the paper bag and had the lipsticked navel.

Afterward, we piled into cars and the veterans took the rookies out. The coaches told us to watch ourselves. In the past, a number of bars and restaurants in the vicinity had been decimated on rookie night, so the veterans had hired an empty hall on the top floor of the Veterans of Foreign Wars building on the main road to Pontiac. Joe Schmidt was in the car. He said how important the rookie night was—how it made you feel you belonged. After his weeks of ostracization because of the veterans' love for the linebacker, Flanagan, whom he replaced, Schmidt was finally accepted in a drinking bout, out on the town, exactly like rookie night. He was plied with liquor. He tried to fake being drunk by reeling around tossing down ginger ale from a shot glass, but they caught him at it, and at two a.m. he was just barely conscious that he was playing the drums in a Salvation Army band. But it was a great night for him.

A tremendous racket was going on when we arrived. We could hear it as we parked the car out in the back lot. Our group, arriving late, hurried up the stairs. Everything had been prepared up there—a large galvanized garbage pail, with a mop handy, was in the middle of an open enclosure of long tables. Within, the rookies sat. In front of them, on the tables, were the big mugs, and the pitchers of beer ready, and around the perimeter the veterans leaned across, shouting at them to stand and drink up. Toasts were ordered—to Bruce Maher's son, born that afternoon, to the president's son, Patrick Bouvier Kennedy, also born that day, and to die the next—the big men standing up on their chairs, the beer soaking the shirtfronts, as they shouted the children's names, and drank to them—and then more names to toast, the coaches, Alex Karras, Dean Rusk, Dinah Washington, Jean Seberg, Pete Rozelle's grandmother, and as the lists went on the rookies began to weave.

Harley Sewell drank down an entire pitcher to show the rookies the proper way to drink—the beer sliding down his open throat as if poured into an open drain. Roger Brown also gave some drinking lessons—pouring the beer from the pitcher into a mouth cupped wide as a hippo's, it seemed, his throat barely working as the beer, like Sewell's, ran unencumbered to his stomach.

For their final toasts, the rookies were subjected to Cardinal Puff—the familiar fraternity drinking game in which the initiate must follow a prescribed ritual, in exact order; if he makes a mistake in word or gesture, or gets the order wrong in the toasting sequence, he must drink his mug down and start again from the beginning. The veterans were strict judges, quick to penalize, and after a while some of the rookies were barely able to get out the first line, which is, "Here's to Cardinal Puff for the first time."

Harley Sewell came by and caught me looking on.

"What you doin' out here, rook? Git on in there."

I got in the rookie enclosure. Bob Whitlow, the first-line center, sat across from me. He had me drink some warm-up toasts—to his hometown; to the high school there, and its football coach; and then Sewell leaned across and I drank a toast to *his* hometown.

"St. Jo, Texas!" I called out.

When Gail Cogdill stopped by, I drank a toast to his hometown without being asked.

"Worland, Wyoming!" I shouted. "Population: fourteen."

It took me almost five mugs to get through the Cardinal Puff exercise. Whitlow was easy on me the last time. When I stood up and left the enclosure, the room was reeling slightly. I went up and concentrated on the wording of an enlarged copy of the Constitution framed on the wall. I went and stood at a window, pulling the rattan shade aside to get some air. Outside the neon lights along the main street beat steadily. The noise behind me was deafening.

I launched myself back into it. At the far end of the hall, a number of the local people were peering in, standing at the head of the stairwell. They crowded the door, quite a few of them; in the back was a row of craning faces, with one in the far back that bobbed up and down, as if the fellow, short of stature, were bouncing on a trampoline to see.

"Wha' you suppose those folks think?" I shouted happily in the uproar. "They look confused and concerned." I went slowly up to them. "Ladies an' gen'l'm'n, the Detroit *Lions*," I announced. "A grand, finely turned, superbly con-conditioned football aggre-aggregation who *here*, in this grand hall of yours, for your eyes *alone,* are doing their daily con-conditioning exercises." I swept a hand behind me. "Gym work," I said bluntly.

Their attention remained caught by the goings-on. I turned. It seemed, at sudden glance, a shipboard scene—a promenade deck, storm-lashed, with an occasional scud of beer flying, the footing difficult as the big men, their shirtfronts soaked, swayed and skidded, shouting, gripping each other for support. A number had succumbed to malaise, two at the garbage pail, a third at the window, the rattan window shade askew across his shoulders as he bent out over the parking lot.

"Boats! To the boats!" I shouted—an alarum that went unnoticed in the confusion.

After a while, the veterans began guiding the rookies down to the cars, supporting some of them, one or two being carried, Reeberg for one, the veterans shoulder to shoulder under him calling out directions, "A little down on your side," as they moved down the narrow stairs like furniture movers.

I drove back to camp with Terry Barr and John Gordy.

"Tonight was a picnic," Barr said. "Some of those rookies were *walking*." He seemed incredulous.

"Oh," I said weakly.

"In Bobby Layne's time, a rookie was never able to get home on his own pins. That was the rule."

They talked about their first rookie night. Both of them had arrived in camp late—from the All-Star game in Chicago in which they'd played—missing a week or so of training, coming in on the day of the rookie night, it turned out, and after a long practice they were taken out on the town with the others. Barr was returned to his room barely conscious. He was put under a shower, briefly, fully clothed, then laid out on his bed, still clothed. They dropped him there as if they were discarding him.

He was there a half hour or so, too miserable to move, though he was conscious of the water squelching in his shoes when he moved his toes. The door to his room swung ajar and he saw the coaches watching him, head coach Buddy Parker with a clipboard. A bed check, apparently. He managed a weak smile. "That's Barr," one of the coaches whispered to Parker.

Down the hall, when Parker and his staff looked in, John Gordy was being sick into a pail as the door opened. He also managed a smile. He recognized Parker. He tried to say "Hi, Coach." He raised himself off the bed, but the coach slapped the door shut before he could get the words out.

Gordy and Barr described the considerable consequences of what Parker saw that night, and its effect on him. The rookie night was on a Saturday. On Monday in Detroit there was a "meet the Lions" banquet, to which over five hundred Lion boosters paid ten dollars apiece to eat a chicken-and-peas dinner; they were to be entertained by introductions to players and coaches, then listen to speeches from club officials, and a guest speaker, Otto Graham, the ex–Cleveland quarterback. Parker, the main speaker, sat at the end of the dais. He sent his chicken and peas away, and sat staring out across the room. Otto Graham got up when his turn came and made a number of jokes about the after-hours deportment of the Lion players, which was a surefire cause for merriment. He said, among other things, "They have an early bed check at Cranbrook so the players can duck on out the windows and get into town for the parties." Everybody laughed hard, and the players looked into their coffee cups with self-conscious grins.

The Detroit sportscaster, Bob Reynolds, who was the master of ceremonies, then introduced Parker, cuing the applause for him by referring to abilities which made him the "best coach in the league."

The applause *was* heavy, the big crowd rising along with Parker as he moved for the lectern, tearing a paper he held in his hand into tiny scraps. He seemed somewhat grim, but that was his manner. Everybody settled in his seat, belts were loosened, smoke rose in clouds from cigars tilted in contentment, and ears were tuned for soothing words about the coming season, perhaps a wry joke or two which would be applauded as much for his attempting it as for its efficacy, Parker not being a man at ease in public.

When it was absolutely quiet, Parker said in a low monotone, "I quit." He did not pause for emphasis, but continued straight on: "I got a situation here I can't handle. These ballplayers have gotten too big for me, or something. I'm getting out of Detroit football—and I'm getting out tonight. So long," he said, and moving laterally along the dais to his seat he sat down.

There was what the press referred to the next day, according to Barr and Gordy, as a "huge silence," finally broken by some incredulous, somewhat tentative, shouts of "What? What?" The master of ceremonies, Reynolds, rose stiffly—his mind apparently set on getting on with the program no matter what—and asked Parker, in that case, if he minded if George Wilson would tell the audience what could be expected of the 1957 Lions. Parker made a resigned gesture, and Wilson, confused and startled, moved to the microphone and mumbled a few words about the team, his mind obviously distracted by Parker's statement, until his feelings got the better of him and he said sharply: "This is serious. I hope Buddy stays and we win the championship. I don't want to get mixed up in any crap, and that's *it!*"

The audience jumped up and began shouting. Reynolds came back on the microphone, still confused, to say that he had never faced such a situation and didn't know what to do. "If I was a newspaperman though," he said, "I'd know enough to start running for the door."

Some of the newsmen did just that, and others stayed around, rushing from group to group of boosters, players, and coaches, trying to find out what was going on, and hearing in the background the voice of

General Manager Anderson booming over the ballroom. "Good old Andy," said Barr. "He took over the microphone and was trying to calm everyone down. But it didn't work out, and he finally gave up." Barr remembered Anderson leaning into the microphone and concluding the evening with just what he would have said had the proceedings sailed along smoothly. "That finishes up tonight's program," he called out to the storming, confused crowd. "Thank you."

"So that was how George Wilson became head coach," I said.

"They gave him the team when Buddy Parker quit," Barr said, "and he went on and won the championship with it."

He turned the car through the gates and into the school grounds.

"There's no telling," he said, "if it was the rookie night and seeing all those players boozed up that *did it*. I mean the guy could have had some tea leaves turn up wrong. He was awful superstitious."

"Listen," Gordy said as Barr parked the car.

Out across the lawns drifted snatches of song, bursts of ribaldry, and occasionally distant hallooing, like the cries of campers lost in a forest.

"From the sound of it, some of them are in the fountains," Gordy said. "Best way to get them sobered up."

Barr said, "Pietrosante spent his rookie night in one of those fountains. He got in there, and the water was warm, like lying in moss, he said, and he dozed off. Somebody came along the gravel walk just before daylight and the sound of the steps woke him up. This guy sees him and stops. A gardener, Nick thinks he was. He looked in at Nick, his face like he's seen a corpse in his fountain, a guy drowned in there, naturally, because it *looks* like that. But then Nick jumps up, big, you know, with the water rushing off him, and I guess he was flailing around because he didn't know where he was, of course, and this gardener or mailman, whatever he was, seeing this in the darkness give a squawk and he *lit out*, I mean to tell you."

A distant splash and a high-pitched yell drifted out at us.

"I wonder if they're up in the Milles fountain," I said, "in there with those nine-foot stick-like nudes."

"Horrible," Gordy said, thinking about the statues. "Of course the rookies might go for those stone gals; or maybe that's Brettschneider up there, giving them the old club rush. A little rough handling by the Badger might improve those statues."

We walked past the gym. "What about George Wilson?" I asked. "What's he make of the rookie night?"

"He doesn't pay this any heed," Barr said. "He shuts his door good and tight. He knows it'll be a better team for it. The rookies are part of it now, they've been initiated—you too," he said, looking over. "Can't you feel it?"

"I feel soused," I said. We went along the gravel walks. "But I know about the other thing too," I said.

CHAPTER 26

It was a happy group that met for the evening classes the next day — a few hangovers perhaps, but there was a new sense of solidarity and purpose. The show and the celebration in the veterans' hall had much to do with that. Perhaps one or two more players would be cut, but the rookies were confident, and felt they belonged. The veterans felt themselves getting into shape, and the enemies now, rather than rookies trying for their jobs, were the Cleveland Browns.

A number of announcements began the session. General Manager Anderson appeared, and he put a crimp in the good spirits by announcing that he did not believe the team was going to be awarded Ford cars to drive during the season. That had been the practice, of course, in the past, he said, but the year before, the Ford Motor Company had struggled until *March,* three months after the season's close, to get their last car back, some three hundred unpaid parking tickets had come into their office, and insurance claims of over ten thousand dollars were under litigation. The insurance company had indicated they would refuse to insure the cars again, and the Ford people were not "brimming over with enthusiasm" — as Anderson put it — to continue the project.

Well, that was Detroit for you, the players said afterward, a dog town. Now take New York. That was a great football town. There wouldn't be any such nonsense there. They talked about pregame ceremonies in Yankee Stadium a few years before when one of the Giants had been honored—gift after gift from New York supporters wheeled out across the grass: golf clubs, a red convertible (driven out by a Miss Rheingold), a Hammond organ, hundreds of dollars' worth of fishing equipment, a television console, a camping outfit with a barbecue stand, other smart accessory gifts, and then a motor yacht on a trailer whose tires left deep twin ruts in the turf. The Lions stood watching from the sidelines, like country cousins, more than one of them remembering Jim Martin "night" in Detroit when his car had been wheeled out for him, a gift from the fans, the only gift, and when he got in it to drive it off he found a payment book attached to the steering column with a ribbon, half the payments still due. The gas tank was a quarter full. Being a man sensitive to the correctness of things, he left the team the next year to play in the American Football League—the niggardliness of Detroit management certainly a contributing factor. He had returned to the Lions, but he was always vocal when representatives of management complained about the team. He snorted when Bud Erickson got up, greeted with a chorus of oo-ahs, the players imitating his speech habits, to complain that the team was inviting too many guests for meals. The evening before, the entire allotment of steaks had been consumed before the coaches, returning late from their liars' poker in their bar down the Pontiac pike, had a chance at them. The chef boiled some eggs for them and there was some iced tea.

Wilson then spoke, and he was in good humor about the steaks. He said, "I'm not a steak man. I'm a pork chop man. The only time I ever got mad was when Layden Miller ate eleven pork chops and Joe Stydahar had nine and I didn't get any. That's the only time I've been real mad...ever!" He grinned at his men. "Of course, we got this Cleveland game coming up, and maybe I could turn up real mad again if you guys don't sit on them good."

Roger Brown then had a film to show he had shot during the Playoff Bowl in Miami the year before. Detroit had played Cleveland, beating them badly. As Brown threaded the film into the projector they remembered him on the practice field with his camera, and the comic routines they worked up for him. Brown had temporary enthusiasms with such gadgets as movie cameras. Two years before, he had a Harley-Davidson motorcycle which was his pride and on which he took Les Bingaman riding around the school grounds. The two of them amounted to over six hundred pounds loaded on that machine, and people who saw them would turn and stare after them for a long while, as if a circus act had materialized and gone by. He had a saxophone that year too, and he practiced assiduously. There were complaints, and if Brown was sympathetic he took the saxophone off and played it out in the pine woods by the lake, the moans of the scales drifting out from the dark line of trees like the high cries of a mournful bird. For the Miami trip he had his new movie camera, and the film he showed the evening class was nearly a parody of the early efforts of the enthusiastic amateur.

His film opened with a long shot of the airplane wing through the window.

"That's the wing there," Brown said. He was seated next to the projection machine, prepared to give a commentary. The camera dwelt lovingly on the wing. Some clouds rolled by underneath. We were given a view of the other wing. The sun was shining on it and the image was pale and underfocused.

"That's the other wing of our jet," said Brown.

The camera panned down below the wing, and for a time the screen showed white, with just a flicker or so to indicate that the film was still running through the projector.

"Clouds," said Brown. "There was some ground down there, but it was quite clouded up."

Then we got another shot of the wing, and the classroom began to get a little out of hand.

"My God, what's that?" someone said.

"That's the wing of our jet," said Brown carefully. He was proud of his film and sensitive to the joking which was beginning about it.

"What's *that?*" someone called.

The screen was suddenly ink-dark with an occasional flash of light, and the sense of movement. We were all squinting to make something of it.

"Coffee," said Brown. "Those are interior shots that didn't quite come out. The stewards on the plane are serving coffee."

"Those close-ups of the coffee, Rog?" someone asked.

"Look," said Brown suddenly. "You guys want to see this film, or not?" He stood up in front of the projector and faced the classroom. His face, shining in the light from the machine, was miserable. The film worked silently and busily on his shirtfront. An airplane wing appeared again, miniaturized on his chest.

"Sit down, Rog," they called out. "It's crazy, man."

"Be a little respectful," Brown said. He sat down; the beam shot forward again to the screen.

We had some more views taken in flight, and then a long ground shot of the Miami Air Terminal, long enough for us to imagine that we were watching color slides, not a motion picture, and that soon we'd hear the lecturer squeeze the cricket, *pick-pock,* so the assistant would push the next slide into view.

"You trying out a tripod or something?" someone asked.

"You really *feel* it, Rog, for that terminal."

Brown, sitting next to the projector, remained quiet and tense, because he knew what was still to come, and sure enough the next shot was the airliner itself, sitting on the ground with some baggage being taken out of its belly. A whoop of laughter went up.

Finally, after some shots of the hotel where the team stayed, some views appeared of the hotel swimming pool, with the players sitting around, and then some shots of the practice field with the players mugging around for Brown's camera, Alex Karras in particular, leapfrogging over his teammates and leering at the camera so that Brown had hardly been able to hold on to it for laughing, and the picture on the screen dipped and swayed.

When the film ended the players applauded Brown, who grumbled as he put it away in its can, and they shook their heads, remembering the pleasure of their Miami trip. It had been almost like a vacation. Practices were kept to a minimum; the players had time to lie around on the beaches. They went out on the town at night; there were no curfews or bed checks.

Paul Brown, the Cleveland coach, had kept his team working as if it were mid-season. He applied his restrictions, which were stringent: curfews, no smoking, no cuts of classes or practices. He meant to show that spartan dedication would triumph. On one occasion, both teams met at a banquet given in Miami Beach, at one of the big hotels on the waterfront. The Lions had beer at their plates, and the air above them was thick with cigarette smoke. To witnesses, it seemed as if a plate-glass partition divided the Lions from the Cleveland area of the banquet room, where the Browns drank water and there was no smoking. Later, one of the Lions told me what he remembered about looking out of the fog bank of smoke at the Browns: "Over there in that clear area, I could make out those guys in their blazers, made you feel like a bum," he said. "But you could see from the guys' faces looking at us, like pleading, how much they wanted to sit with us and cadge a drink, maybe a smoke."

Brown was a stickler on smoking. He had traded a very good defensive end, Bill Quinlan, to the Green Bay Packers, primarily because he seemed unable to abide by the rules, on smoking in particular. Quinlan, loafing around the training room, had spotted a half-smoked cigarette resting on the lip of an ashtray, and he had sidled over and taken a quick hand-cupped drag on it.

"Quinlan!"

He had turned, the smoke escaping in a quick puff as he started back from the cigarette as if burned, and Brown, staring at him from the door, shouted: "What are you doing, Quinlan? Trying to *ruin* my organization?"

Quinlan was sent to Green Bay not long after.

When Roger Brown's film was done, Wilson got up again and began talking about Cleveland. He kept mentioning Paul Brown's name (though Brown had been replaced that year by a new coach, Blanton Collier) as if what was on the line in the upcoming game was the efficacy of one type of coaching as opposed to another—the hard martinetcy of Brown against Wilson's relaxed operation. His psychology had worked in Miami the winter before; he tried it again: he was letting the team know that his system was once again on trial.

Wilson was admired for his oratory. Yale Lary had told me that he thought George Wilson could stir up a team better than anyone he had heard—and he had heard some fine rousers. The coach of his Texas high-school team was in the habit of playing a soothing record as the players trooped into class, or to the locker room; then when they were all seated he would rip the phonograph arm across the record with a fearful amplified screech of the needle against the grooves, and he would rant at them while their nerves jangled.

Whenever discussion of coaching psychology came up, I always thought of my grandfather, who, as a close student of football, was particularly interested in the oracular powers of the head coach. He collected stories about coaches' perorations. He liked the description of Knute Rockne's harangues being "champagne from a battered oilcan." He was fond of telling the story of Michigan's Hurry Up Yost working himself into such a frenzy with his own pep talk that on one occasion he concluded by charging out at the head of the squad through the wrong door of the locker room and tumbling into the field-house swimming pool.

"There was a meet going on in there at the time," said my grandfather, who, though he had not been a witness, enjoyed speculating on the scene, "and there was no end of commotion. Yost was wearing a large capelike overcoat and it hung out in the water like a great bat, his feet beating underneath. To the swimmers it must have seemed that someone had scaled a large Aubusson rug on the pool."

"That is an exaggeration," my grandmother had said.

My grandfather's primary interest was in the fortunes of Harvard, his alma mater; his special hero was Percy Haughton, who coached the team through its early years. "Now the present fellow you've got there, Dick Harlow," I remember him telling me when I was very young and impressionable, "well, he's certainly no slouch. But his hobby is oology, that is he's a collector of eggs, and his approach to the game is what you might expect: delicate, technical, and deft. His predecessor," my grand-father said, "the great Percy Haughton, now he was a different and splendid sort. A dramatic turn was one of his specialties, and on one occasion, pepping up his team just before the Yale game, he strangled a bulldog and tossed it aside to illustrate what he wanted done."

"A bulldog!" I said, my eyes popping.

"That is a legend about Percy Haughton," my grandmother said, "and not necessarily the truth. You should not tell the boy such things."

"Nonsense," my grandfather said. "Of course he did. There weren't any softies around in his day."

I believed my grandfather, of course, seeing the terrible wrench in my mind's eye, and the bulldog sail off into a corner as limp as an empty glove. But then, in a year or so, when I thought about it, the bulldog began to gain somewhat in bulk and stature, so that when the coach called for him ("Charlie, bring me over that bulldog") what was brought through the circle of players was a substantial animal, bowlegged, mean-looking, and rheumy and cynical of eye.

"The opposition," Percy Haughton said, "is soft — a bunch of soft-ies. He reached for the bulldog. "I want you to go out there on that field and throttle them." He hoisted the bulldog up and began applying pres-sure in the neighborhood of the collar. The bulldog got his teeth into Haughton's sleeve and ripped off the cuff. The coach's wristwatch strap was severed and the watch dropped to the floor.

"Not much neck to these things," Haughton said. His breathing was strained. The bulldog began working on the other sleeve. "Give me a hand here, fellows," the coach said. A tackle or two, and a guard, would get up and separate the coach from the bulldog, the three of them haul-ing and the coach straining back, the bulldog in between, and the coach's sleeve separating at the shoulder seams finally and remaining in the bull-dog's possession. They set the bulldog off in a corner with a leash on him.

"Well, that's something," the coach said, shaking his wrist. "Whew! Charlie, that damn thing'd pass as a *mastiff*."

While George Wilson's oratory — of a much simpler variety, and not supported by such artifacts as bulldogs—was admired by all the players, he too had been caught out on a few occasions.

"You remember George's great boner," Wayne Walker had said one night, swinging back in his chair, "the time when he gives us the big halftime speech—was it in Chicago?—when we're a couple of touchdowns down, and he's telling us, just ripping at us, that we can come back, we're a great team, we got the stuff, and he's getting all worked up, red and heavy around the neck, and finally he says, 'Now go out there and *give* it to 'em!' We jump up, and as we start crowding out the door he shouts after us, 'Remember, guys, a good team *never* comes back!' Well, man, *that* let the plug out."

John Gordy, who was sitting in the room, said, "One time George is on television, one of those question-and-answer shows, sitting there looking uncomfortable, and the guy says, 'Mr. Wilson, one of our listeners wants to know the difference between the fullback draw and the halfback draw.'

"Well, George leans forward, much too far so that his face suddenly fills the screen, and then he leans back and you can see him tap his fingers on the table like he was going to say something pro*found*, y'know, and he says, 'You see in the fullback draw the fullback draws, and in the halfback draw the halfback...well, er...*draws*.' Period. That's all he says, and the announcer says, 'Yes, and now we have a question from a viewer in Marquette....'"

Wilson's speech about Cleveland was clever that night, though—with his simple description of Cleveland coaching methods, and the suggestion that, if the Browns won the game, it would mean that the easygoing regimen and the reliance on self-, rather than group, discipline which typified the Lions would be at fault. The implication was that life would not be easy if the Lions lost. It was not a game which was at stake, but a whole way of life, he seemed to be telling us.

When he finished, he looked at us for a while, and we listened to the plush sounds of the fountains playing outside and all of that was made to seem very desirable suddenly.

Then, a game film of the Browns in action was shown. Each play was run over three or four times, Bingaman sitting by the machine in the darkness and hitting the reverse button. In reverse the players would soar up off the ground from the welter of blockers and tacklers and dodge back in a strained backward lope to the sudden pristine order of the teams poised just before the quarterback's snap. On the screen, all twenty-two players were seen at once, a wide-angle view, so that each player would watch his opposition. I could hear John Gordy begin to murmur in the darkness, complaining about the big tackle he would be playing opposite.

"Look at that big whore," he said. He pronounced it "hoo-er."

"What's that?" I whispered.

"Look at him. He's got fifty or sixty pounds on me. I got to play him head-on in the pass plays. He's the biggest horror" (which he pronounced "whore-er") "in the world — a large door with a suit on it."

I could hear Gordy tap his pencil against his teeth. "Tractor foot," I heard him say.

"Can you figure him?" I asked.

Gordy said in the darkness, "If I was him, playing against me, I'd bust out laughing. That's like to be just what he's doing, sitting there with two chairs under him to handle all that goddamn bulk, and watching *our* film and laughing to beat the band...."

We went back to the dormitory rooms after the game films. The player on Cleveland they talked about that night was Jim Brown, the great fullback. Joe Schmidt, shaking his head, said, "He's going to be three kinds of rat poison. How to stop him? Carry a gun."

Many of the descriptions of Jim Brown were platitudes, and they were trotted out about other great players too. But when the reference was to Brown, the players spoke as if the words, however commonplace, were worthy of particular attention for their aptness. A player would say, "Tackling Brown, you try to hold on and pray for help to come." It was a cliché about him and it should have been tossed off and forgotten, but instead what he was saying was so accurate that the scene would play in the defenseman's head, and he would add somberly: "And the help's gotta come fast, or that boy, oh my, he's *gone...*"

Brettschneider had the imaginative idea that defending against Brown one got the notion from his speed and drive that he was running downhill, that somehow the field had tilted to his advantage — there was that sense about him of heavy tonnage in an avalanche. Brettschneider put his hands apart as if the situation were hopeless. He remembered tackling Brown in the Playoff Bowl in Miami the year before. It was near the end of the game, with just a few plays to go, and the Browns got the ball. He remembered cursing as he trotted out to his linebacker's position, and then he began some heartfelt praying that Jim Brown wouldn't be sent around him — it was hot, he was exhausted, the game was safely won, the season gone, and the long months of layoff and lazying around just a moment or so away, and he jiggled around at his position, thinking all this as the Browns broke their huddle. Watching the big fullback settle in his stance for the quarterback's call, Brettschneider had the sudden presentiment not only that Brown *was* coming his way, but that his legs were going to be snapped in the violence of the play. He could barely get himself going when the ball was hiked. Watching his keys, the blockers form, he knew that the ball had been shoveled to Brown on an end sweep toward him, and moving desperately he got by the blockers and to him, and hauled him down, the first time he could remember ever doing it alone, and when he started to get up he discovered the force of the impact and Brown's momentum had knocked the face bar off his helmet and it was lying on his chest.

If the talk wasn't about Jim Brown, Paul Brown became the topic, even though he had retired from the coaching profession. Plum was the authority on him. He said that Brown was the most suspicious man he ever hoped to meet. When airplanes flew over the practice field he would look up, hands on hips, and the players knew that he suspected scouts were taking aerial pictures of the practice. When helicopters flew over, he was sure of it, and the practice was stopped. To discourage ground-level surveillance the practice field had a seven-foot-high canvas fence set around it, and from time to time Brown would walk its perimeter to check for peepholes that might have been drilled in the dark of the night. On one occasion a telephone truck drove up and stopped on the other side of the fence, a crane rose up with a cherry-picker lift on the end of it, and repairmen started work on the telephone-pole transformer. Brown saw them working up in the lift, which in fact gave them a fine view of the field over the fence, and he cried out: "Stop, stop everything!" The coaches blew their whistles shrilly, and the players stood up from what they were doing and watched. Brown walked stiffly over to the fence and looked up at the repairmen. "Don't try to kid me," he shouted at them, cupping his hands. "I know what you're up to— from *Baltimore*, aren't you? Well, don't try to kid me, you'll never find out anything from this practice. Why don't you give up and go home?"

The repairmen looked down at him, too puzzled to say anything, and one of them spun his forefinger near his head, and then pointed at Brown.

But it was curious, Plum said, that what seemed such an obvious paranoia did appear to have, on another occasion, some justification. Brown had stopped a practice because he thought he saw the glint of binoculars from the top story of a building five or six blocks away; an assistant was sent to check, and to everyone's surprise, except perhaps Brown's, it was discovered that the room had been rented just for the daytime, ten dollars a day, and that the landlady had only seen the boarder coming and going at practice time. It was quite likely that the "boarder" was indeed a scout.

I asked, "How much can be discovered that'll help in the game?"

"Enough," Plum said. "Anything about the opposition that you can add to your game plan helps."

But then, shaking his head, Plum went on to say that Brown's suspicions, however justified, were carried to extraordinary extremes. In the locker rooms at halftime Brown would search the corners and run his hands across the walls for microphones, suspecting that the room was bugged, and even his search did not allay his fears. Talking to the team, drawn in close around him, he would diagram a play on the blackboard, but rub it out quickly with an eraser, its name never mentioned aloud.

He would say, leaning in toward his players conspiratorially, "Now in the second half we're going to throw…" and holding up ten fingers three times, he'd mouth "thirty passes."

Jim Martin, who was listening, said appropriately: "He was certainly a man who made you uneasy."

Plum went on to describe him—an extraordinarily competitive man, but an aloof figure, possibly because he had not been a player himself, nor had he coached professional teams before taking over at Cleveland: he had jumped straight from coaching the great service teams at the Great Lakes Training Station, where the environment was military and disciplined, to the professional teams. He seemed almost uncomfortable with his players. He had an office on the first floor of the training-camp dormitories but Plum never remembered him up on the second floor where the players were. Once, he came up to the top step of the stairwell and called a player out of a card game to fine him for abusive language. The player had been trying to fill an inside straight and, when he was dealt an unsatisfactory card, the blue language drifted out into the summer evening and through Brown's office window.

The sense of remove from his players, his concept of them as pawns, was especially evident in Brown's famous practice of sending in the offensive plays to his quarterback, shuttling them in with a relay of his running guards. The guard would whisper the play to the quarterback, who would then repeat it in the huddle.

"He was insistent about that," Plum said. "Even in practice. I remember once he came out to practice with this terrible case of laryngitis. It was cold and damp. They drove him out to the sidelines in a heated car with the windows rolled up. You could see him bundled up in there in scarves. Before every play, he'd crank the window down and he'd croak the play to the assistant coach or the running guard, who'd come out and tell me. Mind, this was just a practice session."

"In those years you played for him," I asked, "didn't you ever call a play on your own in a game?" I recalled from reading that Otto Graham occasionally called his own plays as Cleveland quarterback, though with the compulsion that they had better succeed or Brown would have some stiff things to say. I remembered that George Ratterman, a substitute quarterback for Graham, was once sent in late in a game that the Browns had tucked away, and when Brown's play arrived at the huddle, he said jokingly, "I don't like that one, Joe Skibinski. Go back and ask Brown for another."

Skibinski dutifully trotted away from the huddle on his way back to Brown, and was only hauled back by Ratterman with some difficulty. As Ratterman put it, "The next signal from Brown would have been a ticket to my hometown, which is Fort Thomas, Kentucky."

"Ratterman would have been right. He'd have been out on the next train," Plum said. "I only called my own signals twice. That's all. In fact, when I started out, it wasn't so bad. It didn't bother me and I didn't mind. I didn't know anything and having that responsibility—the whole process of play calling—lifted from me, well, that made things that much easier. But then as I got to learn more what it was all about, and began to understand what I was seeing in front of me as a quarterback, then after a while, which was natural, I began second-guessing—wondering how a play *I* might have called would have compared with what Paul Brown had ordered—particularly if I got piled up with Brown's play. Then, after another season or so, it became frustrating, and that was when I knew I didn't want to play for him anymore."

"What were the two plays?" I asked.

"In Yankee Stadium—'60 I think it was. We got beat bad, and near the end, about two or three minutes to go, the fans came pouring out on the field—fighting, a lot of them, damnedest sight, and Brown took us off."

I had seen that game myself, from high in the upper tiers, and it seemed comic at first: the scurrying of overcoated men (it was a bitter, gray day), among them, I recall, a gawky figure of some elegance, with a chesterfield coat, carrying a tightly rolled umbrella, loping out among the players, but then suddenly he shifted the umbrella so he was carrying it like a club. Across the field one saw the stiff-levered swings of brawling men, then someone down, clumsy in the folds of his overcoat, his legs flailing, and then another, and there was absolutely no reason for it at all. It was not an attack on the players. They stood, huge in their uniforms, stately, near-Olympian figures in that confusion, quite immune, and gazing dumbly at what was going on. Plum described the lunatic stare he saw in the eyes of those tearing by, and the sounds they made, near keening in their eagerness to find someone to hit.

When Brown removed his team from the field, they trotted off with dispatch, those from the bench with their field capes billowing as they hurried past, a few of them lingering in the openings of the locker-room corridors in the dugouts to watch the strange turmoil out on the field. A voice, majestic, and quite implacable, as if announcing the next Sunday's event at the stadium, came over the public-address system, to inform the crowd calmly that if the field was not cleared the game would be forfeited to Cleveland. It was easy to hear the announcement. The huge crowd, after a first great roar at what seemed the carnival attraction of spectators careering out onto the field of play, now watched quietly, almost sullenly, in a mood near introspection, as if aware that what had galvanized the spectators over the box-seat railings ticked quietly in themselves. My man with the umbrella was down. The lining of his coat, half open, was bright scarlet—silk perhaps. The participants in the brawl seemed shabby, though, in that gray light—squat men, quick as beetles, but parodying the grace we had been watching in the game.

The police appeared—a small nervous knot which disintegrated as each trotted onto the field, and then, as quickly as they had appeared, the brawlers stopped, almost in mid-stroke, and each for himself they fled for the rails, the police after them. The crowd warmed to this immediately—flight from authority was explicable—and we stood and yelled cheerfully, applauding each elusive maneuver. It was impossible to clear the field completely, and when the players returned, the spectators trotted along beside them, more coming across the sidelines. For the moment the brawling had stopped, though everywhere there was evidence of the scuffling—hats rocking in the stiff cold breeze, the loops of a scarf convoluting clumsily across the ground, and then incongruous, and quite visible from the tier where I was sitting, an empty saddle shoe lying near the midfield stripe, where it was picked up and used in an improvised touch football game, the shoe flipped from spectator to spectator until a wild toss ended it up in the stands, where it disappeared, flying up rows at a time until I lost it from view under the overhang.

Down near the Giant goal line, the two teams finally lined up, the spectators crowded around, and Plum called two running plays into the line to run out the clock as quickly as he could. The gun went off, and the two teams ran for the locker rooms together, in a big bunch. Those were the two plays he called on his own. Paul Brown never came back onto the field to witness them.

"Something wild?" I asked. "The Statue of Liberty...triple reverse... after all that time following his orders, why...?"

"The crowd," Plum said. "Nobody wanted to fool around. The crowd stood in the huddle with us—maybe forty or fifty in that huddle, I guess the biggest offensive huddle there's ever been. Then they lined up with us, down in the three-point stance, maybe twenty in the backfield, and then a long line up front. But then," Plum grinned, "the defense—the Giants—they had maybe a hundred guys on *their* team. So I just lay down with the ball a couple of times."

"That's too bad," I said. "After all that time."

"It's poor writing when they talk of the crowd as 'the Beast'?" asked Plum.

"Almost surely," I said.

"All the papers seemed to have it on their minds the next day. They would have been right that time. The crowd was standing right in with us. You get used to a crowd yelling—that's as much of the game as your helmet—but to hear it *breathing,* that's something else. I'd been somewhere else, I'm telling you, if there was a choice...."

CHAPTER 27

A few days after the Pontiac scrimmage, Edwin Anderson, the team's general manager, asked me to have lunch with him. I was glad for the chance. I wanted to clear my participation in the Cleveland game. The players had been talking about my playing. They promised me a twenty-point lead, which would ensure that Wilson could let me in without danger of the team losing. We met at the Steakhouse, which is Detroit's equivalent of New York's "21" Club. He met me at the door— a large, impressive-looking man with a squashed-down head, a massive straight jaw, and bushy white eyebrows. His eyebrows were particularly distinctive, and the rookie who played Anderson in a brief role in one of the rookie-night skits had only to come onstage with two thick wads of cotton stuck above each eye for the audience to know who he was.

He came forward, and we shook hands, and I thanked him for inviting me. He was wearing large gold cuff links, a gold bee on his tie clip, a gold watch, and a ring which was large and gold with red stones in it. On the way to the table Anderson did a lot of waving and shaking of hands with acquaintances. When we had got settled we ordered from a menu that crackled stiffly, with a velvet string in the back to hold it together, and it opened up as large as a newspaper. The details of opulence were especially noticeable to me after the relatively spartan existence at the training camp.

Anderson talked for a while about himself. He had devoted himself to the Lions since 1958, when he combined the job with running the Goebels Brewing Company. Then he decided that operating the breweries with one hand and the Lions with the other didn't allow enough attention for either, so he resigned from the breweries to devote his energies to football. His most important function as general manager was to initiate trades beneficial to the team.

He began talking about the art of trades. He thought I'd be interested to know how Milt Plum had come to Detroit. Certainly, I said. Well, at Cleveland, when Plum announced publicly that he thought a team could do better if the quarterback called the signals himself rather than receiving them from the bench, Anderson knew that Paul Brown wouldn't stand for such a breach of authority, and that Plum would be on the trading block. So he called up Brown and offered a straight trade — the Detroit quarterback Ninowski for Plum. Sure, said Brown. Anderson knew that Brown would be riled up enough to lose his sense of values. Anderson went and told his coaches, who wouldn't believe it. When Brown told *his* coaches, they had such a fit that Brown finally called Anderson back and said that things would have to be improved at his end. He wanted Bill Glass, the defensive end, and somebody else, just as a sweetener. OK? Well, that seemed all right, Anderson told him, and for the sweetener he offered up Detroit's running back, Hopalong Cassady.

"He can't make my team," Paul Brown said.

"He's an Ohio boy," said Anderson. "You can sell season tickets on him down there in Cleveland."

Brown thought about it for a while, and then he let Plum go, and raked in the three-player Detroit package. Anderson's coaches wanted Tommy Watkins, and after four additional days of talking it was arranged.

"That poor fellow Cassady," I said.

"What are you talking about?" said Anderson. He raised a hand and a waiter in a resplendent jacket like a hunting coat came and took our order.

"I was thinking that he had a pretty rough career. He got the club rush and they put graham crackers in his bed, and the Coventry deal and Layne hauled him around by the scruff of the neck."

Anderson looked at me oddly. "Graham crackers?" he asked.

I began to explain. "Well, he got into trouble..."

Anderson seemed impatient that I was telling him something about his own team. He probably knew it anyway. "This business is cold," he said abruptly. "And it's cruel. There's no room in it for sentimentality. I wanted Buddy Parker to trade Doak Walker, Cloyce Box, and Bob Hoernschemeyer. He wouldn't. He was a sentimental cuss. Finally, all these three retired and we didn't get a thing. You can't afford to be a sentimentalist. I thought Doak Walker was the greatest credit the game of football could have. The guy never smoked, he never drank, he never even drank a goddamn *Coke* or milk or anything that might cut down his wind. When he retired, they gave him a gold football, and they retired his shirt...and then the next summer he turned up at training camp. He wanted to try it again. It was a terrible thing. Buddy Parker had to argue him out of it. It was too late anyway. For helping the club, he should have been traded when he was still a player of value."

"Firing," I said. "I suppose you have to fire managers."

"Buddy Parker's predecessor," said Anderson. "Of course, Parker walked out on his own. But Bo McMillin, it took me three and a half hours to fire him. He was a great friend of mine and he kept saying, 'You can't do this to me.'"

The food arrived. Anderson tucked a napkin under his chin. He began speaking of the cordial relations he had with the other general managers around the league—they all knew each other on a first-name, backslapping basis, invited each other to their country clubs, and each was aware of the other's football problems. Anderson's manner as he described these relationships was expansive, as if the manipulation involved in running a ball club and trading players was matter-of-fact—conducted, one had the impression, from a leather armchair leaned far back, with a leg, a highly polished shoe on the end of it, up on the corner of a massive desk, a telephone at his ear, and good friends at the other end—golfing companions, good sorts, of course, and talking business with them was just a question of knowing what you had and what they wanted. Of course, he wanted to make it clear that his friends were not limited to football circles. "Civically," he said, "I've got the goddamnedest record of anyone in Detroit, you ask anyone—Red Cross, school drives, community funds, that sort of thing…"

I asked what he felt the relationship should be between the general manager and the players.

"Well," he said, "a big family, and I work for them. I try to find them jobs. Jobs in insurance are the best. Gil Mains, who was a great tackle for us, has sold over a million dollars' worth of insurance. He's a good example. The days of the tramp athlete are over."

Anderson thought about that and then he demurred slightly.

"Well, just *about* over. We have this tramp basketball squad." He described how in the off-season some of the Lions put together a team and played where they were invited. "Maybe that wasn't too many places," Anderson said. Their brand of play was rough, their need for physical contact consuming, and in the town of Belleville, Michigan, the local papers after a game there criticized Alex Karras for a series of what it considered "deliberate backhand blows to the head"—as he remembered the paper stated—one of which left a local player "flat on the floor for five minutes."

"Never know what Karras's going to do," Anderson said. "One time he spent the off-season filling jelly doughnuts in an Iowa bakery for $2.75 an hour."

"What about signing players to contracts?" I asked. "That's your responsibility, isn't it?"

"They're excellent negotiators, the average ballplayer, particularly the veteran," Anderson said. "He comes in and sits down and the first thing he says is that while he appreciates that he's at the peak of his career, never been faster, never been stronger, could move a concrete wall just by *pressing* on it, still he's thinking of the future and maybe that he should quit and become a high-school coach. A *high*-school coach!" Anderson snorted. "He tells me that sixty-six high schools are after him, and twenty colleges, and there have been feelers from a few pro teams looking for assistant coaches. You'd think, listening to him, that his mailbox is choked with requests. Well, maybe. Then recently, of course, management has been having it rough because of these incredible sums of money the rookies are getting — quarter-of-a-million-dollar bonuses. The veterans resent it. I don't blame them. Joe Schmidt came in at $5,800. Well, they were born too early, that's all. You go back to George Wilson's time, and he was playing for $100 a game, and quite often he was playing both ways, offense and defense."

He downed an oyster and shook his head. In the old days a player wasn't allowed to come to training camp unless he'd signed his contract. That was quite a lever for the owners — the player knowing he was falling behind by not being able to attend the classes or the practices or the scrimmages. But then Bert Bell, who was the commissioner then, said that legally the clubs couldn't keep a player away while he negotiated his contract — that an option on his services was included in the previous year's contract. So usually, with the training camp already under way, we have five or six unsigned players."

"It's you they come to see?" I asked. "To haggle."

"I think I've only lost my temper once," Anderson said. "That was when Earl Morrall came in to talk contract and wouldn't say anything. He'd shake his head every once in a while, sitting opposite me there, just looking at me like he had been shot up with some terrible drug. But not a word came out of him, no explanation, no arguing, no nothing, so that I finally whooped with anger, I want to tell you, and damn near went off my rocker."

"What happened then?" I asked.

"He saw that he had got to me," Anderson said. "And then he began to laugh. I think he felt he had to put something over on me. There are all sorts."

"How about Night Train Lane?"

"Well, of course, he's famous around the club for having said: 'Is I under the *consumption* that there ain't no mo' money heah?'" He looked down at his plate and laughed.

"Now John Gordy is a screamer. He comes in so angry you think maybe he's going to wreck the place. You have to be calm and let the steam hiss out of him for a while. Then you get Bobby Layne, on the other hand, who in his year came in looking around for a pen to sign the contract with—hardly giving the terms a glance—and I don't think he scarcely knew what sum of money he was signing for. To be sure, Layne was well-off, he was married to the wealthiest woman in town, so he wasn't in there to spend a lot of time haggling. Then you get someone like Gail Cogdill. You might think that Cogdill, being a country boy, and perhaps younger than his years, and who loves football so much you'd think he'd play for nothing, well, you might assume that he'd be one of the easiest men on the roster to sign. Well, for him, I've practically got to set aside two or three days. First of all, he tells me that he's been checking on the salaries of the other ends around the league. 'Ditka,' he tells me, 'Ditka of the Bears, he gets...' and then he'll name, oh, an astro*nomic* figure. So I say, 'God, Gail, where'd you hear *that* figure?' Gail says, 'He told me so himself. At the Pro Bowl game.' 'He's telling you that to impress you,' I tell him. 'No end in the history of the game has been paid anything like that.' 'Well, I don't believe you,' says Cogdill.

"So we call up the general manager over in Chicago. I get him on the phone and I tell him what Cogdill's been telling me about Ditka's salary. I hand the phone over to Cogdill and I can hear the manager laughing at the other end. He tells Cogdill what Ditka gets. Do you think Cogdill believes him? Of course not. He hangs up the phone with a grunt and he tells me he thinks *complicity* is involved. He says to me, 'That fellow in Chicago is your cousin.'

"So then he brings out a folder of statistics—very complex indeed; after all, he's had the whole off-season to work on it—with charts and graphs and columns of figures which show, oh, I don't know *what* all—

touchdowns scored, yardage gained, percentage of passes caught, key blocks thrown, key *decoys,* by God, in which a certain credit is taken for someone *else's* pass reception, on and on, and then his statistics are matched up against the other ends around the league. Well, on paper, of course, the Lions would only have to field one man—Cogdill—and they'd wrap up the championship."

I said, "I would think that sometimes the statistics would work against him. I mean perhaps he hasn't caught as many passes one year as he did the year before."

"Well, you point that out to him," Anderson said, "and he'll look in his folder and he'll tell you he wasn't *thrown* to as many times. Or if his own statistics don't bear him out, he'll find a generality to fall back on. For example, if you say he scored fewer touchdowns, he'll talk about the general decrepitude of the team and the lack of good downfield blocking. Surely, he says, he can't be blamed for that."

I asked, "What is the actual sum of money that...ah...that all the haggling is over?"

"Perhaps, after a while, five hundred dollars. Pride is involved, you see, and other intangibles—the principle."

"You can't just give Cogdill the five hundred dollars and be done with it?"

"The dialogue is important," Anderson said. "We have to keep our end up."

"I have a question," I said, "which may require some dialogue."

"Sure," he said. "What?"

"I'd like to get in the game against Cleveland," I said. "If the team gets ahead by twenty points, make it thirty if you like, and no damage can be done to the final outcome by my participation, what do you say to my getting in, just for a while? The team's all stormed up about it. They're likely to score a point a minute to get me in there. I don't quite know why. The idea's caught their fancy."

Anderson looked at me. He said, "Why, what do you want to do that for? Didn't you have enough in Pontiac?"

"Well, I was just getting the *feel* of it in Pontiac."

"The *feel* of it. My God, they murdered you in Pontiac."

"Well, that's so," I said.

"Well, I don't know about that," Anderson said. "I don't know if that's possible." He was looking worried. He had been skeptical from the beginning. George Wilson had accepted my participating without telling him, and when Anderson heard I was going to scrimmage with the team, he had said, "Oh no, he can't do that!" Some persuasion had been necessary. A lawyer had been called in to draft a document which absolved the Detroit club of any responsibility if I was maimed or killed. I had signed it, and the paper had been carried away in Anderson's briefcase to be locked up in the club's safe.

"Well, I'll have to think about that," he said.

We drove back from the lunch place to the Lion offices on Michigan Avenue, just up from the stadium. Mounted above the building was a neon lion with a tail that went up and down.

"Very snappy," I said.

"This is the headquarters during the season," Anderson said. "Classes are held in here in the morning and afternoon, and practices, of course, down in the stadium. The procedure for the player during the regular season is quite different from what it is out at the training camp. He behaves like any commuter—leaves the house in the morning, the paper under his arm, his wife and kids seeing him off from the porch, and then he's back for dinner."

He showed me through the building—a modern one-story establishment with Formica floors that squeaked underfoot. It was very well-appointed. There was an exercise room for the players, and classrooms with one wall that slid up at the touch of a button to reveal a motion-picture screen. Anderson punched the button to show me.

"That's terrific," I said.

The classroom chairs were painted blue and highly polished, with kidney-shaped armrests for taking notes. The coaches had rooms. A big mounted pike was hung on Bingaman's wall. Anderson showed me the coaches' conference room. It had a blackboard at one end for diagramming plays, and a long table with chairs set around it. I noticed a scrap of paper on the table—an old gin-rummy score when I looked at it closely.

"This is where the club's season is charted," Anderson was saying expansively.

We walked back to his own offices, passing a blown-up photograph of a heavy-ruffed lion—Majesty, a plate underneath identified him—who once lived in the Detroit Zoological Society. Anderson's offices were spacious. An old half-deflated football sat in a glass case. Some cheerleaders' signs were stacked in a corner. They read GO, GO, GO.

"The Lions are going to use cheerleaders this year—for the first time," Anderson said. Their jerseys, marked with a big C, were piled in a corner. "That's some mistake, isn't it?" he remarked. "What could those people have been thinking, to mark them with a C?"

"Cats," I suggested. "As in 'big cat'? Or maybe 'cubs.' Or maybe you got the Baltimore Colts' uniforms and they got yours."

"Why not?" he said vaguely.

"I hope you can do something about the game, Mr. Anderson," I said. I had my mind on it. "The whole idea is to play against another team—people you don't know, and who don't know you."

"You think they were easy on you in Pontiac?" he asked. He was staring at the cheerleaders' uniforms.

"No," I admitted.

"Well, I'll try," he said. He could see how concerned I was. "I may have to speak to the commissioner."

"That would be fine," I said.

CHAPTER 28

O n the day of the Cleveland game we rode into Detroit by bus, two of them. The rookies kept together, and they got in the second bus. The team was dressed in street clothes, with ties, and almost everyone wore blazers, the regulars with the Lion insignia, a striding lion, snarling, below the breast pocket.

Brettschneider sat on the broad backseat of the bus and read out loud the horoscopes from the morning paper. His own was, "Have a day of relaxation and fun." The players supplied him with their birth months, and he looked them up and read the prognostications. Mine was, "Gad about socially, for today you will be at your best."

He read aloud the daily joke: "They call them bikinis 'cause they hardly cover the girls atoll." A groan went up. Then we had the daily quiz. "Here's a tough one you may want to come back to later," said Brettschneider. "Who said: 'Give me liberty or give me death'?"

Someone said from the back of the bus, "Karras...talking about freedom to say any fool thing that crosses his mind."

With the first game at hand, Alex Karras's name had come up bitterly and increasingly as the team was finding it hard to accept the fact that because of his year's suspension for gambling it was going to perform without his extraordinary skills.

His presence had not only been missed on the field but also in the social life of the training camp — particularly in the dining room, where he put on his skits and monologues, constantly banging the water glass for attention. He had an absolute flow of free association, and his fantasies seemed to spring forth, never set pieces, but spontaneous and extemporized. In California, the following year, when he had been reinstated in the league, I heard him bang his water glass and rise in the role of a high-school coach at the team dinner following a disastrous year. He said, "Thank you…ah…for your…" Then undecided *what* he was thankful for, he looked bleakly out over the dining room through the large black spectacles that gave him such an unsuspecting professorial look. His inflection as the high-school coach was perfect: a somewhat high, nervous, ingratiating voice, not quite a whine, sometimes infused with an abrupt and false boom of confidence—his palms turned up as if the disaster was simply a question of fate.

"We had our problems this year," he said. "For example, we didn't have enough helmets to go around and some of the fellows had to wear coal scuttles. Then, we had the big problem over the shoes, that time we took a trip to play against the Highland Cream Teachers, and the football shoes didn't arrive in the team equipment trunks. The fact was that the team trunks didn't put in an appearance either. Mr. Friday Macklem—where's Mr. Macklem? *There* he is, down at the end, good to have you with us, Friday—well, Friday made the sort of mistake we're all liable to make and he sent the team trunks to Sioux Falls, where he thought we were playing against one of the junior high schools there. That was the mistake. We played Sioux Falls *last* year. We got beat something horrible. I don't know why Friday had it on his mind to send the team trunks to that place rather than to Beverly, Ohio, which is where the Highland Cream school was waiting for us. We stood around on the field for the longest time waiting for the team trunks, and naturally they never turned up. So we played the Cream team in street clothes. Most of the fellows not wanting to get their clothes mussed up or their shoes stepped on, we did not play an especially 'hard-nosed' type of game. We got beat horrible.

"Of course," said Karras, raising a finger for emphasis, "there were some bright moments during the season, very bright. Well, there was a bright moment when the team bus broke down on Route 62, twenty-seven miles from the Pillsbury High School field. They had three All-States in their backfield and if we'd ever got there we would have been beat horrible. There were some other bright moments. But I think the time has come to award the Dan LaRose Memorial Trophy for the Most Desire Shown by a Player on the Pompano High School Team. As you know, the award has been vacant for the past three years—that is, we, the coaches, had a little difficulty finding someone who measured up to the qualities of the late Dan LaRose, whose memory we honor with this grand trophy. Dan, as you know, died of shingles." Karras rapped his glass sharply. "We will all bow our heads in memory of Dan LaRose."

During these monologues the players would drift in to eat, some carrying their empty trays off when they were done, but almost everyone stayed. If Karras wasn't on his feet, the latecomers would say, "Has Alex done anything yet?" pleased to hear if he hadn't and that they were in time. They'd say: "He's a riot, that cat."

When Karras involved the players and the rookies in his skits, calling on them for a speech, they would rise, caught up in the spirit, and do their best. He called on Friday Macklem to explain about the team trunks; also he asked Les Bingaman, the "principal of Pompano High," to say a few words. Often, those called on who were not equipped with such a free flow of imagination would rise half out of their chairs, groping for words, and would murmur, "For Chrissake, Alex," and sit down.

Sometimes, though, the performers were inspired. When I heard the high-school monologue, which was delivered in the team dining room at Ricky's in Palo Alto, California, where the Lions were preparing for two games on the coast, Karras called on a rookie to speak as the elected captain of next year's Pompano High football "aggregation."

"Let's hear it for the new captain!" Karras called, beating his water glass with a spoon.

Dutifully, we applauded. I was a visitor there in Palo Alto for just a day or so, looking in on my old teammates, and I never caught the rookie's name. He rose slowly, his features constricted as he thought of what he might say. I expected him to murmur, "For Chrissake, Alex," and sit down. But instead, he blurted out, "I don't want to be captain," and in the burst of laughter he found time to build a notion, a line of attack.

"I don't want to throw a wrench into the works," he said, "and disappoint all you folks at this fine dinner—but the fact is I came to Pollapo High…"

"Pompano," corrected Karras.

"…Pompano High to concentrate on my music studies. I was coming along just fine on the violin. Then, in one of those beatings we got last year—the one against the high school in Marietta—I lose the use of the forefinger and thumb of my left hand." He held up his hand with the appropriate fingers curled out of sight. He was in control, knowing just where he was going, and enjoying himself. "So I take up the trombone," he said. "I could hold it all right, and pump the slide with my right hand. Then the team gets beat horrible in Duluth and some big crud steps on my right hand and there go three of *those* fingers and I can't work the trombone slide properly. Well, I take up the saxophone. It hangs from a ribbon around my neck, you know, and I got three fingers on my left hand going for me, and two on the right to play the keys. So I'm coming along fine on the sax, playing some simple tunes with some easy fingering, when in the next game the team gets beat horrible and I get me such a fat lip they feed me through a tube and they tell me my jaw's broke. They wire it up so's I can play football, but there's no more saxophoning. I still got my right arm going good, and two fingers on it that work, so I take up the gong, the chimes, and some of those percussion instruments that you can beat, holding the stick or the mallet in the two fingers of my right hand. But then in Beverly, Ohio, in that game where the team trunks don't arrive, I get that arm snapped. So all I got left going for me are my *feet*. What I wanted to tell at this dinner is that I'm continuing my music studies and using those feet to pump the organ for Mrs. Ritchie in the Baptist Church down on Elm Street. The fact is that I'd lose the use of those feet if I played one more year with the Pompano team. That'd finish up my music studies for sure. What would I tell Mom? So I feel I must decline the honor of being captain."

The rookie sat down to a storm of applause.

Karras was delighted. He rapped his glass. "Well, this is sad news," he said. He shook his head. "We've heard the word 'quitter' in this room. I *was* going to award the Dan LaRose Memorial Trophy for the Most Desire Shown by a Player on the Pompano High School Team, and the scroll that goes with it, to the new captain. I guess, under the circumstances, we had better sing the school anthem. Will you please join me in the school anthem."

He rapped his glass and sang in a keening, desperately high voice:

Pompano High, by God,
Fairest of them all...

My year at Detroit, the previous year, I heard so much about Karras that I felt I knew him. I referred to him by his first name. On the bus into Detroit I said to the player next to me, "Well, we're going to miss old Alex this afternoon." The player shrugged. He was Dave Lloyd, the big linebacker from Georgia who said, "Welcome to pro ball" when he smacked me down in my first scrimmage. I could not remember many other words from him. He was the antithesis of Alex Karras. He was a loner, who sat by himself in the dining room and kept clear of the cliques. So there were rumors about him — one of them, of course, that he had killed a man. He had worked a cattle ranch in the West, and he was supposed to have found a ranch hand fooling with his girl under a chuck wagon — that was what they said; it had happened a few years before — and he had hauled this cowboy out and cuffed the life out of him. He seemed a gentle man to me, with a curious habit of nodding whenever he smiled. On the bus trip he told me that what he liked most about playing for Detroit was being left to himself. He appreciated that. At Cleveland, where he had first come up to the pros, it wasn't possible to walk down a corridor without having the coaches leap out at him to quiz him on his game assignments. It was rough on the nerves.

I had my mind on the upcoming game — thinking about my plays — and it was a relief to sit next to someone so quiet.

At first, it was more relaxed on the bus than I had thought it was going to be—with much less tension than there had been on the bus to Pontiac. The players talked easily. Behind me, Brettschneider was talking about an old girlfriend of his who sold yo-yos on the road—a particular model that lit up when it reached the bottom of the string. He was a good storyteller; in the rear of the bus the players leaned over the backs of their seats to listen to him.

But then what was in the back of everyone's mind came rapidly to the fore. As we entered the outskirts of Detroit a silence descended on the bus, quite abruptly, as if we'd suddenly been asphyxiated by the thought of what was coming—thirty men swayed by the bus's motion staring straight at the back of the seat in front of them; it was not the silence of the dumb: the tension was palpable—everyone so keyed up that finally a player could no longer contain himself and he'd bark out, "Get it up, *Detroit!*" and that would set off an explosion of feet stamping on the bus floor and a babble of exhortations, and then just as abruptly the silence would descend again, the quiet bus rocking along, so that one thought of a herd of aroused animals propelled by some nameless dread into a momentary, noisy flurry of motion and milling, and then motionless again, yet still tense, the big heads watching.

The players never tired of talking about the phenomenon of tension building up on the day of a game. If a team was "up," it could perform prodigies, and each ballplayer would be swept along in the effort, playing better than he could even imagine, until everything he did seemed performed in an atmosphere of exhilaration. Before the Thanksgiving Day Green Bay game the year before, when they had won one of their great victories, the team said that the tension had built up so that they could hardly breathe—it was like a ground mist around them—and George Wilson, who usually gave a little locker-room talk to build them up just before they went out on the field, knew that he could break the extraordinary tension if he fooled with it, or said too much. So he called out, "OK, let's get 'em!" quite softly, but hard, and the team rushed out and played such an extraordinary game that the Green Bay players kept looking at them oddly, as if they suspected them of sniffing some sort of elixir.

Sensing the tension, and being part of it oneself, was not necessarily pleasurable. It was trying and difficult to get through the hours before a game, and the players adopted different habits to cope with the wait. Some preferred to go off by themselves. At the nine-o'clock breakfast one could see them eating the game-day steaks and the honey—the sauces locked away—seated almost in the bishops' section of the dining room to remain separate. I was one of them. The reason for our apartness, I think, was a fruitless attempt to keep time from passing. Involvement with others seemed to make the time go quickly, and one would look at one's watch suddenly in the middle of a conversation or a bridge game to find that a great, uncontrolled gulp of time had gone, and that the final confrontation was that much closer. One wanted time *stopped,* at least I did. It seemed to go slower for me if I kept to myself, yawning cavernously, almost caving in on the hollowness I felt in my stomach, and staring every once in a while at the sweep of the second hand on my watch in some woebegone sense that I could control time by keeping an eye on it.

As the day moved on—despite my concern—I became aware of another drift, this a slow, universal move toward the confrontation in Detroit Stadium. In their homes fans were beginning to think about the game, and the officials were packing their striped shirts in kit bags; as we set out for the stadium by bus, so were the Browns sitting around in their Detroit hotel, their bus waiting for them down on the street. It was often a slow, meandering movement, like the progress of a pair of amoebas— often some element of the whole lingering behind (a player walking back across a hotel lobby to buy gum)—but it was always an inexorable motion toward confrontation. Finally the two teams would walk down a corridor and be in a locker room just a couple of *walls* away. Ultimately the confrontation was actual: like hideous magi the Browns were sprung up just a yard away across a line of scrimmage, with all their heft and skill bent on obliteration of the people opposite, who were us.

Other players craved the confrontation and they did what they could to make the time pass—they slept, or organized card games, or there was conversation.

The year after my participation I went down to Philadelphia one weekend to watch the team play the Eagles. After the game-day breakfast with them in the hotel, John Gordy took me up to his room. Alex Karras was his roommate.

Gordy said, "Alex will be telling stories, or doing some damn thing that'll keep our minds occupied. There'll be a bunch of guys up there."

"He takes the day of the game calmly?" I asked.

"Hell no," Gordy said. "He gets sick before every game — violently."

"Well," I said tentatively, "why don't we drop in on Friday, or somebody else. Friday, if pushed, can talk enough to keep one's mind occupied...."

"Alex will be all right," Gordy said.

There were some other players sitting around the room — Terry Barr, Jim Gibbons, and Gary Lowe. Karras was lying on his bed staring up at the ceiling through his big horn-rimmed glasses. His torso was enormous. In his self-deprecatory manner he used to say that if the rest of him was in proper proportion to his torso he'd be eight feet tall. On the field he ran, his teammates said of him, like a "mad duck," but they used to swear softly thinking of his ability.

I had seen him once the year before at the training camp; he was standing in the corridor down from my room, holding his young son, who was just learning to walk, by the hand. He was wearing Bermuda shorts, and what struck me was that the conformation of both father and son was exactly the same — the big torso and the stubby legs, natural in his baby son, but surprising to see in the father, as if in fact Karras was a blown-up image of the boy, done by hauling trick mirrors around. What destroyed the similarity was a cigar set immediately in the center of Karras's mouth, with his lips pursed around it, so that it seemed a comic prop. But the jaunty angle of the cigar didn't disguise his gloom. He was an outsider that year. The players nodded, and called to him in false gaiety. It was obviously difficult for him, and he never came out again.

He also had an uncomfortable year with the Detroit management and the commissioner's office. Good behavior was a prerequisite of his being allowed back to play for the Lions. Both the management and the league disapproved of Karras's ownership of a bar called Lindell A.C. His partners were suspected of underworld links; the place had a flavor and a clientele which were suspicious. Karras was urged to give up both his partners and his ownership of the bar—the intimation being that reinstatement might be impossible if he didn't. Karras was furious. The guarded remark was not one of his traits; nor guile. The lack of these got him into trouble in the first place. "It's normal to make a small bet on yourself," he had said in a radio interview, which, since league regulations prohibited gambling, had forced Commissioner Rozelle's hand and led to Karras's suspension. His banishment did not change his ways; he chafed under it. His defense of his ownership of his little bar was vociferous, and he said the choice of his friends was his own, and not a concern of the league's. The dialogue often got into the papers. His teammates shook their heads when they read about him. They said, "What he says is honest and honorable—but why, just for once, can't he keep his goddamn mouth shut?"

Nor was the Lion management particularly pleased with Karras's choice of professions during his banishment. He had a short career in wrestling, which—as one might expect from Karras—was stormy enough to keep the front office on its toes. For one of his matches he was scheduled to fight Richard Afflis, a former lineman on the Green Bay Packers, who had moved on to villainous roles in the morality spectacle of big-time contemporary wrestling. Afflis fought under the name Dick the Bruiser, and his trademark in the ring was a ferocious countenance usually covered with blood, in fact some sort of red liquid, cow's blood, perhaps, which flowed from a reservoir in a large patch he wore up on his forehead.

A week before the fight Afflis turned up in Karras's saloon to shout obscenities in what was thought to be a publicity stunt to promote the match, and probably was, until things suddenly got out of hand. There was a midget friend of Karras's in the saloon, a forty-three-pounder named Major Little, whose return fire of verbal abuse finally ignited

Dick the Bruiser, and a brawl erupted. The police were called, and the Bruiser, who was wielding a pool cue, was wrestled into submission by eight policemen, one of whom suffered a fractured wrist. They were able to truss him up, binding his hands and feet, and then they moved him out onto the sidewalk, clumsily, like men carrying a large rolled-up carpet, to await the police wagon.

A week later, fed with details on the saloon brawl, a big crowd turned up in Detroit's Olympia to watch the fight—the main event on a card which included Doctor Big Bill Miller, the Sheik, Kit Fox, Moose Evans, and others—many in the general admission seats armed with dried peas to wing at the villains, particularly Dick the Bruiser.

Once again, the midget, Major Little, had a fateful hand in the proceedings. From his front-row seat his height restricted his view of things to the wooden underpinnings of the ring, so in the third or fourth minute of the bout, after fruitlessly trying to see what was happening, he clambered up onto the apron and into the ring itself and crouched in a corner, his back up against the ring post, for a view that though unobstructed was certainly close to. Karras, up to that point, had performed creditably: he had tossed the Bruiser out of the ring four times, and had been tossed out once himself, and he had hit the Bruiser's patch with sufficient force to get the cow's blood dribbling down. He had been less successful at looking fierce. With his glasses off his large, professional face, he simply looked puzzled, and then dismayed, when the shrill imprecations suddenly rose startlingly close at hand, and he looked to see his friend, the midget, up in the ring shrieking at the Bruiser. His attention wandered, and he turned and made some shooting motions with his hands. He shouted, "Major, God damn it, get on down out of there!" his back now turned to the Bruiser, who loomed up close and then in an apparent departure from the script, which usually calls for the villain's defeat, he rushed at Karras from behind and grasped his neck in what is called in the trade an "Adam's-apple choke hold." The Bruiser persevered: he got Karras down and pinned him, and the fight, which was for one fall, was awarded him, his hand raised aloft in a rain of dried peas.

With all this going on, Karras's chances of reinstatement seemed slim. But then he began to change. His teammates said it was his love of football which made him curb his tongue and improve his conduct. He got out of wrestling. Stories about him disappeared from the papers. Finally he quietly gave up his partnership in the bar, and a year from the date of his suspension he was called in by Commissioner Rozelle and reinstated.

"Has he changed?" I had asked Gordy as we walked into the room.

"He's just the same," Gordy said. "But he'd have done a lot to get back—he wanted to so much."

Gordy introduced me to him, and Karras stuck out a hand, remaining absolutely flat where he was on the bed.

I wished him luck that afternoon in the Eagle game. I found a chair in the corner and sat down. He raised up slowly and looked down between his feet at the television set against the wall opposite the foot of his bed. It was on. The sets were almost automatically turned on as soon as one walked into a hotel room, flicked on like pulling up a window shade, not because there was a specific program to see, but to create a second window in those airless rooms to glance at as one might glance out the real window at the walls of the air shaft opposite. "Look at that," Karras said. He was staring moodily at the image. An advertisement was showing—a young man in sharkskin trousers and a yachting jumper sitting on a boulder with the surf piling around, with a girl in close to him, and he was inhaling deeply on a cigarette. "Look at that guy," said Karras. "They always have good-looking guys puffing on cigarettes. They put cigarettes in Milt Plum's mouth and snap color pictures of him for the big magazines and Milt doesn't even smoke—he hardly knows how to hold a cigarette. They had to *teach* him. What about me? I'm a longtime smoker, known how to hold a cigarette since I was eight, I inhale and all, and when the wind's down and I get a little practice, with the pressure really on me, I can put together a smoke ring, think of that. Why not me, then, instead of Plum? The reason is they only pick the good-looking guys, and the good-looking girls. They look at me, blowing away on those smoke rings, and they think, well, he's OK on those rings, but he's got the face of a mechanic who's got squashed working under a large touring car. There ought to be a union of us ugly cruds. I'd like to see an ad, a TV ad, in which this great mountain of a girl comes out, just horrible-looking, with a name like Betty Home, and she's advertising nylons, y'see, and she draws on a pair of nylons over these enormous fat thighs. 'Sheer,' she says, working her lips up the way those thin models do."

"You're beautiful, Alex," someone said.

"Who am I kidding?" Karras said. "I know I'm not very pretty, but then the girls I talk to aren't very pretty either." He groaned. "Even with them I can't make out. I couldn't make out if I had the Hope Diamond hanging from my neck." He dropped back on the bed and stared up at the ceiling. "It wasn't always like that. In my other lives I had some grand times."

It was Karras's fantasy that he had lived a succession of different lives — stretching far back into the past. He had been, among other things, an aide-de-camp to both General Washington and Adolf Hitler.

"What about Hitler?" one of the players asked. "What was your impression?"

"Hitler was not an ordinary Joe," Karras said expansively. "You knew that when you were around him as much as I was. He had this obsession to hold his breath for more than three minutes."

"No! Could he do it?"

"Nowhere near. He got red in the face very quickly, and there'd be this little popping sound when the air came rushing out. He never lasted more than eight or nine seconds — shortest-breathed man I ever saw."

"How about the others? Did you know Rommel, Hess, Goering, and all those...?"

"Certainly, I knew all those cats, Rundstedt, Goering — Bavaria Fats, we called him — and Rommel. He had a terrible weak stomach, Rommel did. He used to get sick all the time. I'd come rushing up to him in the morning to fling the salute at him, and say, 'Hello, hello, heil, heil, good *morn*in', gener'l,' and he'd get sick. Hitler never trusted him for that reason. Why, he'd come striding up to Rommel at head-quarters and say, 'A fine day to mount ze attack against the filthy *Schwein-hund* Monty, the Britisher.' Rommel, he'd lean over and get sick into one of those tall nickel-plated upright ashtrays you find in the smoking section of the railroad coaches — the kind with a button on the side of the stand you push and the trap door opens and the cigar falls down. I carried one of these things around for Rommel when he was at head-quarters, ready, with my thumb on the button. Hitler was suspicious of those ashtrays. 'What is that thing?' he'd always say. I think he had an idea it was a bomb. 'It's an ashtray,' I'd say. 'It's General Rommel's ash-tray.' Hitler'd take a long look, and he'd say, 'Why doesn't the general carry a smaller model around — that thing's three feet tall. What's wrong with those little *pocket* ashtrays, the kind with a hotel name on the bottom? Besides,' Hitler said, 'he doesn't smoke, Rommel, what does he need a big thing like that for if he doesn't smoke, answer me *that!*' 'Well,' I said quickly, 'the general smokes *hemp*.' 'Oh well, no won-der,' Hitler says. 'Why not say so in the beginning?'"

"What about Eva Braun? Tell us about her."

"Eva Braun was my sister."

"No!"

"She was. You may not think so, my looking the way I do, but in that life I was smart-looking, a blond cat, with boots that went up clear to the crotch, shiny as brass, and in company people was always saying, 'Who's that good-looker?' Real Aryan I was."

"Tell us more about Eva."

"She and Hitler didn't get along at all."

"No!"

"My sister had this terrible laugh, a sort of cackle, and when Hitler came fooling around, pushing that mustache at her, why, she'd let out this cackle. Hitler could never figure why she was laughing. 'What's wrong?' he'd ask, looking behind him, thinking some clown back of them was making faces. Her cackling was horrible. 'You laughing at one of Bavaria Fats's jokes?' he'd ask."

Gibbons said, "History books say they were quite a pair."

"That was for appearances," Karras said. "They had to show that Hitler had normal feelings for women. So the public-relations people took a bunch of pictures of the two of them together, she standing under a waterfall bare-ass, and Hitler next to her, getting his uniform wet. You ever see Hitler bare-ass? The answer is no. The fact was, and everybody around headquarters knew it, that Hitler was a woman — my aunt, if you really want to know, Aunt Hilda, and quite a trial she turned out to be to the rest of the family."

"Did Eva know about that?"

"The fact is she *didn't*. And you know what fooled her?"

"What?"

"That mustache. You'd think it was false, Aunt Hilda being a woman and all. Well, that mustache was absolutely real. Aunt Hilda shaved five times a day. After a while Eva got over her cackle, and toward the end she fell for Aunt Hilda. No one wanted to disillusion her, so they got a marriage going there in the Berlin bunker. The Russians were turning up, so the pair committed suicide, which was maybe good for Eva. She'd have found out —"

"That Hitler was Aunt Hilda."

"Her own *mother!*" said Karras. "Aunt Hilda was Eva's mother, you see. Eva didn't know that, of course. She thought she was an orphan. And guess who Eva's *father* was?"

"Who? Bavaria Fats?" someone suggested.

"You're looking at him," said Karras comfortably from his bed.

"You! Come on," said Gary Lowe. "Eva Braun was your sister."

"Both sister *and* daughter," Karras said proudly. "Adolf Hitler was my wife."

"That's horrible," said Gordy.

We sat there reflecting on the tangled family tree of the Nazi hierarchy, the television set murmuring slightly in the background.

"Well, I hope things weren't as horrible as that in General Washington's time," Gordy finally said.

Karras stirred. "General Washington was beautiful. I was at Valley Forge, you know, real cold there, feeding on owls' heads, we were, and such things, and the general would come through the campfires and strike these poses and he'd say, 'Men, we will endure,' things like that. He was just beautiful. But they get a lot of things wrong about him. You recall the cherry-tree story?"

We nodded.

"He *had* to cut that tree down. What did it have but the Dutch elm disease, easiest thing in the world to see, that cherry tree was top-heavy with it, and if Washington hadn't fetched an ax to it, everything around would have been infected."

"Why didn't George tell his father that?" Gordy asked. "He'd have saved himself a whipping."

"Young George had false teeth, you know, a full set, even as a young boy, and when his daddy called him in to ask him about the cherry tree, he *tried* to explain about the Dutch elm disease, but out came a lot of clacking. Washington's teeth fitted badly, and when he spoke he either did this clacking, or sometimes a whistle, a high whistle." Karras demonstrated the whistle. "So when his daddy said, 'Who cut that tree down?' he was only able to understand through all that clacking and whistling that his son, George, had, but he couldn't understand the *reason*. So he took a switch to him. Beat him half crazy."

"How could you understand him saying 'We will endure' and things like that at Valley Forge," someone asked, "if Washington had this speech difficulty?"

"We *couldn't* understand him," explained Karras. "But he got into all these poses, you see. He'd stand around among the campfires, and when he crossed the Delaware he struck a fine pose *that* time, with his foot up there on the bow, so you always knew what the guy had in mind. You know actually who spoke the Farewell Address?"

"Who?"

"You're looking at him," said Karras. "What happened was that I stood right behind the general up there on the platform and I spoke the words for him. He was like a wood dummy, clacking his jaw, but you couldn't tell unless you were right up close that it was me."

"How about his staff? How did they understand his orders?"

"Well, lipreading—they were all deaf-mutes," Karras went blithely on. "That's not generally known, but Washington's closest people—Lafayette (French Fats, we called him), General Gates, and the rest of them—they could hear nothing; but they could *lip-read*. That's why in the portraits of Washington all the generals and the staff people are standing around staring at him. You hear that's devotion they was showing. Crap. They was looking at his mouth in case Washington had it in mind to say something, so they could begin their lipreading and hop to it if there was something to be done."

There had been some other lives Karras hinted at: he had been something during the Civil War—he wasn't sure what. Something low, he thought, a camp follower perhaps.

Between lives, he told us, he would find himself on an airliner flying in heavy cloud banks, or often above them, with the sun shining. The ground was always out of sight, though he would press his forehead against the windows to look for it far down through the clouds, never succeeding, though often the clouds fell away into deep valleys that seemed to drop for miles. The flight was always very smooth and long, with pretty stewardesses coming by and leaning over to offer beef bouillon, and when the evening came their trays had tall drinks on them. He was always very tired on these flights, utterly relaxed; through half-closed eyes he would watch the stewardesses in the aisle, and when they came by he would hold out his cup for the bouillon, or the tall drink if it was in the evening. On the third day, perhaps the fourth, when he was beginning to feel more lively, a mist would suddenly settle in the cabin, increasingly thick, so that it began to take on the same consistency as the clouds outside, the walls of the cabin disappearing in it, and finally the back of the seat in front of him, so that in its thickness he felt himself in the clouds themselves, the wind beginning to sweep across his face, and as he felt himself begin to fall and turn, he knew his time was coming to be someone else and he would cross his fingers and hope to Christ he wasn't going to be a goddamn jockstrap athlete again.

"Well, what would you hope to be?" Gary Lowe asked.

"How the hell do I know?" Karras said. He seemed ill-tempered suddenly. "I tell you nothing can be worse than this—lying around in a little hotel room like a bunch of cruds. Then we get out on some field and knock some guys around for a lousy pile of pennies. What sort of a life is that? It's crud," he said. He raised up off the bed. He looked very sour.

"Let's clear out of here," he said. "I got to find me a place to puke."

When we got out in the corridor, he hurried on down in front of us and began punching at the elevator button.

"That's a mood, isn't it?" I said quietly to Lowe.

"Alex is ready," Lowe said happily. "He's right as rain. He's up for the game."

"Does he mean it when he says he's going to get sick?"

"Sure he will," said Lowe. "Just as George Wilson tells us to go out there and rock them, out in the can we'll hear Alex lose his lunch. Sure. And then in five minutes he'll be out there on the field making the poor fellow from Philadelphia opposite him pay for it."

We crowded into the elevator. No one said anything going down. Karras would sit alone in the bus.

CHAPTER 29

The locker room under Tiger Stadium was a spacious square room with rows of individual dressing alcoves around the walls—a wooden seat set in back of each with a Lion helmet waiting on it, a pair of football shoes underneath, and, above, the rest of the football gear hung up on hangers. Terry Barr and I shared a cubicle. It had the Detroit pitcher Don Mossi's name on a card tacked above it. A three-legged stool stood out in front. I sat on it while Barr changed. There was not room in the cubicle for the two of us. My jersey with the zero had been laundered since the Pontiac scrimmage. Friday and his assistants had put out the uniforms at mid-morning. The big steamer trunks stood in the center of the room, the lids thrown back. Friday circled them, officious, with a big medieval prison warder's ring of keys dangling from his belt, and also a cat's cradle of extra shoelaces and chin straps, swaying as he busied himself around the locker room. The paraphernalia in his charge was varied and voluminous: once, in colder weather, I had seen a dozen or so portable hand warmers being prepared, their wicks flickering like devotional candles as they stood in rows on the floor beside the trunks.

Friday was calling for the players' valuables. Into a set of compartments in a steamer trunk went watches, wallets, rings, key chains, and also their bridgework, wrapped in tissue paper. A substantial pile of teeth came to Friday on game day. The players dressed slowly. There was plenty of time before we were due on the field for the pregame warm-up. Harley Sewell was ready first, as he always was, and he came by with his cleats crashing on the cement floor, his teeth working on a new Chiclets tablet which clicked sharply as he began to break it down to the right consistency. The locker room was quiet, hardly a word spoken, so that one heard the venetian-blind slap of shoulder pads being set in place, and then, increasingly, the sound of cleats against the cement floor as the football shoes were pulled on, and the players walked around keeping loose and in motion to calm their nerves. That was when the behemoth size of football players was most apparent—when they wandered gloomily around the confines of a locker room, their shoulders widened by the pads, and their height stilted up an inch or so by the cleated shoes. The contours of the helmet gave them another inch, so that a player who was six feet three or four, and hardly worth a glance by the fans waiting in the alleys outside the locker room, would come clanking by in gear at six feet five or six, and the fans would gawk and say to themselves, "Holy cow, well, that's something."

An hour before game time we went out for the pregame warm-up. We walked down the alley from the locker room to the back of the dugout, trotting up the wooden steps into the sunlight and onto the field. A small ragged cheer went up from the early spectators scattered through the stands. The Browns were at the far end of the field, just finishing their calisthenics. Their uniforms were brown and orange. I could not resist the assessment one remembered from schoolboy days—a long worried look to see how large the opposition was. That was always the ritual, to pile out of the school bus and inspect the team at the other end of the field. Someone would say, "Look at those guys, they're enormous, look at that one over *there*," and we would stare gloomily at some giant who afterward turned out to be ponderous and of not much use. The Lions, as we walked out, were curious—their heads all craned in the Browns' direction—but for quick assessments of skills rather than size. "There's the Big Stud," someone said at my elbow, Gibbons I think it was, and he gestured at a player going out on a pass pattern. I recognized Jimmy Brown's soft slipping motion, his feet never picked up high, almost as if gliding through the grass on skates, as he cut and gathered in the pass. He was hypnotic to watch in motion. The Brown player nearest us as he backed to the midfield stripe to practice field goals was Lou Groza, "the Toe," they called him, and we watched him, broad and heavyset, take two delicate steps and swing his foot against the ball with a *thunk* that reverberated in the overhangs of the stadium. "Nobody else can get a sound like that out of a kick," said Gibbons. "Hear that sound blindfolded and you'd know it hadda be Groza putting his foot to the ball."

Behind us Terry Barr called for a circle, and we turned away from the opposition and started the jumping jacks, calling out the cadences, the deep gruff shouts from our own people reassuring.

When we got back to the locker room a half hour remained to game time. The players slouched in the backs of their cubicles, or on the stools out front. Some lay on their backs on the floor reading the game programs, or staring up at the long fluorescent tubes that ran the length of the ceiling. Wayne Walker and John Gordy pummeled each other's shoulder pads into position with big jarring whacks. That was traditional between them. On one of the teams, Green Bay, the same ritual took place between Dan Currie and Ray Nitschke, except that in their case, after the blows to the shoulder pads, they would give each other cuffing open-palm slaps to the face, hard enough to twist the head abruptly. They would glare at each other, and then take the hate, which they had generated like clicking on a switch, out onto the field.

A few of the players began circulating, reaching into a cubicle wordlessly to shake a fellow player's hand and wish him luck. "Give 'em hell," they said to me. In the next cubicle was the Roadrunner. I looked in and said, "Good luck, Roadrunner." "I'm not nervous," he said. "I'm just scared to death." Some of the players seemed completely shaken by what faced them, even the veterans. John Gordy sat on his stool, one leg jiggling uncontrollably, his helmet between his legs like a pail into which he could be ill. He looked up when I passed by, and his hand floated up to shield a toothless, sickly grin. With the bridgework wrapped in tissue paper and put away in Friday's valuables boxes, the features of many of the players had changed just infinitesimally: cheeks seemed slightly more sunken, a mouth would have a pucker, and with a smile the vacant gaps of gum would show abruptly and surprisingly.

Milt Plum stood up and began throwing the ball — short, stiff passes half the length of the locker room, in the quiet the laces whistling before the loud slap of the ball into the receiver's hands.

I went back in front of my cubicle and sat back down on the floor. We had about ten minutes to go. Then George Wilson began to talk to us. It was not really a speech. He walked among us as lost in thought as he often seemed on the practice field, and occasionally he would speak, softly and abstractedly, almost as if musing the shopworn maxims to himself: "Just get the idea we can go out there and go all the way," he said. He walked around behind the team trunks. I was lying on my back. I couldn't see him, but I could hear him say, "Keep your lanes on all teams." That was in reference to the defensive specialist teams — the kickoff, punt, and field-goal teams. He came into view again. "Be careful of foolish penalties," he said. "Walk away from a punch." Plum had stopped throwing the ball. It was absolutely quiet, except for the humming of the air conditioners and the dripping of water in the shower room. We had just minutes to go. Down at the end of the room Wilson was saying, "If something goes wrong at the beginning, don't let it bother you. Keep up the momentum." He came by our end again. "Don't let up. Give it sixty minutes." He had a clipboard in his hand. "OK," he said. "Here are the two teams. On defense..." He read off the names rapidly. A thick growling cheer went up. "Now, the offense..." Another cheer went up when he finished the list. An official put his head in the door and said it was time. "OK," said Wilson. The players were all on their feet. I had the sense of a parachute drill, seeing everyone standing up in the heavy gear and beginning to shuffle for the locker-room door. I heard Wilson calling behind us: "Don't fool around. We want this ball game. Go out and play sixty minutes."

We were delayed in the tunnel behind the dugout. The entire team was introduced to the crowd—which took time—each running up the dugout steps and out to the midfield stripe as his name and college were called out over the loudspeaker system. My name was not called. When they had all gone out, I walked out to the bench with Friday and his assistants. Friday sensed my discomfiture. The stands were almost filled. The capacity was over fifty thousand, and on that bright afternoon, with so many there to get their first look of the season at the Lions, I imagined them nudging each other and pointing. I walked with my head down. "Limp a little," Friday said.

"You think Wilson's going to let me in?" I asked. "This is awfully serious stuff."

"He's his own boss," Friday said.

The game began, all of us standing on the sidelines to watch the kickoff, and Detroit scored almost immediately. The Roadrunner caught a pass, the first touchdown he had ever scored in the pro leagues, and he came off the field with his face shining with excitement. He said, "Hot dawg," and he rolled his eyes up. Everyone crowded around. He had gathered in his pass about the fifth play of the game, before anyone had had a chance to settle down.

I did not find it easy to follow the game from the bench. The players, milling in the ruck of a play, were difficult to spot against the multicolored background of the stands opposite, and the intricate patterns of their maneuvers were not apparent. Even the coaches, standing up on the sidelines, often seemed confused if the angle of their vision was difficult, and they'd call out, "What the hell was *that* play?"

Much of the direction of the team was carried on by the coaches up in the rim of the stadium in the spotters' booth. Aldo Forte and Scooter McLean were usually up there, and Don Doll for the defense, and they were connected by phone to the little lightweight collapsible table in front of the bench where they could get on the line to Wilson, or the quarterbacks.

I found myself watching George Wilson. His absorption in the game was complete. He strode up and down the sidelines, his head turned to the field, so that he tripped over telephone and television cables, and swore, and then caromed into his players. He followed opposite the play, so that occasionally he was far down toward the goal line, leaning forward to shout and flap his arms at his players, and often at the referees. Occasionally, he joined his coaches, and their heads would bend over the play charts. Once in a while Wilson picked up the phone to his staff spotting the plays from the top of the stadium. But most of the time I was possessed by the idea that the action on the field was beyond his control, that the triumphs and tribulations of his men rolled on impervious to his presence. What he shouted out to them through cupped hands was not arcane instruction, but exactly what the spectators up in the stadium were shouting—"Hold 'em, gang!" or "Block that kick!" or "Watch the bomb!"—exhortations which not only were commonplace but in the din drifting down from the stands doubtless went unheard.

When Detroit scored a touchdown he made a stiff uppercut of satisfaction, the force of it wheeling his body completely around. "A bitch. A goddamn bitch!" he called to Bingaman. He leaned forward and shouted happily at the offensive team as it came toward the bench, pounding his palm with his fist. When adversity came, he was hardly able to control himself: the temptation must have been overwhelming to tip out onto the field and try to take matters into his own hands. What he did was lean over the sidelines as if an invisible fence were there, and bray. I began to understand why Paul Brown called each play and sent it in to his quarterback: it was not only to keep a grip on the proceedings but so that he had a sense of expectation with each play rather than surprise. It was not easy for a coach to get through a game. Green Bay had a coach, Red Cochran, whose absorption was so complete and frenzied that the head coach, Lombardi, relegated him to the spotters' booth, where he tore up clipboards and play charts when things were going badly, rather than chancing his behavior down on the sidelines.

In varying degrees all the players were caught up in the game. I sat on the bench next to Jim Martin. He kept up a constant roar. Behind me I could hear the swish-swish of the skirts and the rustling pompons of the cheerleaders. They weren't more than ten or fifteen feet behind the team bench. I turned around to catch a look at them. They were facing the field, a long string of them. Under orders never to be in repose, the girls kept up a slow prance in place, the pompons whisking steadily. The one immediately behind me looked at me gravely. I had a glimpse of her eyes, a mouth that shone smooth with pale lipstick, a serene, bored face above the leggy, tart motion, endlessly in place, of her cheerleader prance, and then Martin cuffed me hard on the shoulder pads.

"Keep your mind on the game," he said. I began to grin at him, thinking he wasn't serious, but he was furious. "What do you mean looking behind you like that? What's going on that concerns you is in *front* of you." His voice shook, he was so angry. "Concentrate," he said. "Concentrate all the time on that game out there."

When the next time-out was called, and things were quiet on the field, Martin told me that coaches would get their cheerleaders up close behind a rival bench — anything to take the edge off the opposition's concentration — and have them whisper things, telephone numbers, so that the players would start thinking about where they could find a pencil stub. George Halas of the Bears once put a brass band immediately behind a rival bench, and before it was moved under complaint the players wore their helmets against the noise, which was full tilt, and to protect their ears from the trombone slides that slid between them as they sat on the bench.

The time-out ended. Martin leaned forward and began yelling again. Lucien Reeberg came off the field toward us. He was limping badly. "Jesus!" he said.

"Wipe it off!" Martin shouted at him.

"Jesus," Reeberg said. "I'm getting hit bad — I don' understand how."

"Try to figure it...."

"I don' know. I'm being hit from the side...."

"Well, figure it out," Martin shouted. "You gotta *head* on those fat shoulders."

Reeberg shook his head.

"Figure it, baby," Martin said more sympathetically. "If they're double-teaming you, go low. What is it?"

Reeberg looked at him mournfully. "I'm near *kilt*," he said. "Jesus." He went looking for the trainer, moving his bulk gingerly.

Martin snorted. He kept opening and shutting his hands. It was very hard for him to sit on the bench. When the players came off the field, he was up to shout at them, and to the platoon going out he railed, "Work! Work! Work!"

John Gonzaga came off the field and sat down on the other side. He was wobbling on his feet as he came. Martin saw him, and shouted for Doc Thompson. There was a thickening welt above his eye. The doctor stared at it. "Tough day at the office," Gonzaga said calmly. His voice was very soft. When Thompson had finished ministering to him, Gonzaga said, "I didn't know from nothing out there. When I got hit, I reached out and followed Gibbons into the huddle like he was a Seeing Eye dog, just stumbling along after him, following that blue jersey. Then in the huddle my head cleared. It's crazy how you keep going no matter what."

"You moving them?" It was Martin leaning across.

"Someone's being moved out there," Gonzaga said, grinning enigmatically.

John Simon, the big rookie defensive end from Miami, came off. He had tackled Jimmy Brown, and he said it was like wrestling with the front end of a truck. He shrugged his shoulders.

"The mother went down, didn't he?" Martin shouted at him.

"Sure," Simon said, "sure." He was not sure how to react.

Just then Detroit lost the ball on a fumble, and Wilson was shouting, "Defense! Defense! Get on out there!"

"There's no mother better'n you are, Simon!" Martin yelled after him. "Half ass," he mumbled to himself.

It was exhausting sitting next to Martin. I went and found a place at the other end of the bench. But then Jim Gibbons came off the field and he said, very apologetically, that the end of the bench, that particular seat, was lucky for him, or at least it had been so far that afternoon. One heard of superstitions of that sort. Eddie Khayat of the Philadelphia Eagles had a fixation that the ladles in the water bucket should never be crossed. He was forever looming over the water bucket, snatching it away from the water boy, to get the ladles straightened out. Such things were important. So I slid off the bench and crouched in the grass beside Gibbons.

"We're not going so good for you," Gibbons said.

Groza of Cleveland had kicked a field goal and the score was 7–3. The team was still three touchdowns away from my being allowed to play.

"I'm not sure I'm sad or happy," I said.

But then, just before the half ended, Detroit scored again, which made the chances seem less remote. As the gun went off, and the players rose from the bench, and we began trotting for the dugout entrance at the end of the field, I could feel the nerves begin to collect.

Anderson, the general manager, was waiting just inside the door of the locker room. He motioned me over.

"Listen," he said. "What's the arrangement that's been made?"

I said, "If Detroit is twenty points ahead or so, and the game is out of reach of the other people, then it'll be OK to go in. It doesn't seem very likely at the moment."

"Well, it's off," Anderson said.

"What do you mean?"

"Like I said. It's off," Anderson repeated. "I called up the commissioner, Rozelle, and he didn't go for it. It's OK to have you suited up and all, but you can't go in. I already told Wilson."

"What did he say?" I asked.

"Who? Wilson? He didn't say anything."

"Well, that's a hell of a thing," I said. "What am I all dressed up for if not to play?"

Anderson shrugged. "I called the commissioner. I had to. There might have been hell to pay."

I went back to my cubicle. Barr was sitting in front of it. "What's up?" he asked.

"Anderson won't let me play. He called the commissioner."

"What about Wilson?"

"He knows."

"If things are right," Barr said, "he'll do what he feels like."

"Maybe," I said hopefully.

Quite abruptly, with the news from Anderson, I felt an outsider. Everything remained familiar, but I was no longer a part of it. Opposite, Don Doll was in front of a blackboard, the defensive backs with him. He was chalking up diagrams. With his brown-rimmed spectacles, and his conservative gabardine suit, he could have been a college section instructor working at an equation, except that he wore his hat indoors, a brown felt hat with a red band. Just down from me Bingaman stood amidst his big linemen. "Watch the angle of pursuit," I heard him say. "Joe," he said to Schmidt, "you're calling good plays." Lucien Reeberg stood at the edge of the group. He had taken his football pants down. An enormous mottled bruise covered one thigh. He looked at it nervously. "Lord," he said. Sam Williams said, "Take a towel and wipe it off, rookie." Reeberg looked at him hopelessly. He looked as if he were going to break down and cry.

But all of this—the drama, the discussions, the locker-room bustle, the excitement that permeated even the studious attitudes of the players grouped around the blackboards—seemed far removed, and the temptation, as petulant as a schoolboy's, was to get out of uniform and return to camp.

But I told myself that there was a chance. Wilson was a man of his own convictions. Some of the players, who had heard about Anderson's edict, came by and said so. "We'll get the points, get way ahead, and you'll see," they said.

I went out to the bench without much hope. The second half progressed quickly, with Detroit doing well, its defense, as it always had been, strong and containing Cleveland, and the offense erratic but continuing to press. Then, with one minute to go in the game and Cleveland flailing around on its own ten-yard line, the Detroit team recovered a fumble from the Brown quarterback. The Lions were ahead by a good margin at the time, two touchdowns, the game won, and it would have been a propitious moment for me to go in. I was watching Wilson from my position on the bench, when suddenly he turned and looked directly at me. I could tell immediately that his mind was being tugged slightly. A grin began working at his mouth, and he looked quickly at the scoreboard clock.

My jaw went slack. As I stared at him, mesmerized, my hands grappled blindly under the bench for my helmet. Then abruptly he turned away. I never asked him why afterward. I think he saw the stunned surprise, the look of a man suddenly faced with the abyss—and that perhaps it was sympathy as much as anything which made him turn and concentrate once again on the game. He did not call back Plum. The quarterback ran out and called two running plays, and the game was over.

"He almost did it," I said to Gibbons as the gun went off. "Wilson had it in his mind. Jesus, maybe if I hadn't fouled it up so bad in Pontiac."

"There's always next week," said Gibbons helpfully. "You haven't been cut yet."

I was beginning to get over my disappointment. My heart still thumped with the exhilaration of the last minute of the game. Back in the locker room, the excitement of winning, of getting the season off to a good start, was contagious, and I joined it—whooping it up a little, and whacking people on the back.

"Why weren't you in there?" Sam Williams asked. "Feet too heavy again?"

"Hell no," I said. "The Browns weren't tough enough. You always had the game in hand. No need to send in the special reserves like me."

Lucien Reeberg was nearly overcome with excitement. He gave me a big cuff on the shoulders. "You did terrific!" he shouted.

"I didn't get in," I said.

He didn't hear me. He shouted at another rookie: "You did terrific!"

"How did you get on, Lucien?" I asked.

"I liked it!" he bellowed at me. "It was all right. Two or three plays, I could see that I could play ball up here—*measure* up. I got to the quarterback once—d'ja see that?—and he fumbled." He snapped his fingers. "Nothing to it. I got kicked in the side later, so that made a difference. But I'm three sixteen now. Ten more pounds to go and I'll be down to two ninety-six, and when I'm there I'll be faster and meaner, oh my, real *mean*." He tried to look mean, but his pleasant round face failed to accept it. "I was very happy," he rushed on. "I went out there very curious. Joe Schmidt talked me through the game. Who to watch and what. 'Watch sucker play,' he yells at me. 'Watch takeoff—don't go with him.' I do what he tells me. It works great—just beautiful." He spotted Schmidt across the locker room. "Joe *baby!*" he called out. "You are beautiful."

Schmidt, bending over and lacing up his street shoes, buffed shining black, gave him a long disdainful look.

I asked, "Nothing surprised you out there, Lucien?"

Reeberg, lowering his voice, perhaps surprised at Schmidt's coolness, said, "Well, you know something? The language. The players yell things at the referees, it's something. I thought we was going to be penalized—I mean, man, that language out there is like *blue*."

The Lions did not joke with me about my not appearing in the game. They could tell it was a disappointment. Some of us went down to Alex Karras's bar to celebrate the victory. Karras was in his place. He was in shirtsleeves behind the long bar. The Lions were not supposed to go to the Lindell A.C.—it was declared off-limits—but the rule was broken defiantly. He came out from behind the bar. A table was cleared and he sat down and talked with us. The bar was crowded, but it seemed pleasant. Karras did not talk about the game. The jukebox was turned on, and he began a comic twist dance routine. Someone at the table said that he had been in the stands that afternoon. He had kept himself under control for the first quarter—very blasé, leaning back and puffing at a cigar. But not long after, the cigar had gone out and he was leaning so far forward that his head was practically hanging in the row in front. In the second quarter, at some pivotal play, a yell erupted from him, and he began exhorting the Lions, half out of his seat, his arms flailing—causing a stir around him in the stands from people nudging their neighbors to point him out: "There's Karras—there's the reason we're not going to be copping the title *this* season."

In the last quarter he broke down completely and began crying. He took off his big horn-rimmed spectacles to mop them with a handkerchief, and they fell under his seat. He let them lie there as if the fuzzy dim world of his myopia was preferable to what he would see with them on. They were picked up for him, and the people he was with gathered around and led him away, up the aisle and out onto the ramps behind, one of them holding his spectacles.

Having heard about Karras at the ballpark, I did not mention my disappointment to anyone while we were there in his bar. I *wanted* to complain, just for the satisfaction of it, to ease the chagrin, but I thought better of it. Karras seemed recovered—good-natured enough, and happy to see his ex-teammates; there was yelling and carrying-on with him, and his hand would fly up to contain his high giggle. Often he would break away and dance strenuously to his jukebox. But it was hard to watch him without thinking of him being led from the stadium, with the people looking at him curiously, and someone behind carrying his spectacles.

CHAPTER 30

I went back to Cranbrook early. I decided to leave camp the next day. In two weeks the Lions had a big exhibition game with the New York Giants at Cleveland, part of a doubleheader, but the commissioner's edict was sure to continue. I packed that night and made reservations to leave Detroit at noon the next day. I put the football back in the suitcase, and the high-school coaching manuals on basic principles of team play, which I had not opened. There were some sweatshirts with DETROIT LIONS across the front which George Wilson had given me, and I took those, thinking how when I got back to New York the shirts would look out in the winter pickup touch football games in Central Park.

When I had packed my suitcase, I went down the dormitory corridor to look in on some of the players to say good-bye. It was quiet that night. A few of the players were already asleep. But one or two of the rooms were lively, the players still working off the excitement of the day. I joined them. Hearing that I was leaving the next day, there was some murmuring that I should stay. They knew how much I wanted to get in a league game, and they began plotting how I could be secretly inserted in the Giant game in Cleveland. "We'll just sit on ol' Milt Plum a bit, just *hem* him in on the sidelines," someone said. "And another group doing the same to Earl Morrall, and by the time they're loose, and Wilson's onto it, you can reel off a good quick series."

I knew that if such a thing was done some of them would get into trouble. The temptation was strong, and as we conspired in that small dormitory room the consideration of *writing* about such a subterfuge was almost irresistible. But it would not have sat well. I never forgot that in Pontiac, just before the scrimmage was to begin, John Gordy had shouted as the huddle broke, "Let's everyone lie down, and let him go through, let him get his touchdown." I had shouted, "No, it's got to be straight — no fake, *straight*." Gordy, with the others, not only played it straight, but he shot out of his offensive guard position with such vehemence that he bowled me over. He told me afterward that my being in there at all had upset him. Keyed up as he was by the vigor of his profession, he felt it wasn't *natural* to have an amateur like me involved. That was fooling around. There was no combining the two attitudes — it had to be one or the other.

The talk shifted to the afternoon's game. They began talking about Reeberg's play. "He had a fair afternoon with the guy opposite," someone said. "But anybody good — like Katcavage on the Giants — why the Kat'd rape him."

Just at that moment, quite abruptly, so that a sentence a player was speaking trailed off, the doorway filled, and we looked up and saw the coaches standing there — Wilson in front, Doll on one side, and the Hawk on the other, with a clipboard.

"Bed check," said Wilson.

He had the familiar glum look on his dark face that came when he was forced to do something, usually in the name of discipline, which he felt beneath his dignity.

"Anybody missing in here?" asked the Hawk. He looked at his clipboard. "Where's Whitlow? He bunks in here, doesn't he?"

"He's down taking a shower," someone said without much conviction.

The Hawk made some sort of mark on the clipboard. "That shower's pretty full up tonight, from what I've been told. There's maybe ten, twenty men must be down in there according to my records." He looked down at his clipboard. "That had to be a mighty dusty bus ride coming back from Detroit. We're going to be awful low on soap."

Nobody seemed much amused.

"Where's Morrall at?" the Hawk asked. "That him singing down in the shower?" He cocked a hand to his ear derisively. We all stared sullenly at nothing in particular.

"It's long after eleven," Wilson said. "Can't you men stick to the goddamn rules? You think the coaches like to make Holy Rollers out of you? You think it gives us some sort of goddamn pleasure?"

He turned away abruptly. We heard their footsteps go down the hall, and the murmur rise from the next room where they had stopped to check.

After a while, John Gonzaga said: "This is the time when you want to pack and go back to your wife. At least you don't get some guy turning up with a clipboard and peering into your bedroom to see if you're there."

"What are Holy Rollers?" I asked.

"That's what they call the guys doing the grass sprints," someone said. "You hang around long enough tomorrow and you'll see. The sprints are a type of punishment. It's better than a fine. But not much. A guy will miss a bed check, maybe three or four guys, like tonight, and the coaches'll put them to it the next day. It doesn't sound hard. You have to sprint for twenty yards, then on hands and knees for ten, then down and roll for ten more, then up again and sprint for twenty— keeping this up in succession down the length of the field and back until maybe you've done two hundred yards. It's sort of funny at the start, everybody leapfrogging and grinning, and the spectators all laughing and pointing. But you have to do the drill at top speed, and the rolling in particular gets you dizzy and sick feeling. There're not many who can do a hundred yards of it without puking. Then it's not so funny anymore."

"I can imagine," I said.

Someone said, "George Wilson doesn't call it but once or twice in the training season. But the guy before him, Buddy Parker, he used to have the Holy Rollers performing like it was a weekly benefit. This one time he put the entire squad to it. I've forgotten what for—it must have been bad. Bobby Layne was the team leader then, and he was madder than a tick. He had this gut that poked out, a regular pot, which made it tough on him in the rolling—but he was the leader and the toughest, and while he was rolling himself along, and leaping up and down in those sprints, he was shouting and swearing at the others to keep up with him and finish it out or he'd see to it that they never drew another breath. He pulled them all through, just like he did in the games on Sunday. Then what does Layne do but line up the Holy Roller like a platoon and he's going to march them up towards the gym, singing some damn song, just to show Buddy Parker that he hadn't broken their spirit."

"It's like some sort of bad movie," I interjected.

"Well, Parker was no mild-mannered bozo neither," the veteran went on. "He looked at this singing and marching as indicating some form of disrespect. He blew his whistle and ordered Layne and his guys to do the sprints *again*. There was damn near a mutiny. But they went through it. Layne finished the course; hardly nobody else. He wanted his men to sing and march, but they weren't so sure. And then Layne saw something."

"What was that?"

"Well, he looked over and he saw Parker standing there, calm and collected, wearing a nice shirt, all clean, and a golfing hat, and a whistle on a white cord, and I mean Layne wasn't a complete dummy. I mean it was no contest. All Parker had to do was lift that whistle a couple of inches up to his mouth to blow it, and rolling and sprinting for a hundred yards was no match for *that*. So Bobby Layne lost that one. He just trotted up towards the gym, and the others straggled along behind him."

One of the veterans stirred and recalled that at Chicago when Hank Anderson, an awesome disciplinarian, was there, recalcitrants used to run what were called "fat-man" races, and Anderson had a little wooden paddle he eased onto the posteriors of linemen going by who he felt needed to be picked up in spirit.

"You see," one of the veterans said to me, "you needn't feel too bad about leaving camp tomorrow."

I came in late to breakfast the next morning. A few players were there, and they said that the word was around that I was leaving. "The report is you're chickening out on the grass sprints," they said.

Wilson came up and said that the team and the coaches had planned a little ceremony in which I was to be presented with a gold football mounted on a wooden pedestal that read THE BEST ROOKIE IN DETROIT LION HISTORY. The trophy was not ready, so they would have to send it through the mail. John Gordy, standing nearby, said that the real reason I was leaving was because I didn't have the nerve to accept such an award for the brand of football I had displayed at Cranbrook. "I haven't got one damn trophy," he said with a big grin, "and you're getting one for the worst football I *ever* seen played."

Wilson said he hoped if I had time that morning I'd come down to the practice. When I had the bags in the car, I started through the school grounds for the practice field. I had a half hour or so. It was hot and quiet, the lawn sprinklers ticking back and forth. I thought about the Holy Rollers. I went down past the tennis courts and the pine grove, walking gingerly to keep my street shoes clear of the hot powder dust.

When I stepped out from the sidelines the players all came and crowded around to say good-bye.

George Wilson said, "You want to try one last play. One more?"

"Sure," I said. "Absolutely."

The defense began shouting happily. Joe Schmidt said, "We get one last shot at him. One last shot. That'll do it. One mighty Jumbo, men, that'll do it fine."

Scooter McLean blew his whistle. "OK," he shouted. "Let's get settled. Offense huddle up! George, go on in there and call your play."

The teams separated. The helmets were tugged on. I went in among the offensive huddle, feeling slight in my street clothes. "I expect protection," I said, grinning at them. Their helmets were turned toward me, so as always the faces were hooded and expressionless.

"Let's turn them inside out with a pass play," I said. "Green right, three right, ninety-three on *three!*"

I said it distinctly, and with the right rhythm, and they broke sharply with a crack of hands, and moved up to the line. I went up briskly behind Whitlow. I looked out at the defense. I stood in closer to the center. That had been one of my troubles in Pontiac—standing too far back and reaching for the ball. At "three" the ball came back cleanly, slapping hard into my palm, and I hurried back, sure-footed, seven yards, and turned to look downfield. Just in front I could see the haunches of the blockers around the rim of the protective pocket as they strained forward with their cleats churning up dust, but their bodies bent upright by the shock of the defensive tackles and ends working at them in a flail of arms; beyond them I saw Pietrosante cutting across, downfield about fifteen yards from me; he was looking over. I cut loose the pass, and it hit him just right, so that he could gather the ball in at a height at which the defending linebacker could not reach over to bat it down. With his legs pumping he moved the ball a few more yards downfield before he was brought down.

A great roar went up, not only from the offense, but also from the defensive people. The crowds along the sidelines stirred curiously, craning to see.

I heard the Hawk yelling: "Anything wrong with that? Any complaints about that?"

"Duck soup," I called out. "Damn cinch. Child's play." I snapped my fingers.

"Give him the game ball," said Wilson.

The helmets were off. Everyone was standing around grinning.

"Too bad about this trade with Baltimore—me for John Unitas," I said. "I suppose Bill Ford and Anderson know what they're doing."

I shook hands with some of them. I said what a fine time I had enjoyed there at Cranbrook. Then I left them and walked up through the pine trees, the scent warm and strong in the noonday heat. On the tennis court two girls were playing desultory singles—awkward at it,

It was all right, after a while, to have done it and survived without too much loss of dignity. *(Walter Iooss Jr.)*

using their game for gossip; but they were lovely to watch, both in startling white tennis outfits that set off their tanned bodies. I had a few minutes to spare. Their game consisted mostly of double faults. One of them called to the other: "I tell you Timmy's car seats come *off*—I mean you sit there for a while on that hot leather and it comes off on your legs." She served, a high arched shot like a lob. The other girl set herself, measuring her shot, and when she swung her racquet through she hit the ball with her thumb. The ball glanced off and she dropped the racquet to the court with a clatter. "You absolute fiend!" she said. She inspected her hand. The score went unannounced. One girl served, then the other, in some helter-skelter fashion, whoever held the ball it seemed. "God, at least," said the girl with the bruised thumb, "Timmy plays a banjo. You know what?"

"What?"

"His coat pockets are full of picks—those little fingernail-like things?" She bent and tried to scoop up a tennis ball with her racquet.

"What?" The other girl had her hands on her hips, her head cocked prettily, a bell of hair falling to her shoulder.

"Picks," came the answer. "Those things he *plinks* with. Plink! Plink! Plink!" She began strumming her racquet, her feet shuffling on the court. "He has hundreds."

I stood and watched them. It was quiet in the pine grove. And then an odd sound drifted up from the distant practice field, invisible behind the barriers of trees. I could see in my mind's eye what was going on— the coaches' whistles going, and the players beginning to congregate from the reaches of that enormous field. Then one of them, as he trotted in, offered up a despairing croak, as if he had run too far, or belted the tackling dummies too hard, or his uniform felt soggy and itchy from sweat. With hours more of physical discomfort to come, the anguish erupted from him, and as if empathetic, his yell was caught up by the others, and repeated, so that a chorus rose up through the pine grove— a medley of despair, boredom, frustration, exhaustion—a sound I'd never heard before at Cranbrook. They were the same loud grunts of resentment that went up along the line when troops were called up out of the comfortable roadside grass after a break in a long dusty march. The coaches' whistles began shrilling very loudly, as if to drown out the resentment. I wondered what had happened. Perhaps the players knew that the coaches were going to order the grass drills.

I often thought about the sound, wondering about it. It was an inhuman, melancholy noise. Then it died out abruptly. The players had apparently grouped around the coaches. The hum of insects rose up out of the hot pines. One of the girls began bouncing a tennis ball against the court; the sound was pleasant and summery. "Jiminy, d'ja hear *that?*" she called across the net. "That's the craziest..."

The other girl was still turned, her head tilted, as if the sound would come again, and she could diagnose it this time—her face puzzled and vacant as she waited, her mouth half open. Then, quite abruptly, she seemed to shake herself, a shiver of movement that tossed the hair at her shoulders, and she turned and called: "Who's serving? Who's serving? I'll serve!"—and dismissing the past in a quick rush of breath, she threw the ball so high in the air that she had to maneuver under it, her racquet poised.

EPILOGUE

Detroit had a bad season my year. The team finished fourth in its division — behind Chicago, Green Bay, and Baltimore. Injuries hurt their chances. Eleven of the first-line players were knocked out of the lineup by injuries, most of them on the defensive team. Joe Schmidt and Carl Brettschneider of the linebackers were crippled, and so were Yale Lary and Night Train Lane. Gary Lowe ruptured his Achilles tendon. In one game the defensive secondary was so depleted that Wilson sent in Gail Cogdill at safety, hoping that the superb athlete could adapt himself to a position he had never played before. Cogdill was so startled to be sent in on the defense that he ran onto the field without his helmet, which was not unusual, but on retrieving it, coming out for the second time, he kept calling in his madcap fashion, "What do I do, what do I do, what am I supposed to do?" The rival quarterback, chancing that such a display of ignorance was not a ruse, called for a play that probed at Cogdill's position, a long pass, and it succeeded.

I suffered from afar that season. Once, that autumn, sitting in a waterside café in Bellagio, on Italy's Lake Como, I came across the weekend scores in a *Paris Herald* which turned up down there, and when I read that the Lions had lost a game, I rose in anguish out of my chair, absolutely stiff with grief, my knee catching the edge of the table as I came up, and toppling it over in a fine cascade of Perrier bottles. The following year — though I vaguely hoped the passage of time might ease the frenzy of autumn Sundays—I found that my emotional concern had not been tempered at all. The team had another difficult season, finishing fourth again in the conference, and Sundays were hardly bearable. The Lions themselves were aware of my commitment, and it amused them. They put it to the test from time to time. I tried to see the Detroit games in person when it was possible—at least when they came east to play. One autumn I dropped into their locker room at Franklin Field, Philadelphia—traveling down from New York to watch them play the Eagles in a preseason exhibition game—and when I walked in, already worried about the game, holding up a hand, calling out, "Hello, hello, hello," glad to see everyone, George Wilson, the coach, spotted me and said, "Get that man into uniform, quick." Any citizen with his wits about him would have replied that he was sitting up in Section 24 with an attractive girl, with a crowd down from New York for the game, and beer was going to be sipped from paper cups while the players pushed and heaved in the heat (the temperature was in the high nineties). But I offered a pleased, vacuous grin, willing to do anything they told me to do, and they *did* outfit me, what's more—Friday Macklem scrabbling around in the big team trunks and coming up with a uniform of sorts. He didn't have my zero jersey, but he had a spare one with the number 30, which was George Wilson's number when he played with the Bears. Wilson ran alongside me as we trotted onto the filed and he warned me not to dishonor it. I sat nervously on the bench during the game, knowing that if they ran up the score, the temptation might rise—the commissioner notwithstanding—to run me in as quarterback for one or two plays (Wilson kept asking me if I had my plays straight), and my sense of allegiance being what it was, I *would* have trotted in, absolutely, mumbling perhaps, but shuffling out toward them, seeing the helmets turn to watch me come, and I would have done what I could. As it was, they put me at the quarterbacks' table, with the phones to the coaches on the rim of the stadium, and they would tell me whom they wanted to talk to, and I would motion at the player and he'd come to the table. The game was close, and it was exhilarating to be with the team again, but I thought the girl and the rest of them must be wondering what had become of me. I showered at half-time and returned to my seat in the stands.

"Where have you been?" my friends asked.

"I've been down there on the bench—suited up," I said, just right, the voice absolutely perfect. "You didn't see me?"

"G'wan," they said.

"Whatya mean?" I cried out. "I was number thirty."

"Ah g'wan," they said.

"Whatya mean 'g'wan.' I *was* down there." I was furious. "You didn't see me on the *phones?*"

The people in neighboring seats were craned in toward me, listening, with quizzical looks, as if they thought perhaps the heat had fetched me. I said in a low voice, "Well, never mind." Then, with play under way on the field below, I stirred myself and began calling support for the Lions.

"'S been in the bar," I heard one of my friends say to the girl. "Absolutely blotto."

My behavior began to worry me. I began to wonder if my absorption was absolute and if my commitment would be to hang around the training camp and the practice fields like the superfans I remembered from camp—the Gershes and the Sam Smarts—and I thought once or twice of Jungle Jamey in his autographed car traveling with the teams.

When I went to Times Square on Sunday night to look for the scores in the early morning editions, I would throw the paper skyward if the Lions had won, and whoop, and the people idling around the newsstand would look at me, half grinning, waiting for me to tell them what had brought on such a rage of contentedness, that I'd won a jackpot or something; I knew that I could not satisfy their expectation by saying, "Well, the Lions won." So I would hurry away.

In New York I found a kindred spirit with whom to talk about the problem of being hooked to a football team. He was Mike Manuche, a restaurant owner, and a supporter of the New York Giants. Some years ago he acquired the status of a talisman. He turned up at a Giant practice on a Thursday afternoon, then the following Thursday, and the Thursday after, and someone noted that on the following weekends the Giants won their game. The winning steaks were equated to his appearances at practice, and the Giants, who like so many athletes are a superstitious lot, began to expect Manuche to turn up on Thursdays to ensure victory the following Sunday.

Manuche performed his role rigorously: he was on hand every Thursday, often he went to team meetings, and traveled with the team. As time passed and the winning streaks went on through the championship years he evolved a carefully worked-out system of custom and procedure that he adhered to in order to keep them going: he wore certain clothes (on one occasion, a battered though lucky pair of underpants got thrown out by his mother-in-law and were retrieved from a garbage pail just as a disposal truck was coming up his Scarsdale street), he ate certain foods, and on the day of the game the complexities were staggering. He would leave his house at such and such a minute, follow the same route to the stadium, park the car at the same lot, then, entering through the same gate, he'd go up the same ramp, to his seat—the same seat, of course—showing his ticket stub to the same usher, then getting into his seat in just such a way, backing into it, and at 1:50, fifteen minutes before the start of the game, he would go to the men's room, picking the same stall, willing the team's success as he stood there, and then he had to take the same number of steps back to his seat, often having to hop or mark time to keep them exact, and a hot dog had to be bought at just such and such a time. With all these things to remember, and a host more, it was astonishing Manuche could ever concentrate on the game itself.

The importance of ritual was applied not only by Manuche but by many of the Giant players as well. Before the game, Y. A. Tittle, perhaps the most superstitious of the Giants, and two or three of the others would go to a special food shop to consume one or two meatball sandwiches apiece, not because anyone enjoyed them particularly but for their good-luck value, which was sufficient to keep the players returning week after week until, as the successful seasons continued, the trip to the eatery took on the ritual and solemnity of a pilgrimage.

With the fall of the Giants' fortunes in the mid-sixties, Manuche was hardly of easy mind. I called him up on the phone after one season and asked him about it. Apparently, as the losses continued, with the Giants ending at the bottom of their division, he had tried to establish new patterns of behavior. "We tried all sorts of things — new routes to the stadium, different cars..." he told me sorrowfully. "We thought we had something when we won the St. Louis game — but it was no good, of course. It was a terrible time. I tried all the clothes I had. I had my wife checking all of hers out — to see if there wasn't a Giant win in some combination she had. There was a time, back a year or so, when I was afraid not to show up for those Thursday practices. Then last season, when the troubles started, after all those Thursdays, years of them, I tried a Wednesday, just to see if it would help. It didn't. Nothing worked."

"How about those meatball sandwiches?" I asked.

"Well, when the defeats started," Manuche said, "they thought that perhaps the meatballs were not being *cooked* properly. They had the counterman cook the meatballs just a little longer, then a little less, but nothing helped, and finally we gave up the place entirely. Crazy, it all was," Manuche said. "I mean you'd think there was a screw loose somewhere, the way we behaved."

I said that considering my own behavior, his was perfectly natural.

"You have the trouble too? If you get hooked, you're lost — eat some awful meatball sandwich, fifty or sixty of them, if you thought it'd do the team any good."

Was there any cure for this state of commitment? I asked Manuche.

He was very mournful. He didn't think so — "hooked" was the word he kept repeating.

The Lions were able to get me to do anything for them. The year after my participation they prevailed upon me to represent them at the National Football League draft at New York's Summit Hotel. Nothing much to it, they told me—sit at a phone and give the Detroit office the names of the players drafted by the other teams, and announce the Lions' choice (which they would phone me from Detroit) when their turn came up. It might take some time, they said, and perhaps I should plan to keep that weekend free (the draft was scheduled to start on a Saturday morning). Would I do it? they wanted to know. Absolutely! I shouted into the phone. I had a full weekend planned, but I would cancel it. A tremendous honor. I only wanted assurances that I could not in my official capacity damage the Detroit organization. Would it be possible for me to draft a 132-pound fullback from Ypsilanti High School?

No, they said coldly, that would be impossible.

Bud Erickson met me at a midtown hotel at seven-thirty a.m., a half hour before the drafting session was scheduled to start in the Summit Hotel.

"I'm terribly grateful to be asked to do this," I said.

"It's going to be a long haul," he said. "Twenty rounds, fourteen picks for each round. You'll be in there for quite a spell."

"How do they know who I am? Do I have any accreditation?"

Erickson reached in his coat pocket. He handed me a souvenir key chain attached to a blue disc with the Detroit lion rampant showing on one side.

"You can use this," he said, "for identification."

"It's a key chain," I said.

"Don't put any keys on it," Erickson said. "Just wave it around and it'll do."

The importance of my duties seemed somewhat diminished.

Erickson talked over Detroit news. There had been two deaths which had been almost unbearable to accept—Scooter McLean, the little wiry backfield coach, who had died suddenly of cancer, and then Lucien Reeberg, the big rookie, who had died of uremic poisoning, which came on a month or so after the season's close. He had had a chronic kidney condition which he had kept from the doctors, supposing that it might affect his future with the team. He had made the squad that first season, a reserve at both the offensive and defensive guard positions, which he played with a clumsy élan that was at once the despair and delight of the coaches. I remembered seeing him for the first time as a bona fide member of the team in Baltimore, the only time the team came east that season.

The day before I had been to a game in Cambridge. Princeton was playing there that weekend. The rain was very heavy. Three Harvard graduates died in the stands that afternoon—a headline story in the metropolitan papers the next day. One of them succumbed two or three rows away from where I was sitting; they laid him down carefully in the aisle, and I remember that down in front on the field a cheerleader, quite unaware, kept bellowing cheerfully through his megaphone: "Everybody up! Everybody up for the kickoff!" I drove to the airport after the game and took a flight to Baltimore. Reeberg was the first Lion player I saw when I came into the hotel lobby. He was very nattily dressed. He was wearing a thin-brimmed black hat, like one of Roger Brown's, with an Alpine brush at the side. He was very suave.

I went up to him and said, "Lucien, it's great you made the team."

He barely made a sign of recognition, trying to suggest with his aplomb that making the team was just a matter of course.

"It's terrific, Lucien," I said.

I thought he was going to try to yawn. But it did not work. His Alpine brush began to quiver. He broke down. "Whataya *think?*" he asked breathlessly. "D'ja *believe* it? Well, I'll tell you something true, that *I* can't!" He could hardly contain himself. "You like the blazer?" he said. He pointed at the lion on the breast pocket. "Look at *this,*" he said. He said he wanted to buy me a cup of coffee and tell me about the game he'd played the week before, but some other players came by and I never got a chance to talk to him again.

"He was all enthusiasm," I said to Erickson. "What a mockery."

He shrugged his shoulders and paid for the breakfast.

In the Summit Hotel the league had set aside two large adjoining conference rooms. One of them was set up with a bar, a buffet table, and two television sets, which were tuned to different channels so that a burble of sound rose from them, with an occasional scream or sob from a soap opera, and it sounded as though things were very lively in there.

The larger room, decorated with a deep red wall-to-wall carpet, was devoted to the business at hand—half the room assigned for television equipment and interviews, and the other set up with fourteen small tables, one for each team in the league (the name designated on a placard), and arranged in two long rows of seven each. A speaker's table with its podium from which the draft selections would be announced was at the head of the room. Each table was decorated with a small, fat football-player plastic doll with a painted brown football tucked under one arm, the appropriate team name painted on its jersey. Each had an oversized helmeted head, fixed by a spring, so at the slightest touch it bounced and turned for a painfully long period. One sees such dolls bobbing on the back-window shelves of automobiles. When a draft choice was announced, and the representatives reached for their phones to call the home offices, their dolls, set off by the vibration, would bounce and bob in a little lunatic show of approbation, their faces fixed with the thin half-moons of kindergarten portraiture. I don't know why one of us—in the latter stages of the session particularly—did not reach out to crumble his doll. Perhaps it was in the air, because toward the end someone came by and they were packed carefully away in a valise.

When I arrived the room was beginning to fill: team officials with briefcases sat down at their assigned tables and spread out colored charts and a clutch of sharpened pencils; NFL officials appeared, Commissioner Rozelle among them, who seemed to know everyone—big hellos, and handshakes—and then the big wide-shouldered men who were from the scouting pools, ex-players most of them, who sat at tables at the rear of the room, shucking off their coats first thing to their short-sleeved shirts so the heft of their bare arms was displayed. There were others—and I was among them—who seemed slightly bewildered among these people: superfans, for sure, I decided, who had given up their weekends, as I had, to help their teams. I introduced myself to some of them: "...from Detroit," I said, "the Lions," nervously fingering my key chain. It was hard to say with conviction.

I went to my table with the Detroit placard on it and sat down. The chair was bright leather, the color of a new pocketbook, and air-cushioned, so it whistled slightly as I settled into it. I picked up the phone and called the Detroit office. The football doll bobbed in front of me. The brassy, friendly voice of George Wilson came on the wire.

"I'm ready," I said. "The Giants have first draft choice and they should be selecting very shortly."

"Good," he said. "Bill Ford will be on the phone for us at this end. Call him when the news comes through."

The year before I went to Detroit, William Ford had bought control of the Lions for six million dollars. He would appear on the sidelines to watch the scrimmaging, perched on a shooting stick, his small blond daughters flanking him. As the ball moved on the field, he would pick up his stick, trail it up and down the sidelines after him, set it again, and sit, staring out at his players. He took particular interest in my own eccentric flailings in the Detroit backfield—he was not aware of my privileged position—and I was told later he often described me to his wife over the dinner table. "There's this one fellow," he'd say, shaking his head, "who just isn't going to make it. They keep him on, though; I can't understand it."

I knew what Ford was going to say as soon as I got on the phone to him from the Summit Hotel. "Well, hello, *Bill*," he was going to say. "Hello, is that *Bill* Ford?" and I would laugh, if somewhat hollowly, and say, "Sure, certainly it is."

He calls me Bill Ford because once, when traveling with the team, I made the mistake of using his name to make a reservation in a small fashionable Beverly Hills restaurant named La Scala, and was caught at it. The team had come into Los Angeles earlier that day, and in the evening a few of us began to telephone around, trying for a good place to eat. La Scala was not accepting reservations, they told me over the phone.

"This is Mr. Ford," I said suddenly. "Mr. William Ford in town with the Detroit Lions for the Rams game."

I could hear the clatter of silverware in the background and the hum of conversation. The Ford name helped matters. Someone came on the phone and I was informed that a table had "become clear." We were welcome to appear any time we wanted: it would be held for us. "Yes, indeed, Mr. Ford," they said.

"Right," I said. "We'll be along presently."

We turned up at La Scala, not much later, a group of us, Nick Pietrosante, John Gordy, and Bill Quinlan, a veteran defensive end who had joined the club the year after I left, all of us striding up, hungry, under the little marquee, into the restaurant, and as soon as we were in there I knew something had gone wrong. The owner was waiting for us, eyeing us sharply.

"The Ford table?" I asked.

"Which of you gentlemen is Mr. Ford?"

I looked back at John Gordy. He stared me down. He had heavy, sloping shoulders that make his suit coats ride up high, like an over-grown schoolboy's. Beyond him, Pietrosante had worked himself into a corner of the vestibule, looking out bleakly, and as for Bill Quinlan, with his strong, pocked face, he was chewing belligerently at something, tobacco perhaps, and it was evident from his demeanor that he wasn't going to step forward to pass himself off as the grandson of Henry Ford. He is known as "the Black Irishman from Massachusetts."

"I'm Bill Ford," I said weakly.

"Isn't that interesting," the owner said. "Someone wants to meet you." He put his hand somewhat more firmly than was pleasant on my shoulder and guided me through the restaurant—people looking up as we passed since we were moving at a considerable clip—to a corner alcove, where, sure enough, William Ford was sitting with other officials from the Detroit club, Edwin Anderson, Russ Thomas, the personnel manager, and some others, all looking quite severe, and glancing at Ford so as to be able to equate their reactions with his.

The La Scala owner announced: "Mr. Ford, may I present Mr. Ford."

Ford grinned wildly, the others taking up his reaction on cue, so it was all right, I suppose. But they never allowed me to forget the incident. "Hey, Bill," they all called out when I saw them thereafter. His party had turned up, just by chance, without making a reservation. Naturally, they had been given the "Ford" table, and, curious, had remarked at the restaurant's prescience. They were told someone had phoned for reservations; their eyebrows went up, and, fat cats, they waited to see who the impostors were.

Sure enough, when I got on the phone to announce the first draft choice, Mr. Ford said, "Hello, Bill, that you?"

"Absolutely," I said. "Nobody but Bill Ford. The Giants picked Tucker Frederickson."

"OK, Bill," he said. I could tell from the way he drawled it out softly that the big Auburn fullback had been high on their own list. Detroit was looking for a heavy, hard-running back.

The Giants' choice was made at eight o'clock, their representative striding to the podium with the name, phoned in from Giant headquarters, written on a slip of paper. It was read off by Commissioner Rozelle. Detroit's position was eleventh in the first round, and with each team allowed a half hour to make their choice it was long past noon, and ten players later, when our turn came and the phone rang on my desk with Detroit's pick.

"Thomas Nowatzke," Bill Ford said. "We've picked Nowatzke." The connection was poor and the name arrived as a blur of sibilance.

"Once again," I said loudly. "How do you spell *that?*"

They began snickering at the tables, and I had to cover an ear to get the swatch of consonants in his name straight. I took my slip up to the podium, and he was announced.

Not long after, Nowatzke himself came in with Bud Erickson. An interviewer took them into the television klieg lights, the machine facing them with its long black lens, the twin red lights beneath, and Nowatzke said into a stick microphone that he felt real good to be playing for the NFL, and for Detroit. I looked at him carefully—disappointed in him. If he had been a draft choice for another team I would have been impressed enough—a personable-looking athlete with the power indicated along the width and line of his shoulders—but a first draft choice for Detroit, I thought, *my* team, should have been a titanic figure, carrying away the door in his hand as he entered the room, just by accident, ripping it off the hinges, apologizing then, bobbing his head, not only to apologize, but to clear the ceiling, and when he got to the lights, the interviewer looking up at him nervously, he would take the stick microphone to say into it, "Well, gosh, folks," and it would snap in his hands like a twig.

But some time after Nowatzke's departure my enthusiasm for all things Detroit began to flag. The hours stretched on endlessly. Each round in the draft moved slowly, each team using its allotted time to the limit to make sure through its network of representatives that its choice would sign his contract. It was apparent the session was going to last long into the next day. What had seemed a privilege was in effect a chore—being shackled to a small desk with its telephone and the fat football doll. The league did its best. Meals were sent in, but in the evening I thought of my canceled dinner, and, later, the theater I'd missed and after midnight I thought of the sashaying around town that the Lions had deprived me of, and I began to wonder if perhaps my allegiance had not been pushed too far. Football itself began to seem distasteful, epitomized by the ex-players from the scouting pools wandering about the room in their shirtsleeves. The long hours seemed to have no effect on them. The rest of us slouched wearily at our tables; all seemed scraggly; a sheen of beard appeared on some faces as the dawn came, and the sound of traffic began to drift up from the streets. One of the representatives gave a slight groan, and stretching out on the floor next to his table he slept with his phone on his chest. The scouts grinned and pointed at him. Every once in a while one of them would be called to a team table to advise the home office, Baltimore, say, at the table just in front of me; the scout would amble up, humming, with a stiff, loose-leaf notebook with colored tabs along the side, and when he sat down, the air cushion would whistle shrilly under him. He would talk to the coach on the other end of the phone as follows: "Hey, baby. Bailey Gimbel?" He'd refer to his book. "A real fine kid, this boy. *Big!* Oh, run to two-sixty, quick as a cat—oh, he'll do the fifty in under six, for sure, in gear, and attitude, he's got an attitude you don't have to worry about, real beautiful attitude: hardnose."

That was the gist of it—longer, of course, the patois rich, with the emphasis always on speed ("in gear" had nothing to do with a shift of speed, but with racing in football togs), "hands" came into it always ("he's got a great pair of hands"), and always height and weight. In the early hours of Sunday morning, my attitude sour, with nothing to do, even the television sets dead in the next room, the place quiet, I found myself irreverent enough to be tempted to call the home office, to whisper sharply into the phone as follows: "Bill, this is...ah, Bill. The scout group here has been talking about a real good kid—not drafted yet..."

"What's that? What?"

"He's a tackle from Highland Cream Teachers."

"What's that again? The connection..."

"Courtney Caroline's his name—everybody's agog in here."

"Everybody's *what?*"

"Agog. Everybody's agog. Bill, the kid's big—a real *fat* kid, run up oh maybe five, *six* hundred pounds, as big as a mountain—and big on speed too, Bill, he can tackle you with those feet, great big cat-quick feet, and as for attitude, he's got a real beautiful attitude: he doesn't *smoke.*"

I never called such a thing in. I hadn't the nerve to. But when the twelfth round came along, about six in the morning, a player's name came up, San Francisco's choice, which caught my fancy and gave me a small chance to indicate my newfound attitude of irreverence. When I picked up the phone to report, I said, "Bill, San Francisco just picked up a halfback from Fresno State named Dave Plump."

"Yes, Plump," said Ford. I heard him repeat the name to the others.

They kept charts in the home office, crossing off names as I called in the other teams' choices.

"I think we missed a bet there, a great bet," I said. "You could have worked him into the Detroit backfield with Milt Plum."

"What's that?" asked Ford. "Speak up. The connection's gone sour."

"Plump!" I shouted into the phone. "You could have had Plump in there for Plum's handoffs—Plum to Plump!"

I could hear him murmuring distantly at the other end of the line, but then I heard the rustling in nearby seats, the scouts looking over, and some of the others, so I said, "Never mind, Bill—just an idea," and put up the receiver.

But in the twentieth round something happened which returned me irretrievably to the Detroit fold. About ten minutes before Detroit's choice was due, Aldo Forte, the line coach, called in. He had taken over from Bill Ford, who had finally packed up and gone home. It was one o'clock Sunday afternoon. We had been going for twenty-nine hours. "You all set for our last choice?" Aldo said.

"Sure," I said.

"We got a surprise choice coming up," Aldo said. "Big surprise."

"What's that?" I asked.

"Well," Aldo said, "we've decided to draft *you!*"

"Come on," I said.

"Sure," he said.

"Honest, Aldo," I whispered shrilly into the phone. "You can't do that. The commissioner'll have a fit if he has to read off my name. He'll start suspending people and slapping fines around. He hasn't been to sleep for thirty hours or so, and he looks mean."

"No matter," said Aldo. "You learned five plays when you were training with us. That puts you ahead of someone else we might pick."

"Honest, Aldo . . ."

"The big thing," Aldo said, "is that we don't lose you to the Kansas City Chiefs, or the Oilers, those guys in the other league." He hung up the phone.

The author, back home, with the spoils of victory. *(Walter Iooss Jr.)*

I sat there for ten minutes, waiting. *Drafted,* I thought. Well, what about that? I thought. What a great gesture.

They picked someone else, of course, when the time came. Their last choice was George Wilson Jr., George's son, a tall, young quarterback from Xavier—a natural, they all said. I was relieved that I didn't have to walk up to Commissioner Rozelle with a slip of paper with my own name on it. And yet, not really. I was put out, somewhat. What a shame they had to think of young Wilson. Rank nepotism! Walking home in the bright sunlight that Sunday afternoon I kicked sulkily at the pavement.

And then, oddly, something came to mind which was unexpected. I found myself thinking not of the obvious or pleasurable aspects of my stay with the Lions: not the physical sense of well-being, being toned up and as strong as one would ever be; or the thirsts and appetites and walking up through the pine grove behind the gym thinking of the big tin dippers floating in the iced lemonade in the pails, and the paper cups in their long packages; nor the keenness of emotion that always seemed prevalent, a commingling of fear, exhilaration, and purpose as the team worked up for a game; nor the camaraderie, nor the long stories in the evening; nor the dance nights in town; nor the fine humor; nor the funny vignettes. It was not of these or anything else that would have seemed obvious. Instead, I seemed to hear the odd sound I remembered from my last day with the team when I walked up from the practice field—the long bleat from the players being whistled together by the coaches, almost one of sorrow—and once again I seemed to see the girls with their racquets on the tennis court, the sound catching them in lovely poses of arrest, the bells of hair turning at their shoulders as they stopped their play to turn and listen, peering at the pines, their heads tilted for the sounds drifting up from the practice field beyond.

Appendix

1963 Detroit Lion Roster — Cranbrook Camp

(Numerical)

No.	Name	Pos.	Hgt.	Wgt.	Age	Yr. in NFL	College
0	Plimpton, George	QB	6-4	192	36	1	Harvard
14	Morrall, Earl	QB	6-2	206	29	8	Michigan State
16	Plum, Milton	QB	6-2	205	28	7	Penn State
20	Compton, Dick	OHB	6-1	195	23	2	McMurry College
21	Maher, Bruce	DHB	5-11	190	26	4	Detroit
22	Frantz, Gene	HB	6-3	195	24	1	Brigham Young
23	Watkins, Tom	HB	6-0	195	25	3	Iowa State
24	Schieber, Ron	HB	6-1	190	22	1	Illinois State
25	Studstill, Pat	HB	6-1	180	25	3	Houston
26	Look, Dean	HB	6-0	185	25	1	Michigan State
28	Lary, Yale	DHB-K	5-11	190	32	10	Texas A&M
33	Pietrosante, Nick	FB	6-2	225	26	5	Notre Dame
34	Ryder, Nick	FB	6-0	215	21	1	Miami (Florida)
40	King, Don	HB	6-0	186	23	1	Syracuse
41	Barr, Terry	OHB	6-0	190	28	7	Michigan
43	Lowe, Gary	DHB	6-0	195	29	8	Michigan State
44	LeBeau, Dick	DHB	6-1	185	26	5	Ohio State
45	Lewis, Dan	OHB	6-1	200	27	6	Wisconsin
46	Ferguson, Larry	OHB	5-10	195	22	1	Iowa
47	Martin, Jim	C-K	6-2	230	39	13	Notre Dame
48	Kassulke, Karl	HB	6-0	193	21	1	Drake
50	Scholtz, Bob	OT-C	6-4	250	25	4	Notre Dame
51	Whitlow, Bob	C	6-2	236	27	4	Arizona
52	Lloyd, Dave	C-LB	6-3	248	26	5	Georgia
53	Gaubatz, Dennis	LB	6-2	220	22	1	LSU
54	Messner, Max	LB	6-3	225	25	4	Cincinnati
55	Walker, Wayne	LB-K	6-2	225	27	6	Idaho
56	Schmidt, Joe	LB	6-0	220	31	11	Pittsburgh

No.	Name	Pos	Ht	Wt	Age	Exp	College
58	Archer, Jerry	C	6-4	245	22	1	Kansas State College
59	Clark, Ernie	LB	6-1	220	25	1	Michigan State
61	Reeberg, Lucien	DT	6-4	300	22	1	Hampton Institute
62	Gamble, John	G	6-4	240	21	1	U. of Pacific
63	Williams, Roy	T	6-7	265	25	1	U. of Pacific
64	Lomakoski, John	OT	6-4	250	22	2	Western Michigan
66	Sewell, Harley	OG	6-1	230	32	11	Texas
68	Imperiale, Frank	DE	6-2	245	23	1	Southern Illinois
70	Sanders, Daryl	OT	6-5	250	21	1	Ohio State
71	McMacken, Dick	OT	6-3	250	25	1	Huron
72	Peters, Floyd	DT	6-4	255	27	6	San Francisco State
73	Ward, Paul	DT	6-3	247	26	3	Whitworth
74	Bundra, Mike	DT	6-4	260	24	2	Southern California
75	Gordy, John	OG-T	6-4	250	28	6	Tennessee
76	Brown, Roger	DT	6-5	300	26	4	Maryland State
77	LaRose, Dan	OT-OG	6-5	250	23	3	Missouri
78	McCord, Darris	DE	6-4	250	29	9	Tennessee
79	Gonzaga, John	DT	6-3	250	30	8	No college
80	Gibbons, Jim	OE	6-3	220	27	6	Iowa
81	Lane, Dick	DHB	6-2	200	35	12	Scottsbluff J.C.
82	Greer, Albert	E	6-4	190	22	1	Jackson State
83	Simon, James	E-LB	6-5	235	22	1	Miami (Florida)
84	O'Brien, Pete	T-DE	6-3	238	22	1	Xavier
85	Vargo, Larry	OE	6-3	215	24	2	Detroit
86	Hall, Tom	OE-DHB	6-2	195	23	2	Minnesota
88	Williams, Sam	DE	6-5	235	32	5	Michigan State
89	Cogdill, Gail	OE	6-2	195	26	4	Washington State

Coaching Staff

George Wilson, Head Coach

Aldo Forte, Assistant Coach

Bob Nussbaumer, Assistant Coach

Ray "Scooter" McLean, Assistant Coach

Les Bingaman, Assistant Coach

Don Doll, Assistant Coach

About the Author

George Plimpton (1927–2003) was the bestselling author and editor of more than thirty books, as well as editor of the *Paris Review* for its first fifty years. He wrote regularly for such magazines as *Sports Illustrated* and *Esquire,* and he appeared numerous times in films and on television.

CPSIA information can be obtained
at www.ICGtesting.com
Printed in the USA
LVHW092045191021
700897LV00001B/6